Lecture Notes in Business Information Processing 266

Series Editors

Wil M.P. van der Aalst
 Eindhoven Technical University, Eindhoven, The Netherlands
John Mylopoulos
 University of Trento, Trento, Italy
Michael Rosemann
 Queensland University of Technology, Brisbane, QLD, Australia
Michael J. Shaw
 University of Illinois, Urbana-Champaign, IL, USA
Clemens Szyperski
 Microsoft Research, Redmond, WA, USA

More information about this series at http://www.springer.com/series/7911

Julia Kotlarsky · Ilan Oshri
Leslie P. Willcocks (Eds.)

Shared Services and Outsourcing: A Contemporary Outlook

10th Global Sourcing Workshop 2016
Val d'Isère, France, February 16–19, 2016
Revised Selected Papers

Editors
Julia Kotlarsky
Aston Business School, Aston University
Birmingham
UK

Leslie P. Willcocks
London School of Economics
London
UK

Ilan Oshri
Loughborough Universiry
Loughborough
UK

ISSN 1865-1348   ISSN 1865-1356 (electronic)
Lecture Notes in Business Information Processing
ISBN 978-3-319-47008-5   ISBN 978-3-319-47009-2 (eBook)
DOI 10.1007/978-3-319-47009-2

Library of Congress Control Number: 2016953221

© Springer International Publishing AG 2016
This work is subject to copyright. All rights are reserved by the Publisher, whether the whole or part of the material is concerned, specifically the rights of translation, reprinting, reuse of illustrations, recitation, broadcasting, reproduction on microfilms or in any other physical way, and transmission or information storage and retrieval, electronic adaptation, computer software, or by similar or dissimilar methodology now known or hereafter developed.
The use of general descriptive names, registered names, trademarks, service marks, etc. in this publication does not imply, even in the absence of a specific statement, that such names are exempt from the relevant protective laws and regulations and therefore free for general use.
The publisher, the authors and the editors are safe to assume that the advice and information in this book are believed to be true and accurate at the date of publication. Neither the publisher nor the authors or the editors give a warranty, express or implied, with respect to the material contained herein or for any errors or omissions that may have been made.

Printed on acid-free paper

This Springer imprint is published by Springer Nature
The registered company is Springer International Publishing AG
The registered company address is: Gewerbestrasse 11, 6330 Cham, Switzerland

Preface

This edited book is intended for use by students, academics, and practitioners who take interest in outsourcing and offshoring of information technology and business services. The book offers a review of the key topics in outsourcing and offshoring, populated with practical frameworks that serve as a tool kit to students and managers The range of topics covered in this book is wide and diverse, but predominately focused on how to achieve success in shared services and outsourcing. More specifically the book examines outsourcing decisions and management practices, paying specific attention to shared services that have become one of the dominant sourcing models. The book also explores how to achieve innovation in an outsourcing setting, through country comparison lens. Sharing knowledge and cultural aspects remain among the hot topics for academics and practitioners alike. The need to understand career paths has emerged as a new area for outsourcing practitioners. Last but not least, multiple theoretical lenses have been applied across the studies, among them ambidexterity, dialectics, institutional logic, and more. Topics discussed in this book combine theoretical and practical insights regarding challenges that industry leaders, policy makers, and professionals face or should be concerned with. Case studies from various organizations, industries, and countries such as the UK, Italy, The Netherlands, Canada, Australia, and Denmark are used extensively throughout the book, giving it a unique position within the current literature.

The book is based on a vast empirical base brought together through years of extensive research by leading researchers in information systems, strategic management, international business, and operations.

August 2016

Julia Kotlarsky
Ilan Oshri
Leslie Willcocks

Organization

The Global Sourcing Workshop is an annual gathering of academics and practitioners.

Program Committee

Julia Kotlarsky	Aston Business School, UK
Ilan Oshri	Loughborough Centre for Global Sourcing and Services, UK
Leslie Willcocks	London School of Economics, London, UK

Contents

Why Do Firms Outsource: A Tool for Contextual Ambidexterity 1
   Shivom Aggarwal, Kiron Ravindran, and Gautam Ray

Sharing Knowledge in a Shared Services Center Context: An Explanatory
Case Study of the Dialectics of Formal and Informal Practices 19
   Dragos Vieru and Pierre-Emmanuel Arduin

Towards an Integrated Methodology for Implementing Shared Services 40
   Vipin Suri, Kuldeep Kumar, and Jos van Hillegersberg

Exploring Career Anchors in Shared Service Centres 51
   Stephanie Lambert, Andrew Rothwell, and Ian Herbert

An Examination of the Relationship Between Organizational Culture
Determinants and Retained Organizations Growth Stages 77
   Albert Plugge, Christiaan Kooijman, and Marijn Janssen

The Clash of Cultures in Information Technology Outsourcing
Relationships: An Institutional Logics Perspective 97
   Nikolaus Schmidt, Bastian Zöller, and Christoph Rosenkranz

Outsourcing and Innovation: A Comparative Study of Italy and the UK 118
   Giovanni Vaia and Ilan Oshri

An Accounting Firm Perspective of Offshoring 137
   Silvia Caratti, Brian Perrin, and Glennda Scully

Offshoring in the Wrong Direction? 166
   Paul Alpar

Contract Renewal Decisions in IT-Outsourcing:
A Survey in the Netherlands 178
   Erik Beulen

Exploring Choices of Software Sourcing Methods Among Start-Ups 193
   Björn Johansson, Blerta Deliallisi, and Pien Walraven

Author Index 211

Why Do Firms Outsource: A Tool for Contextual Ambidexterity

Shivom Aggarwal[1(✉)], Kiron Ravindran[1], and Gautam Ray[2]

[1] IE Business School, Madrid, Spain
Saggarwal@faculty.ie.edu, Kiron.ravindran@ie.edu
[2] Carlson School of Management, University of Minnesota,
Minneapolis, MN, USA
rayxx153@umn.edu

Abstract. Why do firms outsource information technology (it)? The literature is divided on whether it outsourcing is a cost-reduction strategy or a growth strategy. We argue that organizations can do both, i.e., they can make choices between exploitative and explorative aspects of it outsourcing, depending on the firm's objective, i.e., to increase revenues and/or decrease costs. Our empirical findings show that it outsourcing has a positive direct effect on revenues and no impact on costs. We also find that the firms with low internal innovation capability use it outsourcing as a substitute for internal research and development (R&D) expenditure to increase revenues while firms with high internal R&D capability use it outsourcing as a complement for internal R&D expenditure to decrease costs. Moreover, in case of less concentrated i.e., more competitive industries firms tend to outsource more in order to increase revenues, while in highly concentrated i.e., less competitive industries firms tend to outsource in order to reduce cost. We reconcile our findings which are partially consistent with disparate perspectives from the literature, using the contextual ambidexterity framework. Our findings suggest that contextual ambidexterity also occurs at organizational level and is embedded in organizational level contexts. We provide important implications for is scholars working on it outsourcing and practitioners from outsourcing firms as well as it vendors.

Keywords: IT outsourcing · Contextual ambidexterity · Seemingly unrelated regression

1 Introduction

The determinants of IT Outsourcing have been argued from a Transaction Cost Economics (TCE) perspective [1–3] such that IT Outsourcing is used to gain access to the economies of scale and specialization of specialist IT vendors [4, 5]. This line of reasoning posits that the receiving end of outsourcing tends to specialize in particular tasks, generating learning and lower costs which are transferred to the clients. This has bolstered the prevalent view that IT Outsourcing is a cost-based strategy where firms tends to compete by lowering costs through outsourcing. However, IT Outsourcing can be used to gain access to capabilities not available in-house. This line of reasoning posits that IT Outsourcing can be associated with increase in revenues as outsourced IT capabilities can be used to explore opportunities that the firm does not have internal IT capabilities for. Consequently, some IS scholars have recently claimed that firms use IT Outsourcing as a growth strategy [6–10] and as an innovation strategy [11, 12] This poses an open question based on divergent prescriptions from literature regarding the impact of IT Outsourcing. Furthermore, the underlying mechanisms for the effect of IT Outsourcing on firm revenues or costs have not been investigated empirically. This study aims to bridge this gap in the literature and resolve the ambiguity concerning the role of IT Outsourcing on firm performance.

This paper explores the fundamental question for firms engaged in IT Outsourcing, i.e., Why firms outsource? And the underlying mechanisms for its effect on firm performance. Although it is a compelling notion that IT Outsourcing is used for reducing costs or increasing revenues, but data tells a different story. Our findings (main effects) suggest that IT Outsourcing has a positive relationship with revenues and has no impact on costs. This is in line with recent literature, (see, [11]), where scholars have failed to find evidence that IT Capital or IT Outsourcing is correlated with firms' operational expenses. However they found a strong positive effect on firm revenues across a large sample of public firms. It seems that the direct effect of IT Outsourcing or IT Capital on firm revenues is positive, but in order to better understand this effect has to be studied within the respective firm-level contexts and objectives. We find that in firms with high R&D capability, high levels of IT Outsourcing is associated with lower costs. However in firms with low R&D capability, IT Outsourcing is associated with higher revenues and higher costs. This suggests that the impact of IT Outsourcing can be exploitative in nature (and can be used to reduce costs) as well as explorative (and can be used to substitute internal R&D capability).

Extant literature has shown that IT Outsourcing can help in reducing coordination costs and may allow firms to conduct their R&D activities more effectively [13–15] and it is possible for firms to reallocate a greater share of their discretionary expenditures to IT if they facilitate R&D activities [11]. Moreover, strategy literature has suggested that firm's posture or relative behavior (to its peers) affects the firm's strategic choices such as innovation [16]. Firms invest in R&D to increase innovation output, which increases the revenues, market valuations and/or stock returns [17–19]. But our study contributes to this literature by showing that for the firms with lower R&D expenditure compared to its industry peers, IT Outsourcing can be used as a substitute to increase revenues by leveraging the explorative aspect of IT Outsourcing. On the other hand, the exploitative aspects of IT Outsourcing can be used by the firms as complement to high R&D expenditure to reduce costs.

The environment of competition within the industry can affect the strategic choices of managers. Prior literature has examined the role of competition within the industry on strategic choices of investment in general purpose IT or IT Outsourcing. So, when considering the moderating impact of industry environment, we find that in concentrated industry environments, high IT Outsourcing is associated with lower costs; and in more competitive (i.e., less concentrated) environments, high IT Outsourcing is associated with higher revenues however accompanied by a simultaneous increase in costs.

We argue that firms tend to be using IT Outsourcing as growth strategy or cost-reduction strategy depending on the environmental context and firm's objective.

The two moderating effects of the industry-specific Industry concentration and firm-specific Relative R&D reflects the notion of industry-level and firm-level factors affecting the organizational decisions including organizational ambidexterity, i.e., organization tend to achieve alignment in its current operations while also adapting effectively to changing environmental demands [20]. The notion of associating IT Outsourcing and organizational ambidexterity has been studied by scholars in disparate contexts and theoretical frameworks, namely, IT Outsourcing governance mechanisms [21], IT Outsourcing effects on efficiency and adaptability [22], IT Outsourcing effects on firm boundaries [23] and Absorptive capacity in IT Outsourcing strategies [24]. While this discourse contributes to the extant literature on ambidexterity using IT Outsourcing as a contextual ambidextrous capability which has both exploitative and explorative aspects to understand the role of IT Outsourcing in performance heterogeneity among firms. The overall effect of pursuing strategy of intra-organizational ambidexterity [20, 25, 26] in general has been empirically investigated in variety of settings and found to be positively influencing firm performance [20, 21, 27, 29–31]. And our results extend the contextual ambidexterity perspective [20, 26, 28] which stipulates that individual employees make choices between adaptation-oriented and alignment-oriented activities in the context of appropriate routine. The adaptation-oriented activities reflect the explorative actions with an objective of building adaptive behavior in decision making, while alignment-oriented activities comprise of exploitative processes that aim to enforce structure and efficiency. IT Outsourcing has an apparent exploitative aspect as it can help firms utilize existing economies of scale and scope enjoyed by the IT vendors, while it also possess explorative effects as it can substitute internal R&D expenditure (a default exploration strategy). The pay-offs from these two courses of action differ in numerous aspects, such as the payoffs from exploitation are earlier, more certain and easier to achieve, while exploration payoffs are subjected to long term, uncertainty and high risk outcomes [33].

Contextual ambidexterity has been argued and studied as an individual-level phenomenon emanating at organizational level in the form of social construction embedded within organizational routines. Our study extends contextual ambidexterity to the organizational level. The organizational level decision of IT Outsourcing provides contextual ambidexterity in the presence of varying degrees of R&D capability and competitive environment. And consequently, the effects on cost and growth can be different. Thus, we find that contextual ambidexterity is a phenomenon which emanates not only at individual-level (within an organization), but also at organizational level depending on the organizational context and contingencies.

The results provide empirical evidence that ambidextrous strategies not necessarily improve firm performance directly and need to be studied in the context of firm's contingent needs. In the next section, we build on the extant literature on ambidexterity and IT Outsourcing. Then we formulate our hypotheses and put forth the empirical analysis using SUR regression (Seemingly Unrelated Regression) and conditional effect plots to understand the moderation ramifications. In the following section, we discuss our results and conclude with future directions and limitations of this study.

2 Hypotheses Development

IT Outsourcing: Cost-reduction Strategy or Growth Strategy: Ambidexterity arises from the firms acquiring the ability to sustain both exploration and exploitation when they are vulnerable to the environment [25, 34]. Many techniques and discourses have been proposed as a mechanism to achieve organizational ambidexterity including building internally contradictory subunits simultaneously [26, 34, 35] and meta-routines modifying underlying processes [20, 36, 37]. For firms, IT Outsourcing is a choice that can lead to decreasing costs or increasing revenues. Therefore it poses an empirical question to study using the ambidexterity framework. Value from IT Outsourcing can be realized at multiple levels such as process, firm, and market [38–42].

IT Outsourcing has been viewed as cost-reduction strategy based on the exploitation principles of leveraging economies of scale and scope enjoyed by IT vendors [1–3]. This stream of literature has found case-based and anecdotal evidence to claim that firm use IT Outsourcing to reduce costs and has been the prevalent view in IS literature in last decades. [43] argued that production outsourcing can help in increasing innovation capabilities of the focal firm by freeing up the resources and giving better incentives to innovate. Similar phenomenon can be observed in the case of IT Outsourcing as the firms can use it to increase access to innovation by investing in building R&D capability. The phenomenon of firms using IT Outsourcing as a growth strategy [6–10] and innovation strategy [11, 12] has also been argued from a capabilities perspective; such that firms can use specialized knowledge of IT vendors to develop capabilities which cannot cultivated from in-house resources. It is an empirical question to find out whether firms use IT Outsourcing to increase revenues or decrease costs as the literature on this issue is highly divided [11, 12, 44, 45].

Hypothesis 1A: Firms do IT Outsourcing in order to reduce costs, i.e., the high degree of IT Outsourcing will be negatively associated with costs.

Hypothesis 1B. Firms do IT Outsourcing in order to increase revenues, i.e., the high degree of IT Outsourcing will be positively associated with revenues.

IT Outsourcing: Contextual ambidexterity: IT Outsourcing can be used as a contextual ambidextrous strategy such that firms can leverage the exploitative nature of IT Outsourcing to reduce costs and/or can substitute the explorative aspects of IT Outsourcing in lieu of internal R&D expenditure, which may increase firm revenues. Exploitative aspects of IT Outsourcing arise from the fact that IT vendors develop economies of scale which help them to have lower marginal costs and outsourcing firms leverage this to reduce their operational costs as well as IT investment risk. On the other hand, explorative aspects of IT Outsourcing can be seen from the perspective of IT investments, which can help in freeing-up the IT resources which are extensively used in disparate business processes in a firm including R&D and can help in increasing the innovation output [46, 47]. Simultaneously, the IT vendors have developed economies of scope and specialization which outsourcing firms can leverage to innovate. Similarly, the firm-specific factor of relative R&D as compared to industry average serves as an indicator firm's internal innovation capability within its industry and can also moderate this strategic choice of outsourcing for growth or cost-saving.

We posit that relative R&D expenditure negatively moderates the effect of IT Outsourcing on firm revenues, i.e., less innovative firms use IT Outsourcing as a substitute for internal R&D expenditure to increase revenues. On the cost-side, relative R&D expenditure positively moderates the effect of IT Outsourcing on firm costs, i.e., more innovative firms use IT Outsourcing as a compliment for internal R&D expenditure to decrease costs.

> *Hypothesis 2A. The relationship between IT Outsourcing and firm costs is positively moderate by relative R&D expenditure of the firm, i.e., a simultaneous high degree of relative R&D expenditure and IT Outsourcing will be associated with lower costs.*
>
> *Hypothesis 2B. The relationship between IT Outsourcing and firm revenues is negatively moderated by relative R&D expenditure of the firm, i.e., a simultaneous low degree of relative R&D expenditure and high degree of IT Outsourcing will be associated with higher revenues.*

Firms are embedded into their environment and the respective strategic choices will be determined and/or affected by these environmental conditions. Digital strategies such as investments in general information technology and IT Outsourcing are major elements of overall business strategy, sometimes allowing firms to differentiate from competitors and other times creating demands to conform with competitive norms (see, for instance, [11, 44–46, 48]). Industry concentration acts as a primary environmental condition for any firm and can significantly affect the organizational level strategic choices such as that of IT Outsourcing. In case of less concentrated industries, firms tend to outsource more in order to increase revenues, while in highly concentrated industries, firms tend to outsource in order to reduce cost. Thus, it can be posited that the Industry concentration acts a contextual factor for the firm's choice of respective ambidextrous aspect of IT Outsourcing:

> *Hypothesis 3A. The relationship between IT Outsourcing and firm costs is positively moderated by Industry concentration, i.e., a simultaneous high degree of Industry concentration and high degree of IT Outsourcing will be associated with lower costs.*
>
> *Hypothesis 3B. The relationship between IT Outsourcing and firm revenues is negatively moderated by Industry concentration, i.e., a simultaneous low degree of Industry concentration and high degree of IT Outsourcing will be associated with higher revenues.*

3 Research Design

We designed an empirical study using three different secondary data sources, namely IT investment and IT Outsourcing data from Information Week, IT Outsourcing Contract level data from Services Contracts Database and firm-level financial data from COMPUSTAT. Information Week, a leading US magazine, collects survey data which has been used in previous studies and has been considered a reliable source of information (e.g., [12, 48]). It is important to note that InformationWeek data do not contain information on IT Outsourcing contracts or deals, rather include information on overall IT expenditure and associated components such as hardware, software, IT labor, IT Outsourcing, etc. Thus, to compliment this with contract level data, we used IDC's (a premier global market intelligence firm complies services deal activity of major firms) Service Contracts Database, which has been used extensively in studying IT Outsourcing (see [5, 49]).

Furthermore, we matched this data with financial data on publicly traded firm from WRDS' COMPUSTAT database. This resulted in an unbalanced panel dataset from 1999 to 2006 with 184 US firms with 523 observations. The mean revenue during our sample period was $34.16 billion with a minimum of $69.2 million and maximum of $207.35 billion, while COGS (Cost of Goods Sold) has a mean of $22.64 billion with a range of $32 million to $157.8 billion. Out of 184, 104 firms are from manufacturing, 32 from services, 29 from transportation & public utilities, 29 from wholesale and retail trade, 30 from finance, insurance, & real estate industry. The corresponding market value of the firms has a mean of $46.8 billion with minimum of $15 million and maximum of $467.1 billion. Within the sample, mean IT contract length is 56 months (4.6 years) with minimum of 3 months and maximum of 156 months (13 years), the market share of the focal firms within a given industry (two digit SIC code) ranges from 0.2 % to 99 % with mean market share of 25.72 %. Note that there are only three companies with market share over 90 %, namely, United Technologies Corporation (UTC), Lockheed Martin Corporation (LMC) and Honeywell International Inc. Since, we consider only large publicly listed firms, very large market share values could be confounded due to elimination of private firms, but still is a commensurate proxy.

We take natural logarithm of Revenues (ln_Rev) as one of our dependent variables as the distribution of revenues in our sample is right-skewed. Similarly, we calculate total operating expenses (Op_Exp) by subtracting COGS and operating income from revenues; and then take the natural log of operating expenses (ln_Op_Exp) to rectify the right-skewness and use it as our second dependent variable. Since we know that the gains of any kind from IT Outsourcing has a delayed effect on the firm-level measures, we also used one-year leads (ln_Rev_Lead1, ln_Op_Exp_Lead1) as our dependent variables for both revenues and operational expenses, along with natural logs respectively. IT Outsourcing is measured as the sum of the contract value of all the IT Outsourcing contracts signed by the focal firm in a given year, but since the distribution of IT Outsourcing also right-skewed, we took a natural log of IT Outsourcing (ln_IT_Outsourcing). Research and Development (R&D) expenditure is captured as the actual value invested in R&D by the firm in a given year and we used this to calculate relative R&D (Rel_RnD) as the R&D expenditure of the focal firm divided by the industry average R&D for the given year (within one digit SIC code). As we know that in a given industry some firms invest a lot in R&D while others do not in a commensurate manner, leading to very high values for some firms compared to others. For instance, Microsoft, Sun Microsystems, Pfizer, Lucent Technologies are some of these firms for which relative R&D is quite high, thus, we have two measures – one truncate measure with relative R&D expenditure values below 50 and other one with all the values for robustness checks (but the main analysis reports results with only the first measure). This is the first firm-level moderator. Next, we calculated the Industry concentration (Ind_Concentr), an industry-level moderator, as the ratio of the sum of revenues of largest four firms divided by the total revenues of the industry for a given year within one digit SIC code. This reflects the concentration of revenues with very few firms (i.e., 4) in a given industry.

In terms of controls, we have considered all plausible confounding factors that were pragmatic within the purview of the data availability and research design. Since we are considering the dependent variables of revenues and operational expenses with similar set of predictors, SUR (Seemingly Unrelated Regression) estimation seem to have best methodological fit. We will first explain the common and revenue specific controls and then highlight the operational expenses related controls. Now, as firms can use their dominating position in the market to appropriate the gains from innovation disproportionately, we first control for Market share (MktShr), i.e., the ratio of firm revenues with total industry revenues (within one digit SIC_Code). As per the prior research on IT Outsourcing, IT Capital of the firm is key factor influencing the decision to outsource [12]. We measure and control for IT Capital (IT_Cap) of the firm as the IT Capital reported by the firm's top management as percentage of revenues, multiplied by the firm revenues and then taken natural log in order to counter for right-skewness and to fit the functional form within our econometric model. Furthermore, IT Outsourcing seem to affect the market value such that the market value reflects some unmeasured or unrecorded assets of the company, which is measured using Tobin's Q (Tobin's Q) as its high values encourage companies to invest more in capital because they are "worth" more than the price they paid for them. Market Value of the firm$_i$

$$Tobin's Q_i = \frac{Market\ Value\ of\ the\ firm_i}{Replacement\ Cost\ of\ Capital_i} \qquad (1)$$

Where, the Market Value (MktVal) of the firm i is calculated as product of common shares outstanding and price per share (at the closing day of the fiscal year end). We also control for the size heterogeneity of the firms by using number of full-time employees (Employees) as the proxy.

In case of operational expenses, we control for firm's PPE (Plant, Property and Equipment), firm's Assets and average industry SG&A (Selling, General and Administrative) expenses apart from IT Capital and size of the firms, similar to the revenue model. A given firm's PPE and Assets is reflection of inherent costs due to specific nature of the business and can add towards the firm's overall operational expenses. Also, the Average Industry SG&A, i.e., the average of the SG&A expenses of a given industry for a given year (within one digit SIC code), is an indicator of industry specific characteristic and need to be controlled for.

From the correlation analysis, we found that the log of IT Outsourcing contract value is positively correlated with log of one-year lead Revenues (0.57, p<0.01) as well as one-year lead Operational expenses (0.57, p<0.01). This signifies that there exist a positive relationship between IT Outsourcing and revenues as well as costs, which is in contradiction to the prior prescriptions of the literature, especially the view of IT Outsourcing as cost-based strategy. But, such correlation does not tell the complete story and needs further investigation by controlling for above mentioned factors while analyzing such relationships. Furthermore, since we know that our both dependent variables are also highly correlated and have similar (not same) set of predictors, there could be a correlation between the errors of the two models. Thus, we cannot conclude about the effects of IT Outsourcing on firm level performance outcomes from these correlations and further analyzed in the following sections.

4 Results

To examine whether firms use IT Outsourcing to increase revenues or decrease costs, we use SUR model specification such that for Firm$_i$ in Industry$_j$ for Year$_t$,

$$ln\_Sales\_Lead1_{it} = \beta_1 ln\_IT\_Outsrc_{it} + \beta_2 Rel\_RnD_{it} + \beta_3 Ind\_Concentr_{jt} + \beta_4 MktShr_{it} + \beta_5 IT\_Cap_{it} + \beta_6 Tobin'sQ_{it} + \beta_7 MktVal_{it} + \beta_8 Employees_{it} + \varepsilon_{i1} \quad (2)$$

$$ln\_Op\_Exp\_Lead1_{it} = \beta_1 ln\_IT\_Outsrc_{it} + \beta_2 Rel\_RnD_{it} + \beta_3 Ind\_Concentr_{jt} + \beta_4 Avg\_Ind\_SGnA_{jt} + \beta_5 IT\_Cap_{it} + \beta_6 PPE_{it} + \beta_7 Assets_{it} + \beta_8 Employees_{it} + \varepsilon_{i2} \quad (3)$$

And $(\varepsilon_{i1}, \varepsilon_{i2}) \in G$

Where, G is a subset of the cartesian product $\varepsilon_{i1} \times \varepsilon_{i2}$.

Table 1. Seemingly unrelated regression estimation results[a,b]

	Model1	Model2	Model3	Model4
Eq1:DV = ln_Sales_Lead1				
ln_IT_Outsrc	0.06***	0.25***	0.11***	0.00
Ind_Concentr	0.23	3.35***		3.87***
Rel_R&D	0.00		0.09**	0.09**
Tobins_Q	−0.08***	−0.05***	−0.08***	−0.07***
MktShr	0.48**	0.84***	0.55***	0.64***
ln_IT_Cap	0.50***	0.52***	0.47***	0.47***
Employees	0.00***	0.00***	0.00***	0.00***
c.ln_IT_Outsrc#c. Ind_Concentr		−0.22***		−0.23***
c.ln_IT_Outsrc#c. Rel_R&D			−0.00**	−0.004**
_cons	2.36***	−0.15	2.02***	−1.03
Eq2: DV = ln_Op_Exp_Lead1				
ln_IT_Outsrc	0.02	0.20***	0.07***	0.00
Rel_R&D	0.02***		0.11***	0.11***
ln_IT_Cap	0.38***	0.57***	0.35***	0.37***
PPE	0.00***	0	0.00***	0.00*
Avg_Ind_SGnA	0.00***	0.00***	0.00***	0.00***
Assests	−0.00***	0	−0.00***	−0.00***

(Continued)

Table 1. (*Continued*)

	Model1	Model2	Model3	Model4
Employees	0.00***	0.00***	0.00***	0.00***
Ind_Concentr		2.74**		2.13
c.ln_IT_Outsrc#c.Ind_Concentr		−0.19***		−0.16**
c.ln_IT_Outsrc#c.Rel_R&D			−0.00***	−0.01***
_cons	3.05***	−1.63*	2.58***	0.52
R2 (Eq1)/ R2(Eq2)	0.8333/ 0.8907	0.8098/ 0.8435	0.8389/ 0.8970	0.8474/ 0.8987
χ2 (Eq1)/ χ2(Eq2)	1167.8/ 1905.33	1600.6/ 2050.7	1198.7/ 2031.99	1249.46/ 2074.55
Residual Correlation	0.6611	0.4832	0.6505	0.6803
Breusch-Pagan test	97.013	87.083	93.943	102.734

[a]All models include industry dummies with SIC one digit code
[b]* $p < .10$; **$p < .05$; *** $p < .01$
[c]All the chi-square tests and Beusch-Pagan tests are significant at p<0.01

Since in our linear system of equations, our dependent variables seem to be correlated and there are some common predictors, it may be the case of contemporaneous cross-equation error correlation (i.e. the error terms in the regression equations are correlated) and thus, we use SUR regression model to take these correlation into account. It is important to note that it is an empirical question, i.e., whether we find any correlation in the error terms of the two equations or not. SUR is implemented using the Feasible Generalized Least Squares (FGLS) method which is a two-step process such that in the first step an OLS (Ordinary Least Squares) estimator is used to predict the residuals from the first part of equation and then use Generalized Least Squares (GLS) estimator using a variance matrix which takes these predicted residuals into account.

From Table 1, we can see that in the base model, Model 1 (column 2), the coefficient for ln_IT_Outsourcing is positive (0.06) and significant (p<0.01) for Revenues, but non-significant for Operational expenses for the next year. This can be interpreted as IT Outsourcing increases revenues (with a lag), but doesn't affect the costs at the firm level. This gives support to our hypothesis H1B and fail to find support for H1A.

Analyzing this relationship further, we included the interaction between relative R&D expenditure (Rel_R&D) and IT Outsourcing (ln_IT_Outsourcing) in both the above specified equations as:

$$ln\_Sales\_Lead1_{it} = \beta_1 ln\_IT\_Outsrc_{it} + \beta_2 Rel\_RnD_{it} + \beta_3 Ind\_Concentr_{jt} + \beta_4 MktShr_{it} + \beta_5 IT\_Cap_{it} + \beta_6 Tobin'sQ_{it} + \beta_7 MktVal_{it} + \beta_8 Employees_{it} + \beta_9 ln\_IT\_Outsrc_{it} X Rel\_RnD_{it} + \varepsilon_{i1} \quad (4)$$

$$\begin{aligned}ln\_Op\_Exp\_Lead1_{it} = &\beta_1 ln\_IT\_Outsrc_{it} + \beta_2 Rel\_RnD_{it} + \beta_3 Ind\_Concentr_{jt} + \\&\beta_4 Avg\_Ind\_SGnA_{jt} + \beta_5 IT\_Cap_{it} + \beta_6 PPE_{it} + \beta_7 Assets_{it} + \beta_8 Employees_{it} + \\&\beta_9 ln\_IT\_Outsrc_{it} XRel\_RnD_{it} + \varepsilon_{i2}\end{aligned} \quad (5)$$

We found that relative R&D expenditure has direct positive effect on firm revenues (0.09, p<0.05), but negatively (−0.004, p<0.05) [Table 1, column 4] moderates the relationship between IT Outsourcing and firm revenues, which can mean that relative R&D expenditure and IT Outsourcing are used by firms as substitutes. This corroborates with our hypothesis H2A. But in order to further understand this moderation effect, we will study the conditional effect plots in later sections. Also, the effect of relative R&D expenditure is positive for operational expenses (0.11, p<0.01), but it positively (−0.005, p<0.01) [Table 1, column 4] moderates the effect of IT Outsourcing on operational expenses (by decreasing them). This can substantiate our hypothesis H2A as the interaction term is negative and it can be argued that the relative R&D expenditure and IT Outsourcing are complements in reducing costs. But we need further analysis using conditional effect plots.

In case of industry-level moderator of Industry concentration (Ind_Concentr), we found a positive and significant (3.35, p<0.01) [Table 1, column 3] direct effect on revenues, but it negatively (−0.223, p<0.01) [Table 1, column 3] moderates the effect of IT Outsourcing on firm revenues. This helps in finding support for our hypothesis H3B, i.e., simultaneous low degree of Industry concentration and high degree of IT Outsourcing will be associated with higher revenues. Similarly, a positive and significant (2.74, p<0.05) [Table 1, column 3] direct effect was found in case of operational expenses. Again, Industry concentration positively moderated the relationship between IT Outsourcing and operational expenses of the firm, as the interaction term was found to be negative (−0.19, p<0.01) [Table 1, column 3]. This lends support to our hypothesis H3A which states that simultaneous high degree of Industry concentration and high degree of IT Outsourcing will be associated with lower costs.

To examine how firms use IT Outsourcing at different levels of innovativeness as firm-level decision to increase revenues and/or reduce costs, we use conditional effect plots and understand the various scenarios for different choices of the firms. From Fig. 1, we can observe that at the lower levels of relative R&D expenditure, high degree of IT Outsourcing increases revenues (p<0.001) [Fig. 1] significantly (as compared to low degree of IT Outsourcing). This means when the internal innovativeness of the given firm is low, the firms do IT Outsourcing as a substitute to increase the firm revenues in the next year. This phenomenon seem to be reversed in case of high levels of relative R&D expenditure. But we found that the 95 % confidence interval of predicted revenues for low and high degree of IT Outsourcing overlap, thus, we fail to conclude the reversed effect in case of high relative R&D. We can also interpret this phenomenon as part of contextual ambidexterity at the organizational level, such that firms tend to use IT Outsourcing as a substitute for lack of internal innovativeness utilizing the economies of scope and specialization of IT vendors, while when the focal firm already has high internal innovation capabilities, then firms don't need IT Outsourcing for increasing revenues.

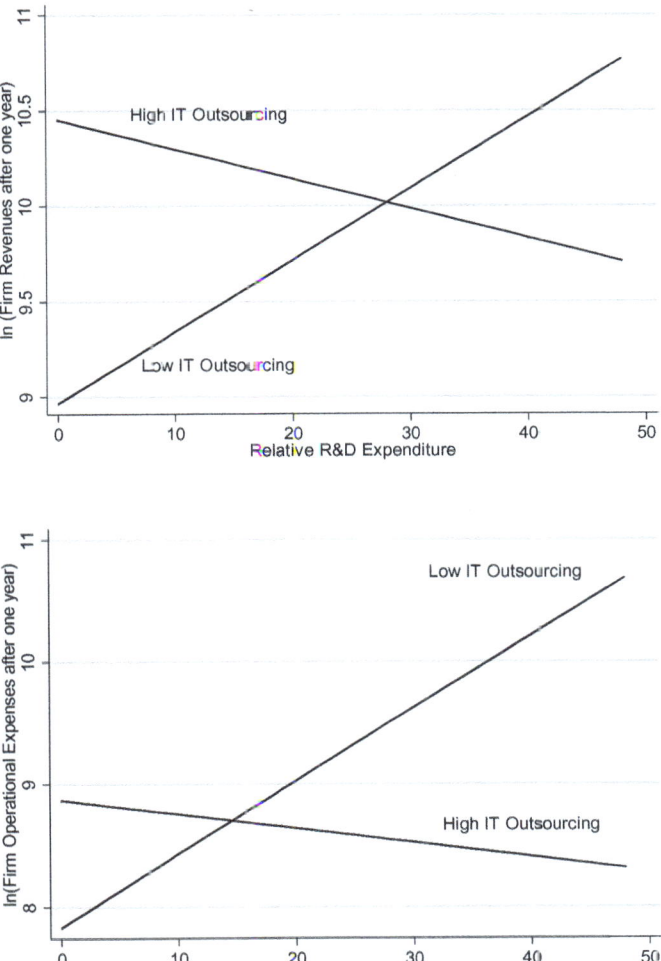

Fig. 1. Conditional Effects plot for High-Low IT Outsourcing with Relative R&D Expenditure

On the other hand, firms tend to use IT Outsourcing to reduce operational expenses when the relative R&D expenditure is high, i.e., firms with high level of internal innovation capability, incurs higher amounts of costs and in order to reduce them, firms leverage the economies of scale of IT vendors. We can observe from Fig. 1 that operational expenses are significantly lower at high degrees of IT Outsourcing as compared to low Outsourcing, when relative R&D expenditure is high. While in case of low R&D expenditure the high degree of IT Outsourcing seem to be incurring higher costs, which can be attributed to the fact that when internal innovation capability is low, firms tend to outsource more in order to increase revenues, but this brings additional costs associated with innovation and are reflected in high operational expenses.

Industry concentration (or Competitiveness) and IT Outsourcing: While considering the industry level moderators such as Industry concentration, we found that firms exhibit contextual ambidexterity by factoring this industry level information in their organizational decisions and use IT Outsourcing accordingly. From Fig. 2, we observe that at low degree of Industry concentration, the difference between revenues from high outsourcing and low outsourcing is positive and significant. This means that firms choose to outsource more in highly competitive environments in order to increase revenues. While as the industries become more concentrated (or less competitive), the returns from high levels of IT Outsourcing diminish. In highly competitive industries,

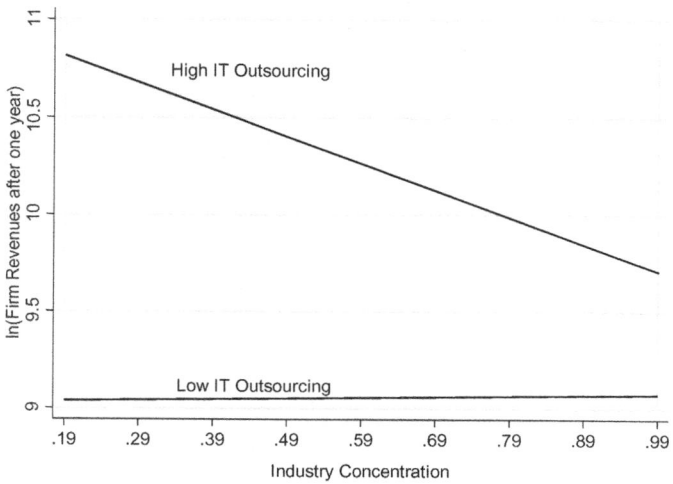

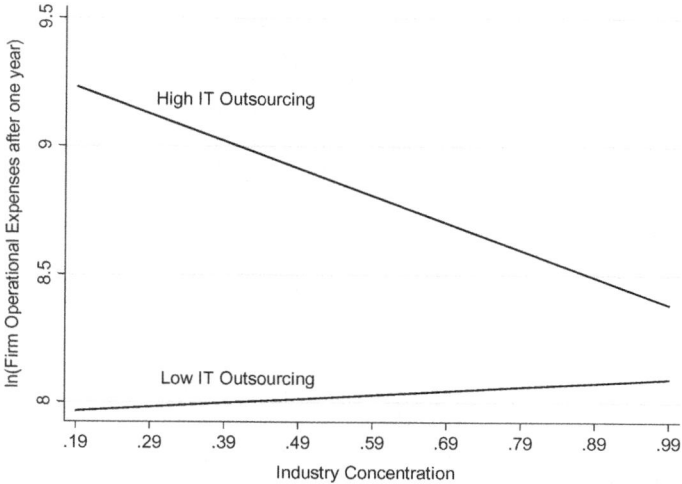

Fig. 2. Conditional Effects plot for High-Low IT Outsourcing with Industry concentration

IT Outsourcing has little impact on cost reduction, as the IT Outsourcing is possibly going largely towards accessing innovation to separate the firm from the competition. While in monopolistic settings, when IT Outsourcing is a choice and not a need, it is possibly directed towards cost reduction activities. But as we know that IT Outsourcing has some associated costs with it and increasing the level of Outsourcing brings additional costs, and these costs are higher for more competitive environments as the cost-based returns from IT Outsourcing are already appropriated. Thus, increasing IT Outsourcing tend to increase costs as the cost reduction arising from economy of scale (or scope) have already been appropriated due to high competition and the Outsourcing associated costs such as contractual costs, administrative and enforcement costs, offsite management costs, etc. increase along with rising level of Outsourcing. We found that difference in operational expenses at different levels of IT Outsourcing tend to be positive and significant for low levels of Industry concentration, while the difference diminishes away when industry become more concentrated.

5 Robustness Checks

As part of robustness check, we used two year leads of revenue and operational expenses for a given firm (apart from one year leads used in the main analysis) and found the results are consistent. Also, we used the complete relative R&D expenditure (not truncated at 50) and found the findings are still consistent. Furthermore, we used average industry IT Outsourcing value as an instrument for firm-level IT Outsourcing in order to check if the results are robust after considering the endogeneity issues with our dependent variable of IT Outsourcing. Thus, we generated an industry-level variable such that for a given $Firm_i$ in the $Industry_j$,

$$Avg\_Ind\_IT\_Out_j = \frac{Total\ IT\ Outsourcing\ Value\ for\ all\ the\ firms\ in\ the\ industry_j}{Number\ of\ firms\ in\ the\ industry_j} \quad (6)$$

We found that results (Table 2) remain consistent and significant for relative R&D expenditure, for both revenues (column 2) and operational expenses (column 3). While

Table 2. Robustness Check – instrumented regression models[a]

	ln_Sales_Lead1	ln_Op_Exp_Lead1	ln_Sales_Lead1	ln_Op_Exp_Lead1
ln_IT_Outsrc	0.09***	0.07***	0.21***	0.07
Rel_R&D	0.10***	0.13***		
ln_IT_Outsrc X Rel_R&D	−0.00***	−0.01***		
Ind_Concentr			2.51**	0.58
ln_IT_Outsrc X Ind_Concentr			−0.18***	−0.05
Tobins_Q	−0.05**		−0.02	

(Continued)

Table 2. (Continued)

	ln_Sales_Lead1	ln_Op_Exp_Lead1	ln_Sales_Lead1	ln_Op_Exp_Lead1
MktShr	0.28*		0.89***	
ln_IT_Cap	0.32***	0.28***	0.50***	0.50***
Employees	0.01***	0.00**	0.00***	0.00
Avg_Ind_SGnA		0.00***		0.00***
PPE		0.00***		0.00
Assests		-0.00*		0
_cons	3.70***	3.22***	0.85	1.14
N	186	168	339	288
R2	0.9041	0.9352	0.8222	0.8513
Sargan's Test	0.370	0.054	0.105	2.738*

[a]Using IVREG2 command in STATA 13, we generated the regression model such that ln_IT_Outsourcing is instrumented by ln_Avg_Ind_IT_Out (Average industry IT Outsourcing) and we have controlled for industry at SIC digit one level in all the models.
[b]* $p < .10$; ** $p < .05$; *** $p < .01$

in case of moderation effects of *Industry concentration*, the results remain consistent and significant for firm revenues (column 4), but the coefficient of interaction term is not significant in case of operational expenses (column 5), although it has the same direction as found previously.

6 Discussion and Conclusion

Our goal in this research was to analyze and understand why firms outsource while considering different confounding factors and contingencies to understand this organization-level strategy decision. We found that a 10 % increase in the level of IT Outsourcing leads to 6.6 % increase in next year revenues for a given firm (on average), while there was no impact on firm-level operational expenses at first glance. This lends support to the line of research which posits that IT Outsourcing is a growth strategy [6–8, 10, 11, 48], but we failed to find support initially for cost-reduction argument. Nevertheless, on further analyzing this relationship with two-moderators – firm-level moderator of relative R&D expenditure and industry-level moderator of industry concentration, we found that firms tend to use IT Outsourcing as a strategic tool to exhibit contextual ambidexterity. Depending on the level of internal capabilities such as innovation capability reflected in the R&D capability [50, 51] which is an apparent exploration organization strategy, firms use IT Outsourcing to achieve organizational ambidexterity by balancing or substituting the internal innovation capability with IT Outsourcing, which seem to be a exploitative strategy at first, but can also have explorative effects. Specifically, firms lacking internal R&D capabilities tend to use IT Outsourcing as a substitute for internal R&D utilizing the economies of scope and specialization of IT vendors, while when the focal firm already has high internal R&D capabilities, then firms do not deploy IT Outsourcing for increasing revenues. It is likely that firms with higher spending in R&D aim to reduce operating costs through IT Outsourcing. However, the firms with lower R&D spend are likely to invest in IT Outsourcing as a more immediate access to innovation but at the cost of increasing operating expenses. This may be considered the market price of innovation.

While considering industry-level factors, we found that firms choose to outsource more in highly competitive environments in order to increase revenues, but as the industries become more concentrated (or less competitive), the returns from high levels of IT Outsourcing diminish. Moreover, the difference in operational expenses at high and low levels of IT Outsourcing tend to be positive and significant for low levels of Industry concentration, while the difference diminishes away when industry become more concentrated. Note that this higher operational expenses at high levels of IT Outsourcing and low degree of Industry concentration, can be attributed to the fact that firms tend to leverage the exploitative nature of IT Outsourcing in order to appropriate higher revenues, but this decision also brings costs associated with investing in innovation. While in the case of highly concentrated industries, firms have enough market opportunities to appropriate revenues gains, and thus, the firms tend to leverage exploitative nature of IT Outsourcing to reduce costs, but due to very low differential bargaining power in outsourcing contracts (among industry peers), the cost differentials are minimum. Here, we again observe that firms are using IT Outsourcing as a mechanism to counter the different industry dynamics such that the decision of outsourcing seem to be contingent on the level of competition in a given industry. This contextualized behavior of firms also reflects the contextual ambidexterity phenomenon from a contingency perspective. Our results extend ambidexterity literature [26, 32] in that we see an organizational level manifestation of this ambidexterity in the choice of a strategic investment such as that in IT Outsourcing.

Furthermore, our results not only aim to resolve the long standing debate in IS literature on decision to outsource IT, but also provide important implications for the two parties – Outsourcing firms and IT vendors.

Implications for IS literature: This research contributes to the rich literature on IT Outsourcing by reconciling the two different perspectives on decision to outsource, i.e., growth perspective and cost-reduction argument. While literature had tended to paint IT Outsourcing with a broad brush we show a multi-dimensional role of IT Outsourcing in both increasing revenues and decreasing costs. The direct effect of IT Outsourcing is shown to be primarily on increasing revenues rather than decreasing costs. However, deeper examination suggests that the impact is affected by the organizational and environmental factors such as the levels of relative internal innovation capability and the degree of competition. Consequently, future research would benefit from this nuanced treatment of IT Outsourcing in the study of its impact on firm performance.

Our findings suggest a close relationship between IT Outsourcing and internal R&D capability. Thus firms may substitute lack of internal R&D capability by high degree of IT Outsourcing. It further provides support that organizations can gain agility by outsourcing their innovation and lowering their investment risk [52].

Implications for Outsourcing Firms: Counter to conventional understanding within practice that outsourcing is a dominant strategy to reduce cost, our research sheds light on the possibility for firms to access innovation through outsourcing. Further, we offer insights on how firms might engage in IT Outsourcing under different environmental conditions to realize different goals. Substituting internal innovation capability by IT Outsourcing can provide agility, speed, lower costs and better returns with lower investment risk contingent on the available innovation capability and industry competition.

Implications for IT vendors: One key insight offered by our findings is that IT vendors can better target customers with IT Outsourcing that is aimed to increase growth or reduce cost depending on the industry and firm level constraints. The internal R&D expenditure and industry concentration values are easily accessible metrics that a vendor may use to better position their service offering.

Limitations & Future Research: Our study focused on the organizational objectives for outsourcing and associated contingencies, but we have not differentiated between different types of services outsourced (although in our sample, a large number of the IT Outsourcing contracts are related to back-end services as well as innovation activities). This is a question for future research and out of the scope of this discourse. We found two different mechanisms for the effect of IT Outsourcing on firm performance, but it is not an exhaustive list and future scholars can find more underlying mechanisms as well as the combined effects of such mechanisms. Some of such factors are industry dynamism, capital intensity, etc. and need further investigation. It will also be interesting to study the organizational skill-set (of employees) of both outsourcing firms and IT vendors and to see how difference in skills (or type of skills) affect the relationship between IT Outsourcing and firm performance. We used two-year lags for our dependent variables and instrumented average industry IT Outsourcing to counter endogeneity, but similar to other empirical studies using secondary data, our study does not claim causality, rather observational effects.

References

1. Loh, L., Venkatraman, N.: Determinants of information technology outsourcing: a cross-sectional analysis. J. Manag. Inf. Syst. **9**(1), 7–24 (1992)
2. Poppo, L., Zenger, T.: Testing alternative theories of the firm: transaction cost, knowledge-based, and measurement explanations for make-or-buy decisions in information services. Strateg. Manag. J. **19**, 853–877 (1998)
3. Ang, S., Straub, D.: Production and transaction economies and IS outsourcing: a study of the US banking industry. MIS Q. **22**(4), 535–552 (1998)
4. Loh, L., Venkatraman, N.: Diffusion of information technology outsourcing: influence sources and the Kodak effect. Inf. Syst. Res. **3**(4), 334–358 (1992)
5. Levina, N., Ross, J.: From the vendor's perspective: exploring the value proposition in information technology outsourcing. MIS Q. **27**, 331–364 (2003)
6. Ang, S., Cummings, L.: Strategic response to institutional influences on information systems outsourcing. Organ. Sci. **8**, 235–256 (1997)
7. Eluinn, J.: Outsourcing innovation: the new engine of growth. MIT Sloan Manag. Rev. Manag. Rev. **41**, 13–28 (2000)

8. Sambamurthy, V., Zmud, R.: Research commentary: The organizing logic for an enterprise's IT activities in the digital era—A prognosis of practice and a call for research. Inf. Syst. Res. **11**(2), 105–114 (2000)
9. Bardhan, I., Whitaker, J., Mithas, S.: Information technology, production process outsourcing, and manufacturing plant performance. J. Manag. Inf. Syst. **23**, 13–40 (2006)
10. Mithas, S., Tafti, A., Mitchell, W.: How a firm's competitive environment and digital strategic posture influence digital business strategy. MIS Q. **37**(2), 511–536 (2013)
11. Mithas, S., Tafti, A., Bardhan, I., Goh, J.: Information technology and firm profitability: mechanisms and empirical evidence. MIS Q. **36**(1), 205–224 (2012)
12. Han, K., Mithas, S.: Information technology outsourcing and non-IT operating costs: An empirical investigation. MIS Q. **37**, 315–331 (2013)
13. Brynjolfsson, E., Schrage, M.: The new, faster face of innovation. Wall Str. J. (2009)
14. Gordon, S., Tarafdar, M.: The IT audit that boosts innovation. MIT Sloan Manag. Rev. **51**(4), 39–47 (2010)
15. Huang, P., Tafti, A., Mithas, S.: Knowledge contribution in online network of practice: The role of IT infrastructure, foreign direct investment and immigration. MIS Q **36**(1), 205–224 (2012)
16. Mol, M., Birkinshaw, J.: The sources of management innovation: When firms introduce new management practices. J. Bus. Res. **12**, 1269–1280 (2009)
17. Lev, B., Sougiannis, T.: The capitalization, amortization, and value-relevance of R&D. J. Account. Econ. **13**, 305–340 (1996)
18. Chan, L., Lakonishok, J., Sougiannis, T.: The stock market valuation of research and development expenditures. Natl. Bur. Econ. Res. No. w7223, (1999)
19. Eberhart, A., Maxwell, W., Siddique, A.: An examination of long-term abnormal stock returns and operating performance following R&D increases. J. Finance. **59**, 623–650 (2004)
20. Gibson, C., Birkinshaw, J.: Contextual determinants of organizational ambidexterity. Acad. Manag. J. **47**(2), 209–226 (2004)
21. Cao, Q., Gedajlovic, E., Zhang, H.: Unpacking organizational ambidexterity: Dimensions, contingencies, and synergistic effects. Organ. Sci. **12**, 54–74 (2009)
22. Weigelt, C., Sarkar, M.: Performance implications of outsourcing for technological innovations: managing the efficiency and adaptability trade-off. Strateg. Manag. J. **33**, 189–216 (2012)
23. Du, W., Pan, S.: Boundary spanning by design: toward aligning boundary-spanning capacity and strategy in it outsourcing. Eng. Manag. IEEE Trans. **60**(1), 59–76 (2013)
24. Rothaermel, F., Alexandre, M.: Ambidexterity in technology sourcing: The moderating role of absorptive capacity. Organ. Sci. **15**(4), 481–494 (2009)
25. O'Reilly, C., Tushman, M.: Ambidexterity as a dynamic capability: Resolving the innovator's dilemma. Res. Organ. Behav. **28**, 185–206 (2008)
26. Raisch, S., Birkinshaw, J.: Organizational ambidexterity: Balancing exploitation and exploration for sustained performance. Organ. Sci. **16**(5), 522–536 (2009)
27. Damanpour, F.: Organizational innovation: A meta-analysis of effects of determinants and moderators. Acad. Manag. J. **34**, 555–590 (1991)
28. Gibson, C., Birkinshaw, J.: The antecedents, consequences, and mediating role of organizational ambidexterity. Acad. Manag. J. **28**(2), 238–256 (2004)
29. He, Z., Wong, P.: Exploration vs. exploitation: An empirical test of the ambidexterity hypothesis. Organ. Sci. **15**(4), 481–494 (2004)
30. Gupta, A., Smith, K., Shalley, C.: The interplay between exploration and exploitation. Acad. Manag. J. **49**, 693–706 (2006)
31. Andriopoulos, C., Lewis, M.: Exploitation-exploration tensions and organizational ambidexterity: Managing paradoxes of innovation. Organ. Sci. **16**, 522–536 (2009)

32. Birkinshaw, J., Gibson, C.: Building ambidexterity into an organization. MIT Sloan Manag. Rev. **19**(4), 457–470 (2004)
33. March, J., Simon, H.: Organizations, 2nd edn. Blackwell, Malden (1993)
34. Tushman, M., Anderson, P., O'Reilly, C.: Technology cycles, innovation streams, and ambidextrous organizations: organization renewal through innovation streams and strategic change. Manag. Strateg. Inov. (1997)
35. Bradach, J.: Using the plural form in the management of restaurant chains. Adm. Sci. Q. **17**, 151–166 (1997)
36. Teece, D., Pisano, G., Shuen, A.: Dynamic capabilities and strategic management. Strateg. Manag. J. **5**(4), 300–310 (1997)
37. Winter, S.: Understanding dynamic capabilities. Strateg. Manag. J. **24**, 991–995 (2003)
38. Davern, M., Kauffman, R.: Discovering potential and realizing value from information technology investments. J. Manag. Inf. Syst. **16**(4), 121–143 (2000)
39. Quinn, J.: Strategic outsourcing: leveraging knowledge capabilities. MIT Sloan Manag. Rev. **40**, 95–106 (1999)
40. Quinn, J., Doorley, T., Paquette, P.: Technology in services: rethinking strategic focus. MIT Sloan Manag. Rev. **46**(3), 41–48 (2013)
41. Kohli, R., Devaraj, S., Ow, T.: Does information technology investment influence a firm's market value? A case of non-publicly traded healthcare firms. MIS Q. **16**, 335–353 (2012)
42. Kobelsky, K., Larosiliere, G., Plummer, E.: The impact of information technology on performance in the not-for-profit sector. Int. J. Account. Inf. Syst. **15**, 66–81 (2014)
43. Glass, A., Saggi, K.: Innovation and wage effects of international outsourcing. Eur. Econ. Rev. **112**(3), 552–580 (2001)
44. Kohli, R., Grover, V.: Business value of IT: An essay on expanding research directions to keep up with the times. J. Assoc. Inf. Syst. **9**(1), 23–39 (2008)
45. Mithas Jr., S., Metzner, H.L.: Are foreign IT workers cheaper? US visa policies and compensation of information technology professionals. Manage. Sci. **56**(5), 745–765 (2010)
46. Tafti, A., Mithas, S., Krishnan, M.: The effect of information technology-enabled flexibility on formation and market value of alliances. Manage. Sci. **59**(1), 207–225 (2013)
47. Kleis, L., Chwelos, P.: Information technology and intangible output: The impact of IT investment on innovation productivity. Inf. Syst. Res. **23**, 42–59 (2012)
48. Sambamurthy, V., Bharadwaj, A., Grover, V.: Shaping agility through digital options: Reconceptualizing the role of information technology in contemporary firms. MIS Q. **37**(2), 471–482 (2003)
49. Lacity, M., Willcocks, L.: An empirical investigation of information technology sourcing practices: lessons from experience. MIS Q. **22**, 363–408 (1998)
50. Acs, Z., Audretsch, D.: Innovation in large and small firms: an empirical analysis. Am. Econ. Rev. **78**, 678–690 (1988)
51. Greve, H.: A behavioral theory of R&D expenditures and innovations: Evidence from shipbuilding. Acad. Manag. J. **46**, 685–702 (2003)
52. Schilling, M., Steensma, H.: The use of modular organizational forms: an industry-level analysis. Acad. Manag. J. **15**, 203–223 (2001)

Sharing Knowledge in a Shared Services Center Context: An Explanatory Case Study of the Dialectics of Formal and Informal Practices

Dragos Vieru[1] and Pierre-Emmanuel Arduin[2]

[1] Distance Learning University of Québec (TÉLUQ), 5800 rue Saint-Denis, Montréal,
QC H2S 3L5, Canada
dragos.vieru@teluq.ca
[2] Université Paris-Dauphine, DRM UMR CNRS 7088, Place du Maréchal de Lattre de Tassigny,
75775 Paris Cedex 16, France
pierre-emmanuel.arduin@dauphine.fr

Abstract. This study focuses on how knowledge sharing across boundaries of merging entities during an information system (IS) implementation project in a shared services center (SSC) context affects the resulting system functionality. Although the literature stresses the growing adoption of the SSC as an outsourcing model, there is a lack of studies that examine shared services as a dynamic process of knowledge sharing across the organizational boundaries. We draw on a sociomaterial practice perspective and on the theory of workarounds to analyze an IS implementation project in a healthcare organization resulting from a merger of previously independent hospitals. The results suggest that new technology can be enacted in different ways as it links up with practices of different communities of users. We propose a multilevel process model that indicates at the end of the project a resulting mix of formal and informal (workarounds) practices that emerged from a dialectic process of resistance to, and negotiation of, the IS configuration during its implementation.

Keywords: Shared services center · Knowledge sharing · Sociomaterial practice · Perspective · Workarounds · Performativity · Sociomaterial assemblages

1 Introduction

Outsourcing arrangements are among the key mechanisms for organizing modern information technology (IT) activities [1, 2]. The literature on IT Outsourcing (ITO) shows that while the first decade of this century was characterized by the adoption of various outsourcing models [3], in the last five years, due to a continued pressure on profit margins linked to the aftermath of the 2007–2009 world recession and to a growing concern regarding data privacy and security, there has been a trend towards insourcing among private and public companies with a preference for the *Shared Services Center* (SSC) model [4, 5]. A report released in 2012 by HfS Research and PwC [6] finds that nine out of every ten firms use a shared services sourcing model.

An SSC is a rather independent organizational unit that provides services to various other organizational units. This sourcing model solves the problem that each business unit is engaged in tasks that do not belong to its core business. SSCs enable efficiency improvement by standardization of services [7]. The main reason for choosing an SSC model stems from the organizational need to manage costs and working capital and have visibility and control over the business processes. The promise of the SSC comes from a hybrid conception of traditional models aimed at capturing the benefits with centralized and decentralized arrangements. For the former, this should result in economies of scale, scope, and standardization. For the latter, this should result into a flexible and efficient alignment of IT with the needs of business [8, 9].

Shared services have received limited research attention [cf. 10, 11]. Prior literature has focused on the motivations and drivers for SSC and its implementation issues [4, 12]. However, little is known about the challenges associated with SSCs. For example, sharing services across the organizational boundaries can be viewed as a dynamic process in terms of knowledge sharing practices. Indeed, any form of outsourcing can be viewed as a knowledge-based activity [13] and efficiently sharing and integrating knowledge is a key challenge [14]. As explained by Davenport and Prusak [15], transmitting information is not sufficient to share knowledge, due to the possibility of meaning variance [16]. Therefore, sharing information is not sufficient to share knowledge. In the same way, within organizations sharing knowledge is a social process in which it is not enough to group together the different 'bits' but instead, collaborative initiatives are required [17, p. 13].

Research has shown that success of IT-based cross-boundary collaborative initiatives highly depend on effective knowledge sharing [18–20]. Although these studies were not conducted in an SSC context, they have shown that cross-boundary knowledge sharing develops collective competencies on building complex information systems [18, 21] and relies on team social bonds during common projects [19, 22, 23].

Several authors have proposed a number of knowledge processes and practices [24–26] for overcoming issues related to knowledge sharing in an ITO context. These practices aim at developing a shared understanding among the firms involved in the ITO, and the literature emphasizes the critical role of understanding the other ITO parties' context. However, this rational approach has limitations particularly when it does not consider internal dynamics. Indeed, employees in organizations may attempt to achieve formal goals through the establishment of formal coordination and role distribution. At the same time, the literature suggests that unplanned processes, such as improvisation or workarounds, emerge in order to fulfill formal objectives [27, 28]. Consequently, these two structures, formal and informal, need not be in conflict with each other. But, aren't they? Or are they complementary?

In the workplace, a workaround represents a goal-driven change to an existing work system in order to overcome a technical or an organizational constrain [29]. Several authors view workarounds as an understudied topic of research [30–32]. Recently Alter [29] proposed a theory of workarounds that includes different perspectives on situations in which actors will either enable or intentionally perform actions going against one or more routines, instructions, expectations, prerequisites, specifications or organizational regulations.

In this research we aim at understanding how knowledge sharing during an SSC-driven IS implementation project affects the resulting system-enabled practices. To do this, we draw on the concept of workarounds [29] and on a sociomaterial practice perspective [33, 34] to provide the theoretical foundation for a case study. The sociomaterial practice perspective, studies information technology as a "technology at work" [33], where the focus shifts from the impacts of technology to the dynamics that attach meaning to a newly implemented system. In this context, the material (the technology in an organizational context) and the social (the users or actors) continuously create and re-create one another while the actors socially negotiate their IT-enabled practices to share their knowledge. The actors share a common set of practices within a field of practice (e.g. business unit or department) in pursuing a joint interest [17] and knowledge is an integral part of these practices [18]. Through practice, actors formalize their membership in a certain field while differentiating themselves from actors in other fields. Because an SSC arrangement involves actors from different organizations, we posit that those organizations represent distinct fields of practice. Where practices are not shared, individuals have different assumptions and interpretations of the organizational context [20]. Thus, cross-boundary collaboration in an SSC context involves the negotiation of multiple domains of knowledge by actors who often understand only part of domains other than their own [35]. A sociomaterial practice perspective will help us better understand the dynamics of cross-boundary knowledge sharing by suggesting that actors engage in formal planned practices and informal workaround practices. This can be illustrated as a dialectical interplay during the process of developing and implementing a new Information System in the context of a shared services center.

We conduct a case study within a large university healthcare center (UHC) resulted from a merger and consisting of two adult sites and a children site. The case is the Laboratory Information System (LIS) implementation project, representing a collaborative effort between the members of a team comprised of site-based lab clinicians and technologists and ITServ (the shared service center) specialists.

The main contribution of this research is a process model explaining the dynamics of the formal (planned) and informal (workarounds) practices during the IS configuration and implementation. The model is based on one of the four types of mechanisms or "motors" that drive organizational change [36]. We are interested by the dialectic motor, which embodies a "pluralistic world of colliding events, forces, or contradictory values that compete with each other, for domination or control" [37, p. 517].

The rest of the paper is organized as follows. We begin by presenting the conceptual foundations of our study. We then describe our research methodology, followed by an analysis of the case data. A discussion of the findings and theoretical explanations follows. We conclude with implications for research and practice.

2 Theoretical Background

2.1 Knowledge Sharing Across Boundaries as a Multilevel Construct

Knowledge cannot be reduced to an object that may be computerized. As a resource giving a competitive advantage [22] and as an individual interpretation [38], knowledge needs practices involving individuals to be actually shared. This is particularly true across boundaries and for Newell et al. [19] "developing these independent Intranets [...] reinforce existing functional and geographical boundaries with what could be described as 'electronic fences'" (p. 94). Thus, developing and implementing a new IS in the context of a shared services center may reinforce such electronic fences, leading actors to engage in formal planned practices and informal workaround practices to share knowledge across boundaries.

Indeed, knowledge transfer is not reduced to the transmission of information and integrates sensegiving and sensereading processes as introduced by Polanyi [39]. Such processes lead someone to create his/her own knowledge from information (sensereading) or to create information from his/her own knowledge (sensegiving). Figure 1 illustrates these processes, i.e. the way we create information from our own knowledge, and vice-versa. Davenport and Prusak [15] stated that "transfer = transmission + absorption (and use)" (p. 101). Then transmitting information is not sufficient to share knowledge, due to the existence of individual interpretation in sensegiving and sensereading processes [39].

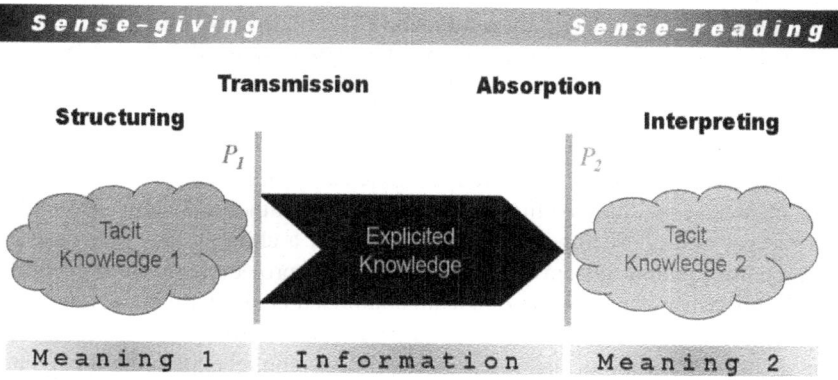

Fig. 1. Sensegiving and sensereading-based knowledge transfer (Source: [16])

Maznevski and Chudoba [40] consider that digital interactions often lead to incidents that may be resolved through face-to-face interactions. In the same way, for Walsham [41] increasing the number of digital communications will not improve human communication. That is notably the reason why we consider that sharing knowledge requires focusing on the way individuals and practices may be managed.

Sharing knowledge relies then on individuals and practices management. According to Stockdale and Standing [42, p. 1091], neglecting social activity leads to "meaningless conclusions". So we cannot be satisfied only with a technological approach and Jordan [43] insists when she stresses that knowledge is not only based on the group but is also tacit, embodied in individual minds: "we believe that there is yet another dimension that needs to be explored and that is the knowledge that is not only group-based but also tacit, implicit, embodied, and not articulated." (p. 18). It is on such another dimension, which is tacit and embodied in individual minds that rely formal and informal practices to share knowledge during the development and implementation of a new information system in the context of a shared services center.

Organizations are complex and multilevel phenomena [44] and therefore, IT-driven organizational change (such as the implementation and adoption of a new information system) is best framed as a process theory that explains how a sequence of events that unfolds through time leads to some outcome and provide explanations on how one micro-level event leads to and affects the ensuing one [36]. *Events*, the main elements of the sequence, can be defined as being instances of social action relating to the IT adoption process. The resulting view of the process tells a rich and comprehensive story of the events taking place within a specific situation by explaining how significant conditions interact, such as user perceptions and institutional factors, IT functionality, and the nature of knowledge (tacit or made-explicit knowledge) that needs to be shared during the IT implementation /adoption, how they collectively lead to future action, and what constrains them.

Important change processes in organizations, such as the introduction of a new IS that significantly changes organizational practices, can be explained over time by four different theories of change or "motors": life-cycle, teleology, dialectic and evolutionary [37]. Life-cycle and evolutionary are prescribed modes of organizational development and change because the process unfolds in a pre-established order; teleology and dialectic are constructive modes of change as the development is discontinuous and unpredictable. Moreover, life-cycle and teleology depict the development and change of a single organizational entity, while evolutionary and dialectic depict multiple organizational entities.

With regard to the implementation of a new IS, the multilevel process of IT-driven organizational change can be considered as being managed by a dialectic motor. At the individual level, during the configuration and implementation process each team member forms his own perceptions about the new technology and the relevant knowledge that needs to be shared in order to collaborate. These perceptions are continuously adjusted according to the individual's values, assumptions, goals and aspirations [45], while using a new technology. The individual-level decisional events influence further how the user community in the organization uses the new technology. Moreover, group-level events shape those individual-level events given the reciprocal influence between technology and its social and historical context [34, 46].

2.2 The Sociomaterial Practice Perspective (SPP)

The introduction of a new information system triggers a set of complex interactions. In particular, users' practical appropriation of a technology, which is strongly influenced by an organization's values and institutional characteristics, affects whether the "technology-in-use" becomes collaborative or not [47]. Thus, the characteristics of a specific technology do not fully determine its ability to entice individuals to use it. There is a dynamic process created by recursive interactions among the technology, human agency, and institutional norms and values. Emerging sociomaterial practice perspectives [33, 34, 48, 49] have accepted the challenge to focus on both social context and the materiality of the technological artifact. A central assumption of these approaches is that neither technology nor social agency can be constituted independently. Rather, social and material phenomena should be theorized as inextricably interrelated [50]. Sociomateriality represents a commitment to holding meaning and matter together in the conceptualization of technology [34].

Two different sociomaterial approaches have emerged in the literature. One perspective, called the *agential realism*, is normatively attentive to how technology defines the ways in which actors and meanings come to matter in sedimented organizational practices [33, 34]. It is based on the tenet that there is no social that is separate from material and therefore, there is only the sociomaterial. In explaining her view on sociomateriality, Orlikowski [33] adopts Barad's [51] argument that "we have tended to speak of humans and technology as mutually shaping each other, recognizing that each is changed by its interaction with the other, but maintaining, nevertheless, their ontological separation. In contrast, the notion of constitutive entanglement presumes that there are no independently existing entities with inherent characteristics" [51, p. 816].

The other perspective, the *critical realism*, is instrumentally concentrated on how users use technological affordances in situated organizational practices [48] and considers time as a determinant factor in the process of sociomaterial "becoming". The main conceptual difference between the two perspectives is that on one hand, critical realism's main tenet is that the social and the material are indeed separate entities that are put into association with one another, but they become inseparable only through human agency occurring over time. On the other hand, agential realism considers the "sociomaterial" as something that is already ingrained in individuals' perceptions of technology [49]. Each approach highlights important aspects of sociomaterial practice. While critical realism perspective highlights how sociomaterial practices have a trajectory, or a forward moving direction [49], the agential realism perspective focuses on how sociomaterial practices have boundaries, or are defined inside and outside [33, 34]. Both approaches are essential to forming a sociomaterial explanation of technology use. Orlikowski [34] rejects the so-called "ontology of separateness," arguing instead that no a priori assumption of separate agencies exists. Technologies are theorized as an apparatus of the ongoing process of interaction where boundaries, such as "subject" and "object," get created.

In this study we adopt an agential realism perspective to sociomateliaty because we are interested to understand how sociomaterial practices have *boundaries*. Boundaries show how practices have an inside and outside as technology defines what "counts" as a problem worthy of solving. A certain boundary formed by a sociomaterial practice can generate subjectivity for certain agents at the expense of others. For example, Barad [52] showed how high-resolution ultrasound images enact subjectivity for unborn fetuses by creating powerful visual representations. Rather than seeing a computerized image, people see the ultrasound image as a correspondence with the fetus in the womb. This taken-for-granted meaning is made by the technology which performs here as an apparatus, part of an already entangled practice that makes normative distinctions.

The agential realism perspective advances the concept of *sociomaterial assemblage* [51] which illustrates this constant agency shift between the material (IT) and the social (practices performed by the organizational members). In this view, an information system represents a sociomaterial assemblage that "emerges from practice and defines how to practice" [46, p.279]. In order to make sense of their practices, the sociomaterial assemblages reflect individuals' shared understandings within the organizational context [53]. Here we define *practices* as referring to coordinated activities of individuals and groups in doing their 'real work' as it is informed by a particular organizational or group context [46]. Through practice, agents formalize their membership to a certain field of practice and, at the same time differentiate themselves from agents from other fields. A *field of practice* may represent business units, departments or goal-driven groups, in which individuals who share practices are in pursuit of a joint interest [17]. In order to make sense of their practices, members of these fields develop sociomaterial arrangements that would reflect their shared understandings within the organizational context [53].

An information system is configured based on the belief that a collection of practices (i.e., industry-based best practices) can be extrapolated from general to particular settings. According to SPP, the dynamic relationship between organizational actors and ISs is reflected in practices and is referred to as *performativity*. This is a dialectic process of resistance and accommodation that produces unpredictable *reconfigurations* of the sociomaterial assemblage [46]. In the SPP view the intimate entanglement of technology and human elements are both made of matter. Hence, separation between humans and non-humans is radically challenged; their micro-entanglements need studying so as to understand the constitution of meaning. The SPP focuses attention on the flow of practice and by using the term *performativity* it provides a new vocabulary to describe how actors, technologies and meanings are dynamically brought into being through the continuous flow of practice.

In their analysis of an enterprise's information system implementation, Wagner et al. [46] clarify the concept of performativity by comparing the differences between sociomaterial assemblages of the same IS to the differences between the games of American football and rugby. The American football game, as a sociomaterial assemblage, emerged from the UK game of rugby, as those playing the game altered over time the sociomaterial assemblage that we call rugby. The former is quite different from the latter in terms of rules, equipment, physical skills required for the athletes, and the discourse that surrounds the practice of the game. Thus, from the standpoint of the SPP, professional-based communities tend to promote practices that have a local character based on an departmental or goal-based context despite their engagement in the same shared practices [54]. This is to stress the fact that there are always differences even when organizational members are supposedly engaging in the same practices.

Information systems are subjective and bear within them the traces of their social history. Individuals draw differently on their experience to transform and create different organizational patterns [33]. In this sense, an IS represents an adaptive assemblage of material and human components that assumes a practical meaning when it is used in a specific situated social and material context [45]. Best practice routines are not rooted in an IS, but rather are enacted by users that draw upon the software in their situated practices. Practices are emergent and often improvised during the complex process of adoption that precedes a working information system [27]. By engaging in improvisations or workarounds during organizational change, employees take advantage of existing technological resources in new ways to enact new practices [55].

2.3 The Workarounds Theory – an Informal Approach to Organizational Practice

A workaround represents a goal-driven change to an existing information system in order to overcome a technical or an organizational constraint [56]. Alter [29] proposes a theory of workarounds that includes different perspectives on situations in which actors will either enable or intentionally perform actions going against one or more routines, instructions, expectations, prerequisites, specifications or organizational regulations. This theory attempts to address two types of workarounds. The first takes place during a work process, when one or more actors face an obstacle that prevents the execution of an optimal performance during a work assignment. Barriers may be a result of anomalies, exceptions, lack of information, knowledge and skills on the part of the actor, or lack of technological capacities. The second represents a misalignment between objectives and incentives of actors, principles and stakeholders (e.g., lack of understanding, inadequate communication, confusion or inattention). The latter usually emerges during an IT-driven organizational change [cf., 27, 56].

The persistence of workarounds in a work environment is explained by the need for balance between bottom-up constraints (operationalization of the daily tasks) and top-down pressures (regulatory entities, physical constraints) [31]. There is a dichotomy between the negative perceptions and the need for workarounds that deepens in highly standardized work environments. Indeed, lower level management in these environments will often tolerate workarounds [32, 57]. Organizational challenges during the process of change are due to a combination of different perspectives on workarounds. These perspectives are comprised of the ability to operate despite the obstacles, adopt an interpretative flexibility, balance between personal, group, organizational and authorized interests and learning emerging changes.

Some researchers consider workarounds as violating and resisting managerial expectations [29] and business process activities [58]. The main assumption of this perspective is that employees tend to resist top-down pressure due to conflicting goals. Others suggest that workarounds represent a problem-solving strategy [59]. In this perspective, workarounds are presented as creative acts and sources of future improvements. Workarounds can be essential sources to analyze and learn policies, procedures and issues [60], or necessary for generic IS and as a part of the daily tasks [55]. Workarounds can also enable positive resistance by ensuring the continuity of an IT-based work task [61].

3 Methodology

We adopted an explanatory theory-building-from-cases approach [62]. Explanatory models seek to find relationships between an "observed state of a phenomenon and conditions that influence its development" [63, p. 428]. Given the research objective of this study, the first author spent a significant period of time at a purposely chosen company, focusing on the subjective descriptions of users' practices and knowledge sharing activities. The subjective and context-dependent nature of knowledge implies that interpretations of reality depend on individuals' thoughts and feelings and on other influences that may operate within the social context.

The selected organization was the University Health Centre (UHC – not its real name), a Canadian 1,400 beds-tertiary care teaching institution. The UHC is the result of a "merger of equals" of three independent teaching hospitals with over 1 million patient visits per year: two Adult hospitals (the Downtown and the Midtown) and the Pediatric Hospital. The merger, announced in 2001, had the goal of creating a mega-hospital to provide 21st-century health care by implementing a "best practices" business model for coordinating care. The shared services center, ITServ (fictive name), was founded as a non-profit corporation with 150 employees in 1992 by the Downtown and Midtown hospitals. Its role was to provide information technology services to the two hospitals. ITServ was considered as being a necessity to centrally manage the two hospitals that, albeit remained independent, were using the same platform (mainframe) for the Patient Care System and the same software (ADT – Admission-Discharge-Transfer). After the merger was announced, the Pediatric site IS department was taken over by ITServ and its director became one of the associated directors under the newly appointed CIO. The newly merged technology architectures triggered a major structural reorganization of the SSC in order to clearly define the boundaries between the skill-based services offered. User-centric authentication was implemented based on a "contextless" concept with a "no site"-bound user authentication. This approach imposed a unique organizational identity.

Although studies have shown that the participants in organizational processes do not forget key events in these processes (the interviews for this study were carried out during spring-fall 2010), it is possible that a participant-informant in a retrospective study may not have judged an event as important when it occurred and therefore may not remember it later [64]. To avoid these shortcomings, we obtained access to a number of emails that team members exchanged during the system implementation. We also followed Leonard-Barton's [64] recommendation to engage in informal conversations (e.g., at lunch or in hallways) with individuals who were members of the project teams because useful data may emerge from this type of interaction. Interviews were the main method of data collection. Informants were selected using a snowball sampling procedure. We interviewed key stakeholders, in particular project development and implementation committee members (i.e., department managers, ITServ professionals, project managers, and clinicians) who had participated in the ISD project. The interviewees were significant as agents, since they influenced the knowledge sharing process due to their roles, status, power and experience. Fifteen interviews were conducted on site, and lasted between 45 to 90 min. We interviewed five lab physicians, three lab technologists, three lab managers, three ITServ professionals and the ITServ project manager.

The interview protocol combined three interview strategies [65]. Each interview started with an *informal conversational strategy* in which questions surfaced from the context and usually were tailored to each individual. This approach was followed midway through the interview by a *guide strategy* with a standard format that clearly spelled out the topics and issues that needed to be covered. The interviews ended with a *standardized open-ended interview* in which respondents answered the same basic questions in the same order. This last part was necessary to get systematic data, thus increasing comparability of responses that allowed cross-case comparisons [66]. The interviews were recorded and transcribed. In a few instances, when clarifications were required, follow-up questions were asked via phone or email.

Interview questions focused on understanding, from the participant's standpoint, the history of the IS implementation project's collaboration practices, differences in practices, claims of relevant knowledge, and differences in IS's functionality between the initial and the go-live phases of the project. Data collection was terminated when the interviews revealed no new information. The data were triangulated using archival sources, including project documentation, organization documents (management strategy documentation, communication plans, and emails). We used the case narrative for the data analysis. The coding process involved the creation of a list of categories and codes prior to the interviews.

Most of the coding categories were based on the three theoretical constructs introduced in the previous section on the sociomateriality practice perspective: *practice*, *performativity*, and *reconfiguration*. The interview transcripts were entered into a database, read carefully and relevant portions highlighted. The highlighted portions were then keyed into the database into a field called "evidence" as chunks of rich text. The interview data were analyzed in NVivo, in an iterative process by cycling between data and relevant literature [62]. This approach provided us with a rich understanding of the case.

4 Main Findings and Analysis

4.1 The Laboratory Information System (LIS)

In 2004, upper management acquired a software program package to provide common best practices for its unified Laboratory departments. The software, developed by Labsys, was based on formal industry standards and provided flexibility to accommodate, to a certain degree, idiosyncratic practices. The role of a software package is to "meet general needs of a class if organizations, rather than unique needs of a particular organization as is the case in custom software development" [67, p. 2]. Thus the initial design of the LIS embedded a set of practices based on Labsys' approach to best practices and on UHC upper management requirements. It was expected that these practices would be implemented in all three laboratories with the help of the shared services center. Concretely, the UHC wanted to develop a common test index for the three laboratories in order to standardize the collection of statistics and reporting, and create a unique test index for the future LIS.

In a hospital an LIS automates laboratory clinical, financial and managerial processes and enables lab staff to maintain accurate tracking, processing and result recording, while avoiding lost and misplaced specimens. UHC's three laboratory services were using three different workflows supported by different legacy ISs. At the outset of Phase I, in order to supervise the implementation work of the project team, a Clinical Consultative Committee (CCC) was set up. Its role was to decide on the project scope and direction. The CCC included representatives from the upper management and lab physicians and proposed guidelines for the standardization of practices in the three main laboratories.

In collaboration with ITServ, the committee created an LIS project team that included laboratory technologists, physicians and IS specialists from the SSC. During Phase I, the three lab services were asked to standardize their practices (lab request workflow). Even though the typical lab workflow (scanning barcodes that include laboratory number, patient identification and test destination – hospital department/physician) seems to be straightforward, each of labs was using different sequence steps and different legacy ISs. During this phase, the lab clinicians struggled to find common ground in the specimen management processes. Consequently, the team members decided to adopt a "retain" approach, i.e. to try to accommodate as many old procedures and workflows as the new system would accept. At the end of 2005, Labsys advised UHC that it would provide a new version of the LIS.

Early in 2006, Phase II commenced with the ITServ's members of the LIS team restarting the process of programming the system's database from scratch on the new LIS platform. During Phase II, the nature of the group dynamics changed, as upper management brought several well-known laboratory physicians into the project, hoping they could bring about the much-needed collaboration between team members. Not only was upper management exercising constant pressure to speed up the development, but also the team members realized that they should agree on common procedures reflecting industry standards. Therefore, the weekly team meetings produced a mix of compromises and executive decisions that influenced the final system functionality.

After almost three years of testing and implementation, the new LIS was deployed at Downtown, followed by Midtown and Pediatric after 6 months. While the initial functional configuration was based on best practice standards, the final system configuration revealed a blend of industry standards and local pre-merger idiosyncrasies.

4.2 Data Analysis

Fields of Practice and Boundaries. For UHC upper management, the new LIS would bring best practices to laboratory and standardize them across the sites. Even though a typical medical lab workflow seems to be quite forthright, the lab services at the UHC were presenting a different reality. The three site-based lab services were using three different workflows, each with a different set of practices:

> "We had Downtown working one way, Midtown working another way, Pediatric working a different way. That was as if 'Joe' works at this bench. 'Jim' works on the same bench [...] You take these two people with different visions of doing the same work, and you multiply it by three sites." (Downtown laboratory technologist)

Labsys provided the members of the project team with a remote access to a mockup LIS database at the company's headquarters. The database was populated with fictive organizations and patients. The ITServ specialists were able to learn or to verify their knowledge about how to build and configure the new system by using this tool. On a regular basis they were testing LIS prototypes and organizing simulation sessions with the lab technologists. Not only did the ITServ specialists have to learn the programming language of the Labsys-based platform, but they also had to understand the labs' workflow and procedures. The importance of the latter aspect is emphasized by one of the interviewees:

> *"LIS is supposed to help lab people to do their work so we [ITServ specialists] need to understand that everything starts on the bench. It's what you do in the lab that you should be able to do a good programming to get, it's not supposed to be Labsys that will tell you what to do."* (ITServ manager)

At the beginning of Phase I, the context of the project featured a high level of novelty that prevented the project team members (the agents) from correctly assessing differences in knowledge of each other's practices and the dependencies between the team members.

> *"When it came to building the system, this was something new for everyone. This was having three feeder systems go into one feeder system. This was the first time..."* (Downtown laboratory technologist); *"I felt sorry for them [LIS team members] because they were thrown in cold. This was very novel for most of them."* (ITServ specialist); *"I looked at it as a complete new challenge"* (Midtown laboratory technologist); *"I was working with people that I didn't know."* (Pediatric lab technologist)

The level of dependence among the members of the project team was also high:

> *"We we're very dependent on the technologists because [of] what they do – so the assistant chief tech even to this day when we have a protocol meeting they're still included because they know exactly at the bench level what's going on."* (ITServ specialist)

Under these conditions, sharing knowledge was not possible until team members understood the differences between the practices of the three laboratories (end of Phase I).

> *"It was seeing how the other person thinks. If you come with an understanding of how institutions work – and not all institutions work the same – and ours is different for a lot of reasons, the way we've evolved. Just as blood taking has evolved totally differently at the Downtown site."* (Midtown laboratory technologist)

At the same time, different interests emerged among the lab clinicians when they realized that they must transform the knowledge they had invested in their own practices.

> *"Physicians from different labs in the same discipline could not agree on what to do with tests, or with procedures. They couldn't standardize."* (Downtown laboratory technologist)

The need for a unique set of lab practices was clearly conveyed by the upper management to the laboratory clinicians:

> *"Not only do they [management] count they're going to start using the same system, but the system will work the same way for all of them. Suppliers are not going to develop a specific need for a specific site."* (ITServ manager)

The evidence suggests that resistance arose right from the outset due to the new LIS imposing a new sociomaterial assemblage upon the lab clinicians. This set up a need for negotiations and adaptations if the new LIS were to be adopted and used by the labs user community.

Dialectics of Resistance and Accommodations (Performativity). During Phase I, the agents reluctantly engaged in knowledge sharing to identify shared understandings about how to standardize their work procedures.

"It was difficult because the members selected for the LIS team were not selected by the manager of the LIS at the time. Upper management selected them, so there was this "keeper of the knowledge" mentality, and trying to gather information was difficult." (Downtown laboratory technologist)

The general feeling among the team members was that they should not have to change their respective laboratory procedures just because upper management had decided to replace the three legacy systems with a single common laboratory IS.

"Physicians from different labs in the same discipline could not agree on what to do. So why? Probably politically, because they did not have any background information on why they're doing a test in a certain way." (Pediatric lab technologist)

Some of the agents saw the implementation of the new LIS as a means to reify their loss of organizational identity. They felt that by using the system they would eventually lose the control over the rules of the game within their respective fields of practice. Some of them felt like "immigrants" in an adoptive country. They were not comfortable engaging in a game based on unfamiliar rules.

"They didn't give us a chance to mourn [...]. We were losing the identity that we had as stand-alone areas" (Midtown laboratory technologist); "You always recognize yourself with the site that you're at, but also being part of a bigger [entity], let's say you're an immigrant. You move to a place and you're part of where you are but you're also part of what you were as well." (Downtown laboratory pathologist)

During Phase II, the sense of urgency to standardize practices, along with pressure from upper management, made the agents engage in negotiations of trade-offs to ensure that eventually some of their pre-merger practices would be preserved while a number of new laboratory procedures would be adopted.

"What we did is that if there were some different clinical practices, we allowed some exceptions. The Pediatric site had very different protocol, and we've had to make more exceptions. So we had fights, and finally we agreed to some exceptions, but for the Adult sites we did a lot of work to try to get to a consensus." (Midtown microbiologist)

During lengthy meetings, proposals emerged on how to standardize some practices or keep them unchanged. However, in order for them to be successfully embraced, care was taken not to present these trades-offs as ideas that came from one of the three fields of practice.

"It's always about being careful that it's not taken as a Midtown idea or a Downtown idea. This was during meetings. You didn't say, 'You know, at the Midtown site we do it like this and it works, or at the Downtown site we do it like this and it works'... Industry standards! This would be the better way to go." (ITServ manager)

Our data analysis suggests that the negotiation process resulted in accommodations that enabled emergent sociomaterial assemblages, some of them based on workarounds implemented by the ITServ specialists. The following example is illustrative:

"We do syphilis tests, typically about 100 a day. At the beginning, I'm laughing because they would have to click each individual syphilis results. I was getting calls, 'this is impossible!' because you could be here until night doing the results. Finally I called one of the [ITServ] specialists who figured it out that we could verify it without doing a hundred clicks. So what

normally would have taken about two hours of signing, it took ten minutes now." (Downtown physician)

LIS-based Resulted Practices and Workarounds. While neither the UHC upper management nor the lab user community got their wishes - the former to impose new practices and the latter to keep its pre-merger workflows - the new sociomaterial arrangement gained enough support from both sides to reach a stable environment:

"What we did is that there are some different clinical practices we allowed, but we tried not to make too many because it's too difficult to keep on with quality." (Midtown physician)

In a CCC post-implementation report it was mentioned that every task performed with the new LIS was taking more steps and time to complete than before with the old system. Workload had increased, lab technologists were working a maximum amount of overtime, and physicians were not receiving reports in a timely fashion. Some lab clinicians informally were asking the ITServ specialists to create workarounds to 'get their job done'.

"We thought that there was one way of working with the system, common to all the sites. But a year after the implementation, we did a follow up. We found out that some people were expressing their concerns about the functionality and we found out that they [ITServ specialists] resolved it. But they didn't tell anyone about this. So we found out that there were some different practices ... workarounds depending on the problem." (Downtown lab manager)

The workarounds implemented by the ITServ specialists enabled the three lab communities preserve some pre-merger practices (i.e., the order entry), while accepting new practices (i.e., the lab requests and access to results). Thus, the new LIS unified all laboratory protocols across the sites and linked the laboratories in one common system. Also, the laboratories had to change how their staff was managing the laboratory requests because the LIS imposed one set of common practices. However, at the same time, the workarounds made it possible for the Pediatric site to keep its pre-merger order entry procedures and for a number of laboratory technologists from the Adult sites to accommodate some pre-merger practices.

5 Theoretical Explanation

This research investigates how social and material dynamics influence activities of knowledge sharing during an IS implementation project that affects the combination of formal (planned) and informal (workarounds) practices in a context of a shared services center. Two important themes emerged from these results.

Performativity: An Outcome of the Social and Material Dynamics. The evidence suggests that the formal practices based on industry best practices adopted by the UHC upper management involved the imposition of new practices and shaped the context of the LIS implementation project. At the outset of the project there were three different fields of practice, each defined by historical and local information management-based norms. Therefore, significant differences were between the pre-merger site-based practices on one hand and between these practices and the new planned formal practices on the other hand. Moreover, the ITServ specialists that were involved in the project were not aware of the differences in practices between the three labs. Resistance from physicians and lab technologists from the three merging entities ensued. Negotiation was critical to introduce modifications and keep some of the pre-merger sociomaterial assemblages.

The concept of performativity clarifies how relationships between agents and technology were never fixed. Although the adoption process happened in the same organizational context and regarded the same technology, the resulted sociomaterial assemblages varied unpredictably across the three sites. The sociomateriality practice perspective, thus, emphasizes the process, and assumes that practices are constantly changing even when agents are supposedly engaging in the same practice: "Pursuing the same thing necessarily produces something different" [68, p. 894]. It also shows that new technology can be enacted in different ways as it associates with practices of different fields of practice.

However, these different enactments were influenced at the UHC by the technical limits imposed by the technology (material) and by the common interests and field-based values that were at stake (social). While what the new technology *is* did not change during the implementation process, what it changed was what *it does*. In all three lab communities, performativity depended on the material properties of the LIS, as well as on agents' perceptions of whether that materiality afforded their ability to engage in effective lab practices. This situation triggered resistance that was followed by negotiations with the management. The resulted arrangements undermined the planned outcomes of the implantation project.

A Multilevel Process Model of Sociomaterial Assemblages. Our findings suggest that at the individual level, agents' actions were formulated by their understanding of others' practices while engaged in knowledge-sharing activities and of what the new LIS can and cannot do. The workarounds were supposed to reflect what the new technology should do taking into account the idiosyncrasies of the three fields of practice.

The lab clinicians and technologists followed a similar process, in which individual actions (resistance, negotiation, accommodation, acceptance of practices, etc.) were the product of the interplay between opposing forces: the formal practices imposed by the material properties of the new technology *vs.* the informal practices based on team members' knowledge sharing practices. Our multilevel process model, presented in Fig. 2, illustrates the operation of the dialectic motor of change during the process of a post-merger IS implementation.

First, we posit that the decision to impose new formal practices will reveal existing pre-merger practice-based field boundaries. Then, we conjecture that users affected by the IS-enabled changes in practices, will resist system's implementation. In this context, team members will negotiate and propose accommodations through reconfigurations (workarounds) of the system during implementation. Thus, the initial functional design of the IS may be different from the final functionality at the end of the implementation. The resulting view of the process tells a rich story by explaining how the dynamics of performativity (individual level) generate new sociomaterial assemblages, which collectively lead to future action (organizational level). At UHC, the upper management through its shared

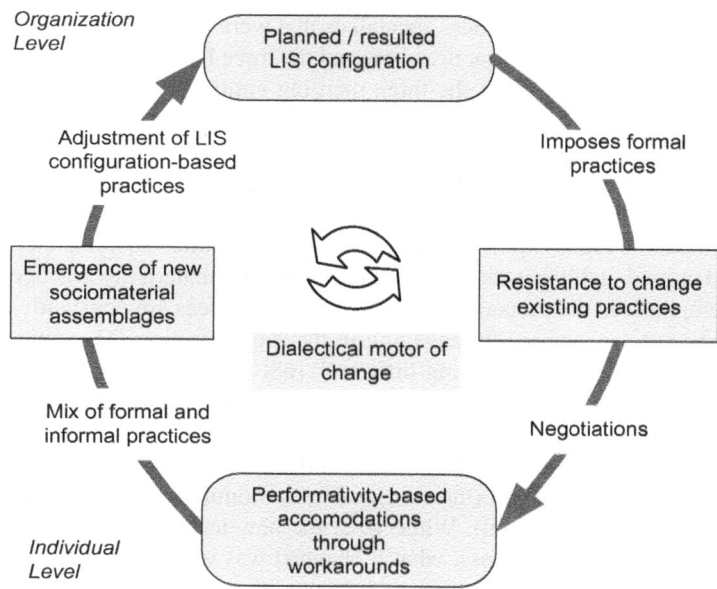

Fig. 2. A process model of dialectics of formal and informal practices

services center, decided to implement a common LIS that caused resistance from the site-based lab services clinicians (struggling to come up with a standardized lab workflow). The subsequent negotiations resulted in a workable system that enabled a common set of formal lab practices and accommodated some pre-merger practice idiosyncrasies via workarounds (mix of practice transformation and preservation).

Moreover, the lab clinicians were able to use the new LIS in unintended ways, which proved to be beneficial to them. The resulting dialectic leads to an iterative process of resistance and negotiation of common interests (at the individual level), followed by a change of the existing sociomaterial assemblages (at the organizational level) implemented by the SSC, which reflects a mix of formal and informal practices in contradiction with the original, planned ones. Agents' actions and technology's materiality are distinct from one another, and it is only once they become assembled in specific ways that they can then create new or recreate existing sociomaterial assemblages [33]. Thus, at the organizational level, change of practices is driven by the actions of agents, who seek to negotiate their field-based lab practices (see Fig. 2). Depending on whether they perceive that a technology affords or constrains their goals, the agents made choices about how to link social and material agencies based on practices and norms defined at the organizational level.

Thus, the multilevel process model depicted in Fig. 2 provides a more complete explanation of the different outcomes regarding the adoption of a new technology at the organizational level. In this view, emergent outcomes are products of indeterminate interplay among opposing forces and are difficult to predict a priori [69].

6 Conclusions and Future Research

Through sociomaterial assemblages, agents and technological artifacts meet in a particular manner. Such a manner is notably induced by the context, the situation and the purposes agents and artifacts interact for. While authors such as Oshri et al. [25] and Hawk et al. [26] insist on the importance of formal practices during the implementation of a new IS to support knowledge sharing, others such as Orlikowski [27] and Pavlou and El Sawy [28] suggest that informal practices like workarounds are at the basis of efficient knowledge sharing.

The main contribution of this article is to consider the dialectics of formal and informal practices during an SSC-leading IS implementation project in the context of a merger. Formal practices may have been imposed by the material properties of some new technological artifacts, whereas informal practices may be based on team members' knowledge sharing practices. This is particularly true in the context of merging entities and a shared services center, where organizational and/or country boundaries are crossed. Our study highlights two important topics: (1) the concept of performativity, which clarifies how relationships between agents and technology were never fixed, and (2) the process of emerging sociomaterial assemblages, which provides a more complete explanation of the different outcomes regarding the adoption of a new technology at the organizational level. By proposing a multiple-level process model, our research provides new insights on the adoption of a technology in the context of shared services center-driven organizational change. The results demonstrate that negotiated practices are part of a normal course of action in a new technology implementation across the boundaries of merging entities and that it is therefore preferable: 1) not to have a strict "formal" approach at the outset of a project; and 2) to take into consideration the unavoidable emerging "workarounds". This study also sheds light on how knowledge is shared in the context of a SSC. These are important takeaways for practitioners that may provide interesting insights to the management of an organization engaged in a process of a merger.

The main limitation of this study might be that it attempts at generalizing only from empirical statements to theoretical statements in developing a process model from a case study [70]. However, it has been shown that statistical, sampling-based generalizability may be an unbefitting goal for qualitative studies [71]. The UHC case is built on strong historical foundation and deals with issues of central importance to our research, which makes it purposeful [65].

Future research avenues could further build on the SSC and IT-enabled organizational change literatures to investigate other contexts and extend our multilevel process model in order to better and deeper understand the dialectics of formal and informal practices.

Acknowledgements. The authors would like to gratefully acknowledge the FRQSC funding (no. 2015-NP-180713) received for this project.

References

1. Sambamurthy, V., Zmud, R.W.: Research commentary: the organizing logic for an enterprise's IT activities in the digital era - a prognosis of practice and a call for research. Inf. Syst. Res. **11**(2), 105–114 (2000)
2. Dibbern, J., Goles, T., Hirschheim, R., Jayatilaka, B.: Information systems outsourcing: a survey and analysis of the literature. ACM Sigmis Database **35**(4), 6–102 (2004)
3. Oshri, I., Kotlarsky, J., Willcocks, L.P.: The Handbook of Global Outsourcing and Offshoring. Palgrave Macmillan, New York (2011)
4. Joha, A., Janssen, M.: Public-private partnerships outsourcing and shared service centers: motives and intents for selecting sourcing configurations. Transf. Gov. People Process Policy **4**(3), 232–348 (2010)
5. Amiruddin, R., Aman, A., Sofiah, A.A., Auzair, M., Hamzah, N., Maelah, R.: Mitigating risks in a shared service relationship: the case of a malaysian bank. Qual. Res. Acc. Manage. **10**(1), 78–93 (2013)
6. HfS Research and PwC: The Future of Global Business Services, Survey Findings, HfS Reaserch Ltd and PwC (2012). http://www.pwc.com/en_US/us/outsourcing-shared-services-centers/assets/pwc-future-global-business-services-summary.pdf. Accessed April 28, 2016
7. Bergeron, B.: Essentials of Shared Services. Wiley, Hoboken (2003)
8. Janssen, M., Joha, A.: Motives for establishing shared service centers in public administrations. Int. J. Inf. Manage. **26**(2), 102–115 (2006)
9. Niehaves, B., Krause, A.: Shared service strategies in local government – a multiple case study exploration. Trans. Gov. People Process Policy **4**(3), 266–279 (2010)
10. Rothwell, A.T., Herbert, I.P., Seal, W.: Shared service centres and professional employability. J. Vocat. Behav. **79**(1), 241–252 (2011)
11. Howcroft, D., Richardson, H.: The back office goes global: exploring connections and contradictions in shared service centers. Work Employment Soc. **26**(1), 111–127 (2012)
12. Herbert, I., Seal, W.: Shared services as a new organizational form: some implications for management accounting. Br. Acc. Rev. **44**(2), 83–97 (2012)
13. Peppard, J.: The conundrum of IT management. Eur. J. Inf. Syst. **16**(4), 336–345 (2007)
14. Kien, S.S., Kiat, L.W., Periasamy, K.P.: Switching IT outsourcing suppliers: enhancing transition readiness. MIS Q. Executive **9**(1), 23–33 (2010)
15. Davenport, T., Prusak, L.: Working Knowledge: How Organizations Manage What They Know. Harvard University Press (1998)
16. Arduin, P-E.: On the measurement of cooperative compatibility to predict meaning variance. In: Proceedings of IEEE International Conference on Computer Supported Cooperative Work in Design, Calabria, Italy, pp. 42–47 (2015)
17. Levina, N., Vaast, E.: The emergence of boundary spanning competence in practice: implications for implementation and use of information systems. MIS Q. **29**(2), 335–363 (2005)
18. Orlikowski, W.J.: Knowing in practice: enacting a collective capability in distributed organizing. Organ. Sci. **13**(3), 249–273 (2002)
19. Newell, S., Tansley, C., Huang, J.: Social capital and knowledge integration in an erp project team: the importance of bridging and bonding. Brit. J. Manage. **15**(S1), S43–S57 (2004)
20. Vieru, D., Rivard, S.: Organizational identity challenges in a post-merger context: a case study of an information system implementation project. Int. J. Inf. Manage. **34**(3), 381–386 (2014)
21. Suchman, L.: Practice-based design of information systems: notes from the hyper-developed world. Inf. Soc. **18**, 139–144 (2002)
22. Liebowitz, J.: Knowledge Retention: Strategies and Solutions. CRC Press, Boca Raton (2008)

23. Prax, J-Y.: Manuel du Knowledge Management: Mettre en Réseau les Hommes et les Savoirs Pour Créer de la Valeur, Editions Dunod (2012)
24. Grundstein, M.: From capitalizing on company's knowledge to knowledge management. In: Morey, D., Maybury, M.T., Thuraisingham, B. (eds.) Knowledge Management Classic and Contemporary Works, pp. 261–287. MIT Press, Cambridge (2000)
25. Oshri, I., van Fenema, P., Kotlarsky, J.: Knowledge transfer in globally distributed teams: the role of transactive memory. Inf. Syst. J. **18**(6), 593–616 (2008)
26. Hawk, S., Zheng, W., Zmud, R.W.: Overcoming knowledge-transfer barriers in infrastructure management outsourcing: lessons from a case study. MIS Q. Executive **8**(3), 123–139 (2009)
27. Orlikowski, W.J.: Improvising organizational transformation over time: a situated change perspective. Inf. Syst. Res. **7**(1), 63–92 (1996)
28. Pavlou, P.A., El Sawy, O.A.: The 'Third Hand': IT-enabled competitive advantage in turbulence through improvisational capabilities. Inf. Syst. Res. **21**(3), 443–471 (2010)
29. Alter, S.: Theory of workarounds. Commun. Assoc. Inf. Syst. **34**, 1041–1066 (2014)
30. Safadi, H., Faraj, S.: The role of workarounds during an open source electronic medical record system implementation. In: Proceedings of the 31th International Conference on Information Systems (2010)
31. Azad, B., King, N.: Institutionalized computer workaround practices in a mediterranean country: an examination of two organizations. Eur. J. Inf. Syst. **21**(4), 358–372 (2012)
32. Röder, N., Wiesche, M., Schermann, M., Krcmar, H.: Why managers tolerate workarounds: the role of information systems. In: Proceedings of the 20th Americas Conference on Information System, Savannah, GE (2014)
33. Orlikowski, W.: Sociomaterial practices: exploring technology at work. Organ. Stud. **28**(9), 1435–1448 (2007)
34. Orlikowski, W.: The sociomateriality of organizational life: considering technology in management research. Cambridge J. Econ. **34**(1), 125–141 (2010)
35. Boland, R.J., Tenkasi, R.V.: Perspective making and perspective taking in communities of knowing. Organ. Sci. **6**(4), 350–372 (1995)
36. Poole, M.S., Van De Ven, A.H.: Theories of organizational change and innovation processes. In: Poole, M.S., Van De Ven, A.H. (eds.) Handbook of Organizational Change and Innovation. Oxford University Press, New York (2004)
37. Van de Ven, A.H., Poole, M.S.: Explaining development and change in organizations. Acad. Manage. Rev. **20**(3), 510–540 (1995)
38. Arduin, P.-E., Grundstein, M., Rosenthal-Sabroux, C.: From knowledge sharing to collaborative decision-making. Int. J. Inf. Decis. Sci. **5**(3), 295–311 (2013)
39. Polanyi, M.: Sensegiving and sensereading, philosophy. J. Royal Inst. Philos. **42**(162), 301–323 (1967)
40. Maznevski, L., Chudoba, K.M.: Bridging space over time: global virtual team dynamics and effectiveness. Organ. Sci. **11**(5), 473–492 (2000)
41. Walsham, G.: Knowledge management: the benefits and limitations of computer systems. Eur. Manage. J. **19**(6), 599–608 (2001)
42. Stockdale, R., Standing, C.: An interpretive approach to evaluating information systems: a content. Context Process Framework Eur. J. Oper. Res. **173**(3), 1090–1102 (2006)
43. Jordan, B.: Ethnographic workplace studies and computer supported cooperative work. In: Shapiro, D., Tauber, M., Traunmüller, R. (eds.) The Design of Computer-Supported Cooperative Work and Groupware Systems, pp. 17–42. Elsevier, The Netherlands (1996)
44. Tsoukas, H., Chia, R.: On organizational becoming: rethinking organizational change. Organ. Sci. **13**(5), 567–582 (2002)

45. Wagner, E., Moll, J., Newell, S.: Accounting logics reconfiguration of ERP systems and the emergence of new accounting practices: a sociomaterial perspective. Manage. Acc. Res. **22**(3), 181–197 (2011)
46. Wagner, E., Newell, S., Piccoli, G.: Understanding project survival in an es environment: a sociomaterial practice perspective. J. Assoc. Inf. Syst. **11**(5), 276–297 (2010)
47. Orlikowski, W.: Using technology and constituting structures: a practice lens for studying technology in organizations. Organ. Sci. **11**(4), 404–428 (2000)
48. Leonardi, P.M.: When flexible routines meet flexible technologies: affordance constraint, and the imbrication of human and material agencies. MIS Q. **35**(1), 147–167 (2011)
49. Leonardi, P.M.: Theoretical foundations for the study of sociomateriality. Inf. Organ. **23**(2), 59–76 (2013)
50. Dulipovici, A., Vieru, D.: Exploring collaboration technology use: how users' perceptions twist and amend reality. J. Knowl. Manage. **19**(4), 661–681 (2015)
51. Barad, K.: Posthumanist performativity: toward an understanding of how matter comes to matter. J. Women Culture Soc. **28**(3), 801–831 (2003)
52. Barad, K.: Meeting the universe halfway: quantum physics and the entanglement of matter and meaning. Duke University Press, Durham (2007)
53. Orlikowski, W., Scott, S.V.: Sociomateriality: challenging the separation of technology work and organization. Acad. Manage. Ann. **2**, 433–474 (2008)
54. Cetina, K.: Epistemic Cultures: How the Sciences Make Knowledge. Harvard University Press, Cambridge (1999)
55. Gasparas, J., Monteiro, E.: Cross-contextual use of integrated information systems. In: Proceedings of the 17th Europeean Conference on Information Systems Proceedings, Verona, Italy (2009)
56. Berente, N., Yoo, Y.: Institutional contradictions and loose coupling: post-implementation of nasa's enterprise information system. Inf. Syst. Res. **23**(2), 376–396 (2012)
57. Davison, R.M., Ou, C.X.: Sharing knowledge in technology deficient environments: individual workarounds amid corporate restrictions. In: Proceedings of the 21st European Conference on Information Systems, Utrecht, The Netherlands (2013)
58. Boudreau, M.-C., Robey, D.: Enacting integrated information technology: a human agency perspective. Organ. Sci. **16**(1), 3–18 (2005)
59. Koopman, P., Hoffman, R.R.: Work-arounds Make-Work, and kludges. Intell. Syst. IEEE **18**(6), 70–75 (2003)
60. Cooper, R.B., Zmud, R.W.: Information technology implementation research: a technological diffusion approach. Manage. Sci. **36**(2), 123–139 (1990)
61. Ferneley, E.H., Sobreperez, P.: Resist, Comply or Workaround? An examination of different facets of user engagement with information systems. Eur. J. Inf. Syst. **15**(4), 345–356 (2006)
62. Eisenhardt, K.M., Graebner, M.E.: Theory building from cases: opportunities and challenges. Acad. Manage. J. **50**(1), 25–32 (2007)
63. Avgerou, C.: Explaining trust in it-mediated elections: a case study of E-voting in brazil. J. Assoc. Inf. Syst. **14**(8), 420–451 (2013)
64. Leonard-Barton, D.: A dual methodology for case studies: synergistic use of a longitudinal single site with replicated multiple sites. Organ. Sci. **1**(3), 248–266 (1990)
65. Patton, M.Q.: Qualitative Research and Evaluation Methods. SAGE Publications, Thousand Oaks (2001)
66. Miles, M., Huberman, M., Saldana, J.: Qualitative Data Analysis. SAGE Publications, Beverly Hills (2013)

67. Brehm, L., Heinzl, A., Markus, M.L.: Tailoring ERP systems: a spectrum of choices and their implications. In: Proceedings of the 34th Hawaii International Conference on System Sciences, Maui, HI (2001)
68. Nicolini, D.: Stretching out and expanding medical practices: the case of telemedicine. Hum. Relat. **60**(6), 889–920 (2007)
69. Pfeffer, J.: Organizations and Organization Theory. Pitman, Cambridge (1982)
70. Lee, A.S., Baskerville, R.L.: Generalizing generalizability in information systems research. Inf. Syst. Res. **14**(3), 221–243 (2003)
71. Denzin, N.K., Lincoln, Y.S.: The Sage Handbook of Qualitative Research. SAGE Publications, Thousand Oaks (2005)

Towards an Integrated Methodology for Implementing Shared Services

Vipin Suri[1,2], Kuldeep Kumar[2], and Jos van Hillegersberg[2(✉)]

[1] SGS Global Solutions, Po Box 217, 7500AE Enschede, The Netherlands
vipinsuri@ssinsights.com
[2] Department of Industrial Engineering and Business Information Systems, University of Twente,
Po Box 217, 7500AE Enschede, The Netherlands
{k.kumar,j.vanhillegersberg}@utwente.nl

Abstract. Setting-up hybrid shared services is not a straightforward and requires methodology support. To learn more about current practices and experiences with shared services delivery models and methodologies to setup shared services we conduct survey research among companies that deploy shared service centres. In this research paper we report on the findings of our research. Based on the results we outline initial requirements and present building blocks for an integrated methodology to effectively support implementing shared services.

Keywords: Business support services · Shared services · Service delivery models

1 Introduction

The origin of the term "shared services" and its related concepts is somewhat unclear. As early as 1986, General Electric, USA, formed an organizational group called Client Business Services, which is still often used today as a model for what we know as shared services. Bob Gunn of the consulting firm Gunn Partners believes the term was coined when he led a best practice study at A.T. Kearney [1].

Service delivery models for Shared Services can be seen as strategic instruments which are dependent on organizational business objectives. The most common models are Centralized, Shared Services (Insourced), Outsourced, Offshored, Collaborative and Decentralized. More recently, a hybrid model called "global business services" has emerged in industry. This model uses a combination of internal shared services and external service providers. It aims to allow companies to operate with greater efficiency and enables business growth, as well as supporting global standards and compliance. The goal of this model is to optimize service delivery and drive process improvement across the entire company.

1.1 Implementing Global Business Services

While this model holds high promises for shared service delivery, setting-up hybrid shared services is not straightforward and requires methodology support. To provide seamless services to the business units, the various service delivery models need to be integrated.

To implement a service delivery model successfully, companies must decide how to select strategically among various service management strategies. Most companies have been experimenting with various service delivery models, such as, decentralization or centralization of services, shared services, offshoring and outsourcing of services, etc. through which they manage their business support services. These models have been changing significantly over the past decade. A number of methodologies have been used to implement a combination of these models but a lack of adequate integration has resulted in varying degrees of success of their implementation and acceptance.

The implementations of shared services are usually linear processes. Although linear and sequential, there is often a need to revisit previous steps taken to make corrections and to revisit decisions when more information becomes available. While there is little research available into success of shared service implementations, several sources report that implementing shared services has often not been successful [1]. Typically, reasons for limited success reported point at a lack of effective methodology support for the design and implementation of shared services. Thus, there is a need to study in more detail what methodologies are being used to support shared service implementation, what current issues with implementation of shared services are, and to what extent these are effective.

1.2 Research Questions and Method

Using a combination of literature study, focus group discussions with practitioners, surveys and in-depth interviews we address the following research questions:

1. What are benefits and issues in implementing shared services delivery models from an academic and practitioner perspective?
2. What are current methodologies and tools in use by service delivery organizations during the planning, design, implementation and operation phases?
3. What are the shortcomings of the methodologies and tools that are/were used
4. What are requirements and building blocks of a comprehensive methodology for shared services design and implementation

The paper is organized in following sections: Sect. 2 is a brief review of selected literature related to business support services. Section 3 presents data collection methods. Section 4 provides findings and conclusions of data collected and Sect. 5 discusses requirements of the new methodology and presents the building blocks and the roadmap for integrated methodology for shared services. Section 6 outlines the conclusions and future research.

2 Brief Literature Review

2.1 Shared Service Delivery Models

Welke [2] defines a service as a mechanism to enable access to one or more organizational capabilities. This access is provided using a prescribed interface. It is exercised consistent with constraints and policies specified by the description of the service. A service is provided by an entity called the service provider, which is provided for use by others; however, the eventual consumers of the service may not be known to the service provider, and may sometimes demonstrate uses of the service beyond the scope originally conceived by the provider [2]. Organizations increasingly establish Shared Service Centres, either for transactional (administrative) or transformational (organizational change) purposes. Their popularity originates from a combination of efficiency gains and an increase in service quality, without giving up control of the organizational and technical arrangements. The belief is that shared services should maximize the advantages of centralized and decentralized delivery of business functions [3]. Shared services integrates centralization and decentralization models and shared services value follows from user characteristics such as their product-specific human capital that enables them to create value out of service delivered by service providers. The creation of value is a joint activity to which suppliers, clients and end-users contribute. In order to understand how shared services creates value, the focus needs to be on the intersection of supplier, client and end-user resources and on their co-creation activities [4].

A service delivery model is an arrangement of resources for delivering business support services within an organization, for example, centralization, shared services and outsourcing. The models through which organizations deliver and manage their core operating services (e.g. Information Technology (IT), Finance & Accounting (F&A), Human Resources (HR), customer care) have changed significantly over the past 25 years. Leading organizations today employ a broad range of service delivery models and techniques, including alternative delivery models such as shared services centers (SSCs), offshore captive operations, Information Technology Outsourcing (ITO) and Business Process Outsourcing (BPO). There is a renewed focus on optimizing services and driving process improvement across the entire organization using domestic and offshore captive SSCs augmented, extended, and often improved by external service providers [5]. After the emergence of shared service centres, shared services became most common in the fields of Human Resources Management and Finance. The fields such as Information Technology and Supply Chain Management are also on the rise [6].

2.2 Inter-organizational Shared Services

Sharing services increasingly extends beyond intra-organizational concentration of service delivery. Organizations have started to promote cooperation across their boundaries to deal with strategic tensions in their value ecosystem, moving beyond traditional outsourcing. The challenges of inter-organizational shared services (ISS) are: why organizations want to get and remain involved in ISS and what are the implications of ISS for (inter) organizational value creation? The key motivation of ISS lies in the fact that independent service partners together may create an added value level far beyond each individual's service [7].

Shared services is one of the most popular organizational forms of the last two decades and has emerged in a variety of businesses. While most studies of shared services investigate their benefits and risks; even though organizational structure has a strong influence on the performance of a firm, often much less insight about the actual structural design of shared services is examined. Typically, goals and strategy for shared services dominate the existing literature [8]. Companies are no longer looking at alternative delivery models, function-by-function or process-by-process. To help maximize the impact of service management, they are looking across their portfolio of business services for both stand-alone as well as cross-service integration opportunities. In some cases, companies are turning to global multifunctional shared services to drive an integrated portfolio. In other cases, they are creating enterprise-wide systems and organizations to develop the service delivery strategy, execute the plan, and manage ongoing relationships between service providers and users. Given the variety of options available and the complexity of establishing and maintaining relationships, the new groups charged with realigning and integrating business services require a unique set of skills and tools typically not found in the same individuals or group of individuals who have traditionally managed business services in the organization so far [9].

Building a mature, value-producing Global Business Services (GBS) organization requires many integrated elements and practices, one of the most critical elements being the ability to measure and monitor performance to guide continuous improvement. The GBS model includes shared services, outsourcing, optimized processes, technology, performance management and governance [10].

2.3 Shared Services Implementation Challenges

Organizations can encounter a number of diverse technological, managerial and organizational challenges while developing shared services [11]. The technological challenge of complex and diverse processes and IT systems refers to processes and IT systems that are difficult to analyze, improve, standardize and harmonize. The managerial challenge of alienation refers to a distant relationship between shared services and end-users, a loss of face-to-face contact and depersonalization with formalized procedures. The organizational challenge of ownership and responsibility refers to a lack of clarity of or different views on ownership of problems and responsibility when operating shared services across organizational boundaries which can result in employees feeling that a clear structure, of who to turn to with problems, has faded after shared services is established.

A methodology is an approach to "doing something" with a defined set of rules, methods, tests activities, deliverables and processes which typically serves to solve a specific problem. A service delivery methodology is defined as a body of service delivery guiding principles, standards, procedures and rules, a set of working methods and management practices including tools such as software solutions necessary for design, implementation and operations. The methodology needs to provide sequential steps during various phases of the journey. Methodology represents a system of methods used to conceptualize, design and implement the integrated model for delivering business support services. Essentially, a methodology must be determined so that it follows the constraints established by the governance system [12].

3 Data Collection

The first research question stated in the introduction was addressed by conducting a "shared services value potential" survey as part of the activities of the Asia-Pacific Shared Services Council of The Conference Board. A list of companies who have implemented shared services was compiled and the survey was sent to over 100 shared services leaders globally and 34 respondents from companies with primary business in 10 industries participated in the survey. The second and third research question were addressed by conducting a "Methodology and Tools" survey. A total of 47 respondents from companies with primary business in various industries participated in the survey. To get additional insights, in-depth interviews and an updated version of the "Methodology & Tools Survey" were conducted. This research has primarily focused on the perspectives of service leaders and functional leaders responsible for governing and operating service organizations in various companies. Figure 1 shows that in addition to the focus group session, three sets of data were collected and analysed:

1. Shared Services Value Potential Survey (2009)
2. Methodology & Tools Survey (2009)
3. In-depth Interviews and Methodology & Tools Survey (2011)

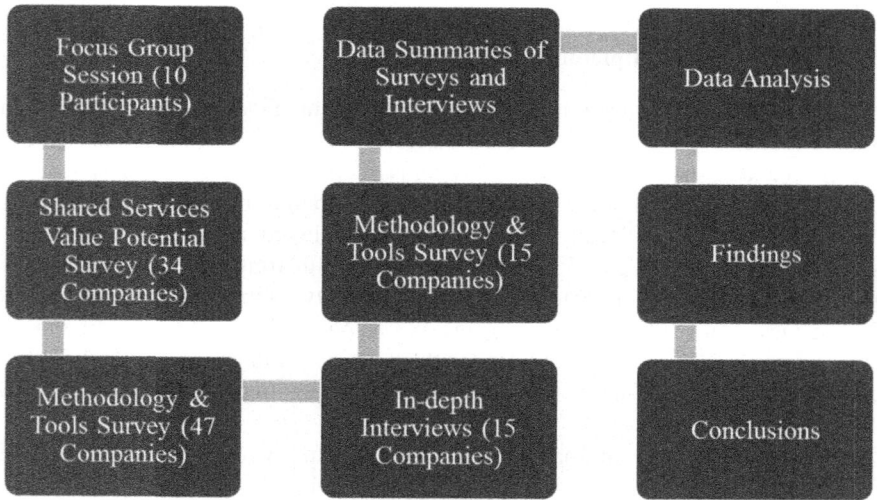

Fig. 1. Data collection and Analysis

4 Findings

Here we present the key results related to the practitioner's part of our first research question: (1) what are benefits and issues in implementing shared services delivery models from an academic and practitioner perspective?

4.1 Findings of the Shared Services Value Potential Survey

Key findings of the Shared Services Value Potential Survey include that shared services is viewed as a business strategy to increase service satisfaction and quality and to reduce cost, and that the scope of shared services can potentially be applicable to all scale and expertise services in business support functions. In addition, the shared services model allows business units to focus more on market and competitive issues. The value proposition of shared services is improvement in quality and reduction in cost. The respondents indicated that:

- Shared services creates a platform for satisfying internal customers and reducing cost effectively
- Shared services results in clarification of accountabilities for both providers and customers
- Shared services providers are primarily responsible for improving service quality and decreasing total cost of services
- Enterprise resource planning (ERP) systems are key enablers for increasing the value created by shared services.
- Management practices, change management, performance targets and vision, values and operating principles are foundational elements for shared services and focus should be on meeting customer needs and not on what providers want to provide.
- Areas which are important in managing functions and business support services include pricing/cost to serve, process standardization and service quality

The survey further reveals that customer satisfaction and business value contribution measures must be included when assessing the performance of shared services implementation and customer satisfaction is directly proportional to the commitment of employees to shared services values. Also, Shared Services Organizations (SSOs) must adopt a service based culture and a commercial culture in order to operate "like" a business as SSOs must communicate their value to their business units on a regular basis.

The training programs for shared services employees must include training in customer service, communications and change management, and change management programs should equally focus on service providers and internal customers. In addition, the change management programs should focus on changes in service delivery, in processes and in organization structure. Also, the communications programs must be based on a fact-based "no surprises" approach.

Next, we present the results of the Methodology and Tools Surveys that address our second research question - What are current methodologies and tools in use by service delivery organizations during the planning, design, implementation and operation phases and the third research question - What are the shortcomings of the methodologies and tools that are/were used?

4.2 Findings of the Methodology and Tools Surveys and In-Depth Interviews

During the data collection process, over 70% of the respondents indicated that there were limitations and shortcomings in the methodologies used by their companies. These methodologies were identified as those acquired from professional consulting firms, developed in-house or adopted from other companies. The key shortcomings of these methodologies in use are no comprehensive roadmap to success, inadequate coverage of essential management practices, difficulty to implement, as tools are critical for optimizing the performance of functional and service organizations, most companies are developing in-house tools, the current tools in use are complex and not integrated, most of the respondents indicated that their methodologies did not provide clarity about the sequence of steps to be followed.

In order to improve efficiency, the tools used during various phases of the shared services lifecycle need to have interface capabilities with company ERP and other systems. Between 70% and 80% of the surveyed companies indicated that there were limitations and shortcomings in the tools used by their companies during their shared services journey. The key shortcomings of the tools in use are lack of automation, lack of appropriate functionality and no interface capability with ERP and other systems. Moreover, the companies are having difficulties with the following type of tools performance measurement tools, customer satisfaction measurement tools, service-based costing tools and service level agreements tools.

The surveys conducted, using a different sample of companies, further reveal that a disciplined approach is critical for optimizing the performance of functional and service organizations. Current methodologies used by companies have limitations and are not providing clear instructions. The Shared Services Methodology & Tools Survey and follow up in-depth interviews resulted in a number of experiences and recommendations that we grouped below in (1) Implementation Considerations, (2) Roles and Responsibilities (3) Communication and Change Management and (4) Change Management:

4.3 Implementation Considerations

- A "big bang" approach should be avoided when virtually all staff are inexperienced.
- Inability to attract key personnel is a challenge.
- Partnerships with consultants were a significant source of conflict, as they maximized fees and did not optimize SSC implementation. A partner is important, however, it is best to engage with a strategic partner rather than one who is fee focused.
- Conceptual essences should be converted and applied for practical use, a copy-book approach should be avoided.

Precise human resources planning based on work measurement is difficult in services processes. Advanced methodologies/tools such as Lean Process and BPMS software should be considered to increase the precision of implementation. An ideal methodology needs to be simple and provide step-by-step instructions and a clear roadmap for success. The scope of an ideal methodology should include performance management, service level agreements and demand management. Currently, most of the organizations do not use a service management to design and operate their service strategy. Methodologies used by companies do not assist them effectively in simultaneously achieving all of the following performance optimization goals:

- Reduction in function/service cost
- Increase in service quality
- Increase in customer service
- Increase in compliance and control
- Process standardization
- System standardization

The current methodologies have many operational limitations and do not provide clear instructions for implementation and change management.

4.4 Roles and Responsibilities

The confusion between roles and responsibilities of ERP implementation teams, ERP development teams and shared services implementation teams should be avoided to increase probability of successful implementation. An integrated effort should be planned to split between functional-led re-engineering and IT-led ERP development.

4.5 Communication, Change Management and Governance

Change management, risk minimization and functional versus service orientation are principal shortcomings. Fact-based approaches are not sufficient in and of themselves to engender the necessary support and alignment to implement step change solutions. Internal control should be present in the implementation environment.

5 Requirements and a Proposal for a Shared Services Methodology

Based on these results, in our discussion below we present initial requirements for an enhanced methodology for implementing shared services. To address recent developments in hybrid models, it should consider the extent to which a mixed economy model (hybrid) utilizing both in-house service delivery and third-party provided delivery is appropriate for optimizing an organization's service delivery operations. It should provide criteria for integration of internal and external services providers. The methodology should also be able to measure customer satisfaction and identify service quality improvement goals. It should provide the most effective sourcing mix for the service delivery operations. Furthermore, it needs to provide a resolution of issues that arise in integrating and managing in-house and third-party services and provide criteria for identifying opportunities for outsourcing.

The requirements for a new methodology for integrated delivery of business support services have been developed based on conclusions drawn from the data collected, application of theories studied to understand the phenomenon of business support services, claims from the literature review and experience of the authors. These requirements are:

- The methodology should provide the most effective sourcing mix for the service delivery operations. It should consider the extent to which a mixed economy model (hybrid models) utilizing both in-house service delivery and third-party delivery are appropriate for optimizing an organization's service delivery operations.
- The new methodology should provide a technology strategy to drive efficiency by leveraging the ERP systems and internet functionality. In addition, the ideal tools should focus on key improvement opportunities and extract data from company databases economically.
- It should be simple and provide step-by-step instructions and a comprehensive roadmap for success.
- The methodology should include management practices to address processes, systems, cross-functional change management and work measurement.
- The tools used should capture data economically and integrate all required data elements.

In particular, a shared services design and implementation methodology should cover the:

- Role of the service organization in supporting companies in achieving their business objectives
- Initiatives that organizations will be taking in future years to enhance their service operations
- Drivers & inhibitors and benefits achieved from incorporating third-party business process outsourcing services within an organization's service delivery model
- Criteria that service organizations need to use for identifying appropriate areas for use of outsourced services
- Success criteria for integrating internal and external services within the service delivery model
- Key governance mechanisms for managing combinations of internal and outsourced services within the service delivery model.

Based on the identified requirements, the building blocks and the roadmap for the new methodology are shown in Fig. 2:

- *Define (D)* - Governance Model, Functional Scope, Work in terms of Services & Activities, End-to-End Global Processes, Service Strategy, Success Criteria and Performance Metrics
- *Measure (M)* - Baseline Costs and Performance Metrics, Criteria for Outsourcing, List of Services to be Insourced or Outsourced, Internal Customer Requirements, Internal Customer Satisfaction Baseline, Outsourced Service Providers and service catalogue

- *Explore (E)* - Feasibility Study and Business Case for Change, IT infrastructure and Architecture, Change Readiness and Barriers to Change
- *Develop (D)* - Change Management and Continuous Improvement Plan, Organization Structure and Roles & Responsibilities Integrating Multiple Service Delivery Providers, Service Management Office Structure, Enabling IT Systems Ensuring Integration with Processes, Required Skills and Competencies for each Position, Talent Pool, reward & Recognition System, Career Progression Paths, Training Programs, Performance Metrics and Regular Performance Reports
- *Implement (I)* - Locations for Insourced Service Delivery Centers, Workplace Requirements, People to Identified Roles, Customer Account Managers, Customer Help desk, Self Service Technology, Contracts with Outsourced Service Providers, Service Level Agreements, Control Plan and Validation Plan Post-Implementation

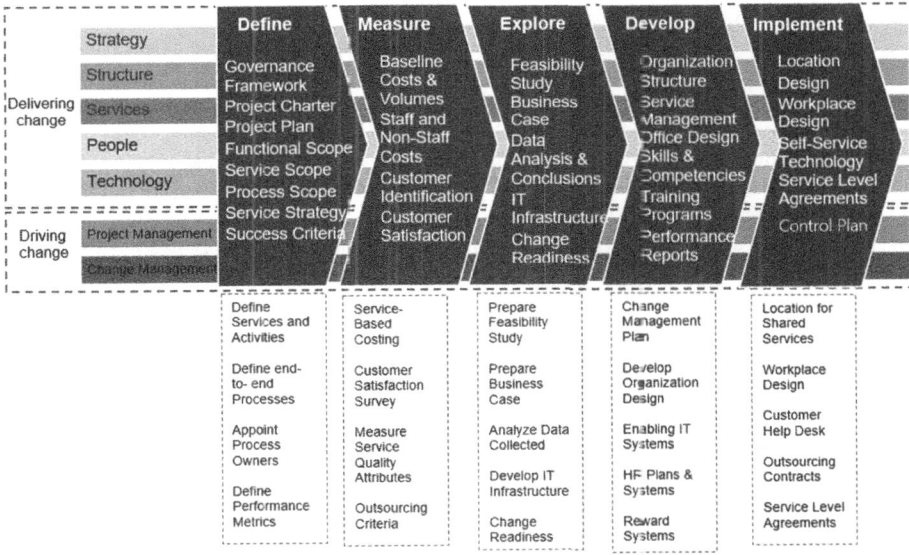

Fig. 2. Building blocks of the methodology

6 Conclusions and Future Research

Clearly, our surveys and in-depth interviews reveal that shared services are seen as a strategic value proposition and have the potential to improve quality and reduce cost. Also, shared services, if implemented, monitored and measured well, can make responsibilities and accountability clearer. However, companies should adopt appropriate culture, change and training programs to reap the benefits of shared services. Post-implementation, a control plan should be put in place to ensure verification of effectiveness and sustainment of desired results on an ongoing basis.

Implementing shared services is not straightforward and current methodology and tool support has several limitations. They do not provide clear steps, lack elaborate practices and metrics and can be highly complex. Tools lack functionality and are often poorly integrated with the enterprise systems landscape.

Based on our empirical results, we outlined requirements and presented a proposal for a disciplined approach to establish shared services implementation methodology. In our current research efforts this methodology is being further developed and evaluated using an action design research approach during implementation of Finance and HR Shared Services at one one of the largest Oil & Gas Companies in China.

References

1. Quinn, B., Cooke, R., Kris, A.: Shared services: mining for corporate gold. Financial Times, Prentice Hall (2000)
2. Welke, R.J.: Think Service, Act Process: Meeting today's demand for innovation and agility. HowDoUPress, 37p. (2005)
3. Bondarouk, T.V.: Shared Services as a New Organizational Form. Emerald Group Publishing Limited, WA, UK (2014)
4. Meijerink, J.G.: Beyond shared savings: a multilevel analysis of the perceived value of HR shared services. Ph.D. Thesis, University of Twente (2013)
5. KPMG Sourcing Advisory 2Q11 Global Pulse Survey. Trends in the outsourcing and third-party business and IT service markets, gleaned from KPMG's own field advisors and leading global service providers (2011)
6. Loges, M.N.A.: Shared services in information technology and supply chain management (2013). http://essay.utwente.nl
7. van Fenema, P.C., Keers, B., Zijm, H.: Interorganizational Shared Services: Creating Value Across Organizational Boundaries, vol. 13: Shared Services as a New Organizational Form, pp. 175–217. Advanced Series in Management. Emerald Group Publishing Limited (2014)
8. Friebe, C.M.: Specialties of organizing shared services: standardization, formalization & control. BSc thesis, University of Twente, The Netherlands (2013)
9. Cecil, B.: Sustain competitive advantage by rethinking your business services models. In: KPMG International (2011)
10. Huber, B., Danino, S.: Global Business Services: Taking Business Support Functions to the Next Level, TPI and Compass, Information Services Group (2011)
11. Knol, A.J., Sol, H.G.: Sourcing with Shared Service Centres: Challenges in the Dutch Government: Ecis 2011 proceedings (2011)
12. Erl, T., Bennett, S.G., Carlyle, B., Gee, C., Laird, R., Manes, A. T., Venable, C.: SOA Governance: Governing Shared Services On-Premise and in the Cloud. Prentice Hall Press (2011)

Exploring Career Anchors in Shared Service Centres

Stephanie Lambert[✉], Andrew Rothwell, and Ian Herbert

School of Business and Economics,
Loughborough University, Loughborough, UK
{S.Lambert,A.T.Rothwell,I.P.Herbert}@lboro.ac.uk

Abstract. New ways of professional working associated with new organisational forms such as the shared service centre (SSC) are challenging the ways in which careers exist and are perceived by finance professionals. Schein's original concept of career anchors has proved to be a helpful and robust framework for understanding career motivations over time, culture and context. Nonetheless, the theory is still largely based on career motivations and personal expectations prevailing in the 1970s and updated in 1990. Empirical testing of new anchors is rare and proposals for refreshing anchors tend to be conceptual. Using mixed methods this paper investigates the underlying constructs of career anchors for finance professionals in the contemporary SSC environment. Exploratory factor analysis (EFA) is used to explore a number of issues arising from interviews in a global multi-national organisation. The results suggest that a six-factor model, which blends traditional and new ideas about career motivations, can better represent career anchors in new organisational contexts than original theory.

Keywords: Shared services · Professional work · Finance · Career anchors

1 Introduction

The notion of professional work is changing from the traditional 'learned' occupations, in which an exclusive body of knowledge and access to practice was controlled by a privileged minority. Nowadays, many more vocational groupings enjoy professional status although, the locus of control over standards and behaviours is moving from professional bodies to organisations in which access to, and use of, knowledge is embedded in information systems. Such changes are epitomised by a new organisational form; the shared service centre (SSC) where business support functions are aggregated into business process centres so that efficiency and quality of service can be improved through task simplification, automation and the adoption of multidisciplinary process working. A consequence of the new factory-style environment is that work becomes polarised between a small number of senior professional personnel, who design and monitor work systems, and the vast majority of workers who perform low-level, transactional tasks. In the hollowed out middle, a career 'bottleneck' develops meaning that workers have little chance of progression and, moreover, the nature of lower level work may not equip them for senior roles potentially dulling aspirations of a long term professional career. The purpose of this enquiry is to explore the impact of these changes for the careers of finance professionals working in the SSC and understanding how far a traditional career theory can explain trends in new organisational forms such as the SSC.

2 Background Literature

2.1 Careers

During the 90s the literature on the nature and form of careers shifted away from traditional notions of organisationally structured careers [1] towards a more individual view adopted by 'boundaryless' careers [2]. A growth in market forces, globalisation and new working forms (exemplified by outsourcing, SSCs and organisational restructuring) were considered a catalyst for this change [3]. Careers were no longer assumed to follow a linear upward progression pattern; individuals were seen to be making lateral and multidirectional moves and basing career decisions around their personal needs rather than chasing objectively defined career success within a single organisation [4, 5]. The frequently cited 'boundarylessness' of individual workers suggested higher levels of mobility in relation to career direction, geographic location and inter-organisational movement.

Although mobility seems to have increased on some of levels (i.e. the mobility of the younger workforce), empirical evidence in this area suggests it is not as prevalent as hypothetical literature suggests [6]. More recently, boundaries have regained a level of relevance in response to the domination of 'boundaryless' careers in literature which may be muting important organisational aspects [3, 7]. Careers are still bounded by constructs; for instance achieving professional qualification for finance workers may reduce boundaries and punctuate a professional career together with providing an element of structure to their working lives. The SSC also demonstrates boundaries existing in modern day careers, in this case the flat structure and constrictions in careers in terms of organisational mobility and upward progression [8]. This raises the question how do individuals' understand their careers in this context? Are they as boundaryless as previously suggested? And what role does the organisation play in bounding careers. There is suggestion that the organisational career is alive and well [7] (in response claim of 'the organisational career is dead' [5]) but just exists differently to its original conception.

The existence of the 'organisational man' [9] may no longer be an expected norm for careers but whilst individuals are taking more responsibility for their careers there has also been research that suggests organisations are becoming more involved in career development and management [10]. Indeed, individuals are seeking a level of job security but are also desiring the training and personal growth that facilitates their 'boundarylessness' and creates opportunities for their career progression whether that exists internally or externally to their organisation [11]. For instance, pursuing professional qualifications and accreditation, such as the Chartered Global Management Accountant (CGMA) designation, develops both technical competencies and business skills that are relevant to contemporary working contexts.

The relationship between professional individuals and the organisations employing them shape both the institutions they work for and their own personal career paths in this way. The work of Edgar Schein [12–16] has consistently advocated the interplay between the individual and organisation in terms of understanding careers. His seminal work on career anchors provides an explanatory tool that "serves to guide, constrain, stabilise and integrate the person's career" ([14], p. 127). According to Schein's original work [14], career anchors are consistent throughout a career (as a stable syndrome) but are subject to changes in the first three years of work and experience as the anchor stabilises. There are a number of theories that seek to identify different types of career orientation [14, 17–19] with Edgar Schein's career anchors [14, 15] perhaps presenting one of the more robust models [20–22]. Career anchor theory encapsulates a range of factors in individual career paths and enables researchers to organise and make sense of values, motivations and competences that guide these.

Edgar H. Schein's career anchor model developed from longitudinal research on men and women in different occupations [12, 14, 15]. Despite the age of the original concept, Schein [16] argues that understanding career anchors is more important than ever, given the transitional nature of work and a rapidly evolving global economy, so that individuals are able to make intelligent plans for their future. Changes in work and structure of work such as downsizing, delayering, rightsizing, globalisation, new technologies and an increased emphasis on knowledge based work means that traditional job descriptions may become increasingly irrelevant [16].

The concept of a career should be understood as a dynamic process whereby individuals are able to define and redefine their changing roles as structure and networks change around them [16] Understanding careers in this way may encourage individuals to adapt to turbulent working environments and may prompt managers to examine roles and changes to allow for responsive succession planning. The concept of a career anchor promotes the understanding of a career as the steps and phases of an individual's occupation anchored by a self-image of competencies, motives and values which have been constructed internally from experience [14]. The definition emphasises self-discovery and the importance of feedback in shaping the development of an individual vocationally [23]. This provides a framework for articulating what each person's values and motivations are within their overall conception of self across a range of career anchors - see Table 1 for summary.

Anchors have also been described as 'careers within careers' [14, 24] whereby individuals can pursue a number of different types of career (in line with career anchors e.g. managerial, technical, entrepreneurial) within a single occupation (e.g. accounting, HR, IT, etc.). For example, an accountant may be an individual with strong technical knowledge and competence who builds credibility through practice. But, another accountant may be more suited to leading and managing others in the profession (thus, reflecting a managerial competence anchor). Bodies of professional accountants are emphasising the need for individuals to have a mix of technical and managerial competencies [25, 26].

Whilst Schein's anchors have been studied across contexts, industries, sectors and cultures which vary over time [20–22], there has only been a single instance where the original COI has been updated to incorporate a new anchor. An internationalism anchor [27] has been empirically tested by Lazarova, Cerdin and Liao [28] and was found to

Table 1. Schein's career anchors [14, 15]

Schein (1978)					Schein (1990)		
Security and Stability	Autonomy and Independence	Technical/ Functional	Managerial	Entrepreneurial and Creativity	Service and Dedication	Pure Challenge	Lifestyle
The desire for security of employment and benefit	The desire for freedom to pursue career interests	The desire for enhance technical competence and credibility	The desire for managerial responsibilities	The desire to create and develop new products and services	The desire to engage in activities that improve the world in some ways	The desire to overcome major obstacles and solve almost unsolvable problems	The desire to integrate personal and career needs
Need based	Need based	Talent based	Talent based	Talent based	Value based	Value based	Need based

be the most prevalent in a sample of French expatriates; the items that formed the score for the anchor were heavily focused on the physical mobility of individuals in response to unique characteristics surrounding expatriate work and careers. The prevalence of this as a primary anchor over the sample highlights that there are opportunities to develop Schein's work to incorporate and represent contemporary career motivations.

2.2 Changes to Professional Work

Traditionally, professional work has been exclusive to elite groups of [29], in which the highly qualified practise in a 'learned' profession (such as medicine, law or accountancy [30]). They apply their technical skills in a practice based setting with predictable and clear linear pathways through their career [31]. Currently, what we understand to be professional work has changed considerably since this establishing theory, with only some themes remaining relevant.

However, the prediction and awareness of changes to professional work was not far behind. In 1973 Haug proposed a theory of deprofessionalisation whereby professional workers (specifically within the medical profession) would lose their monopoly over exclusive knowledge because of processes of codification in medical knowledge and subsequently patients being able to access this information [32]. Whilst Haug's hypothesis has not been overtly supported in subsequent research, there are elements that resonate with more general changes to professional work (such as technology increasing availability of professional knowledge to lay individuals).

Similarly and writing at the same time as Haug, Oppenheimer's proletarianization thesis acknowledged that professional work can be broken down so that some staff could perform parts of a task (considered as deskilled work) whilst a smaller number of individuals took administrative and bureaucratic control over the whole process [33]. Professionals operating within large organisational settings were subjected to this (exemplified by the case of modern hospitals in his thesis) with aspects of bureaucratic control undermining professional autonomy.

More recent research has addressed the notion of professionals 'embedded' within organisations [34]. Some claim that professionals working towards organisational goals could lead to a form of 'corporate professionalisation' where pleasing customer, clients or stakeholders takes greater importance over upholding professional responsibilities [35]. These views appear to be superseded by more positive perspectives on professionals within practice. Professionals have become increasingly strategic and have been key drivers of institutional change because of their position of power and role as "brokers of varieties of capital" [36, p.436] in business settings. Rather than a play off between organisational and professional values, the modern view is that of an interconnection of occupational and organisational principles [34, 37].

2.3 Shared Service Centres and Professional Work

New organisational forms such as SSCs and business process outsourcing (BPO) are redesigning and re-engineering professional work around multi-disciplinary processes such as the so-called 'Order to Cash'. Process working along with other new working methods such as team working, empowerment, Lean, etc., drive efficiency and hence, the flow of information between organisational departments. This not only has an impact in terms of the professional work that is engineered out but that the changes to management accounting within SSCs meant that some professionals were released from transactional work and are now providing support for management decisions in new strategic roles [38]. (Note: in terms of the effect on professional work the forms of SSC and BPO are essentially synonymous and herein the issues of BPO are subsumed in the SSC model).

SSCs denote the "concentration of company resources performing like activities typically spread across the organisation, in order to service multiple internal partners at lower cost and with higher service levels, with the common goal of delighting external customers and enhancing corporate value" [39, p. 71]. Here support functions are taken out of individual branches or businesses and located together in one unit as a 'business within a business' [40], see Fig. 1.

M-form model
(support services embedded)

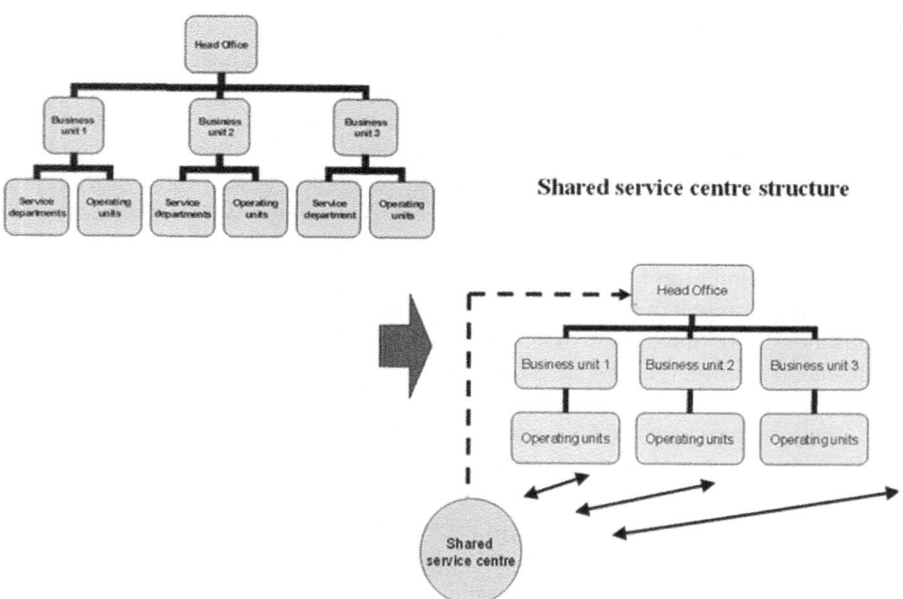

Fig. 1. Moving to a shared service model [8]

Typically many lower level professional processes are simplified and automated, driving efficiency and potentially reducing the cost of these activities for the parent organisation [33]. This activity becomes enabled by technology with the professional process becoming embedded in systems (such as ERPs) [32]. Ultimately this means that the deep professional understanding that comes with professional education or accreditation is not needed to perform some tasks.

At the other end of the scale, senior and established professionals are engaging in strategic work in the SSC [36]. Whilst the work of the finance professional in the SSC is founded on their technical knowledge and professional values, there is a requirement to build skill sets that are increasingly suited to their organisational context [41].

Delayering of management in the SSC means that the centres have a workforce consisting of large numbers of employees carrying out lower level tasks and a smaller number of professionals engaged in the strategic work [42] reflecting Oppenheimer's proletarianization thesis [33]. It is this structure coupled with the polar nature of roles in the SSC that has led to a skills gap for finance professionals working in the SSC [8].

Following on from the background literature, the following question was formulated to guide the empirical enquiry:

- Can the use of a traditional theory (Schein's career anchors) aid in understanding the values and self-perceptions of professional workers in the SSC?

3 Method

The researcher adopted a mixed method approach to examine these constructs in line with the exploratory nature of the research questions. The first phase of the empirical work was to conduct a series of face-to-face interviews to capture the complexity of the SSC as a new relatively understudied context and build up a more detailed understanding of professional work and careers in the new environment of the SSC. Guided by the interview data, the second, quantitative, phase sought to explore the underlying assumptions of career anchors in a contemporary working context. Data was collected in the form of 18 semi-structured interviews with key informants (11 face to face and 7 via telephone) and an online survey disseminated to 500 individuals yielding a response rate of 63.8 % (n = 319).

All data was gathered from a single organisation which will remain anonymous and herein referred to as 'Oilco'. Oilco is a global group of energy and petrochemical companies with around 94,000 employees in over 70 countries and territories. Oilco operate five SSCs across the world based in Europe and Asia and are considered well established against their peers in terms of their SSC operation which began in 1999. The finance function in the SSC performs over 55 % of the financial and accounting based work for Oilco's entire business. Overall there are over 10,000 employees working with or as part of the SSCs operating in finance, HR, customer service, procurement, IT, supply and distribution with 23 languages spoken across the centres.

Both Oilco and the interviewees featuring in this work were recruited through a purposive sampling strategy [43]. Sampling was confined to specific groups of people that fulfilled a number of criteria surrounding their work in a SSC, management accountancy and finance and their role. This was facilitated by senior staff at Oilco.

11 interviews were initially conducted in one of Oilco's SSCs located in the UK; these were recorded with the consent of the interviewees, transcribed verbatim and then checked (and in some cases amended) by interviewees. Each interview lasted between 20 min to 1 h. Before the interviews commenced each participant was able to have an informal discussion with the researcher surrounding the nature of the work. This also involved a full explanation of ethical guidelines. Before beginning the interviewees were given a hard copy of the interview prompt and made aware that this acted as a guide rather than an exact script and that the semi-structured approached to interviews meant that additional questions may be asked [43]. Consent forms were signed and collected before recording began.

The interview prompt was organised and ordered into 5 sections with the intention of collecting a coherent and detailed story for each participant; these areas were background, role and structure, the organisation, personal progression and anchor related questions from Schein's career planning interview questions [16] which supplement his career anchor inventory (COI) [14, 15] used in the quantitative part of this research. The purpose of this research stage was also to inform the quantitative survey and understand how a tool developed in the 1970s may need to be adapted for the needs of research new organisational contexts.

There were two outcomes from the interviews; firstly splitting Schein's original security/stability anchor into 'organisational security/stability' and 'employability security/stability' (both of which had previously been suggested by factor analysis on Schein's COI [4, 44]; and secondly, the inclusion of a new measure for global working (notions of internationalism as an anchor were originally suggested by Suutari and Taka, 2004). A notable empirical study testing internationalism as a career anchor was published by Lazarova, Cerdin and Liao [28], however their measure for an internationalism anchor was deemed unsuitable for studying global work in the SSC because it focused too heavily on physical, geographical mobility.

The online survey consisted of two sections which aimed to capture different types of data from 70 different items. The first section sought to capture information on demographic factors (accounting for 20 of the items); this was followed by an updated version of Schein's career anchors inventory (COI) consisting of 49 items which included items to measure two different types of security/stability (organisational and employability) and a global working anchor. The final item of the survey was an opportunity for respondents to add 'further comments'. A five point Likert scale was adopted (as it has been in many career anchor studies, e.g. Lazarova, Cerdin and Liao [28]) to allow for a null option and increase the variety of responses to give a better indication of the strength of a response.

The survey was disseminated to 500 staff working in finance at Oilco's SSCs. This was distributed as an online survey using Bristol Online Surveys; it was disseminated over five countries; UK, Poland, India, Philippines and Malaysia; this process was facilitated by Oilco once the sample requirements (as outlined previously in this chapter) had been clarified with the organisation. The link to the survey was sent out via email to participants work email addresses from an internal email address with the sponsorship of management at Oilco SSC. The survey yielded a response rate of 63.8 % (n = 319).

Once the survey results had been collected, a final set of seven interviews were conducted with employees at Oilco's Malaysia SSC[1] (Pacific-Asian countries are host to many SSCs [45]). The purpose of these interviews was to clarify any anomalies between the first set of interviews and survey data, to ensure the survey data was interpreted correctly and contribute further meaning and understanding to the survey findings. There was an element of progressive focusing [46] in the methodological design. This allowed for a degree of flexibility to enable the researcher to move between theory and fieldwork, making modifications in between, in order to generate meaningful theory and insights. Quantitative analysis using exploratory factor analysis (EFA) was used to examine constructs of career anchors in this context, along with correlation analysis.

4 Results and Discussion

4.1 Demographic Statistics

The data collected on demographics, when taken as a whole, represents an evenly spread population in terms of sex, previous shared services work, location of work and professional membership. It is clear that Oilco's mature centre houses a highly educated workforce across the globe. Respondents falling within generation Y and X age categories are prevalent with most falling in the former, younger age range. The range of demographics here should provide a varied range of responses (and individual experiences) to the career anchors section of the survey.

The survey was distributed across five SSCs to a total of 500 workers at varying stages of careers in finance. The survey yielded a response rate of 63.8 % (n = 319). The majority of the sample had been working within the case organisation's SSCs for between one and six years. 41.4 % of the sample had previously worked at a SSC prior to their work at Oilco; 58.6 % had not worked at an SSC before. In terms of professional membership, across the entire data set, 55.5 % did not belong to a professional body, 0.9 % had previously (but were not a part of one now) and 43.6 % had a current and active membership.

All of the participants were based in their country of work (see Table 2); only 3.6 % (n = 12) of the sample reported that their home country was different to their current location of work.

The majority of respondents were aged between 25–34 years, representing participants categorised as generation Y [47, 48] followed by those aged between 35–49

---

[1] Cultural differences were acknowledged by the researcher, however the standardised nature of SSC work across the globe (in terms of type of work, structure of roles and the general operation) meant that these effects may have been lessened; the construct under study was professional work and careers not cultural factors, however this is an opportunity further research into SSCs. The researcher sought to reflect reality which in this case was a seamless global operation that did not distinguish work by the country in which it was completed.

Table 2. Current location

		Frequency	Percent	Valid percent	Cumulative percent
Valid	India	146	45.8	45.8	45.8
	United Kingdom	85	26.6	26.6	72.4
	Malaysia	49	15.4	15.4	87.8
	Philippines	21	6.6	6.6	94.4
	Poland	18	5.6	5.6	100.0
	Total	319	100.0	100.0	

years representing generation X [49]; only 2.5 % of the sample represented 'baby boomers'.

Nearly the entire sample reported being educated beyond secondary school. Table 3 shows the highest levels of education reported by the sample. The participants that reported other education levels all stated that their professional qualification was their highest education level.

Table 3. Education levels

Highest reported level of education	%
High school/secondary school	1.6 %
College	11.9 %
University or higher education	40.4 %
Postgraduate education	31.7 %
Other	14.4 %

The sex of the respondents was fairly evenly spread with 52.7 % male and 47.3 % female making up the sample. Table 4 shows the roles of the respondents.

The population pyramid below (see Fig. 2) demonstrates the structure of the reported roles within the centres which has been split by gender. There is constriction in vertical progression which is described by the interviewees:

> SG10: *I would say that as you get up in the centre in Glasgow the career roles and the grades become fewer and fewer and therefore realistically to expand you would have to move into business.*

The narratives of individuals suggest frequent movement between roles, but that most of this is lateral rather than vertical.

Figure 2 reflects the entire sample across all five centres however there are individual differences between them. For instance the spread of gender differs considerably for each SSC (see Table 5), for example the centre in Chennai employs a greater number of males whilst the centres in Malaysia and Poland have a higher population of females. This may reveal aspects to do with national culture and work.

Exploring Career Anchors in Shared Service Centres 61

Table 4. Roles of respondents

Role	%
Team member	57.4
Technical expert	2.4
Team leader	10.4
Manager	14.4
Senior manager	9.4
Global manager	0.7
Other	5.3

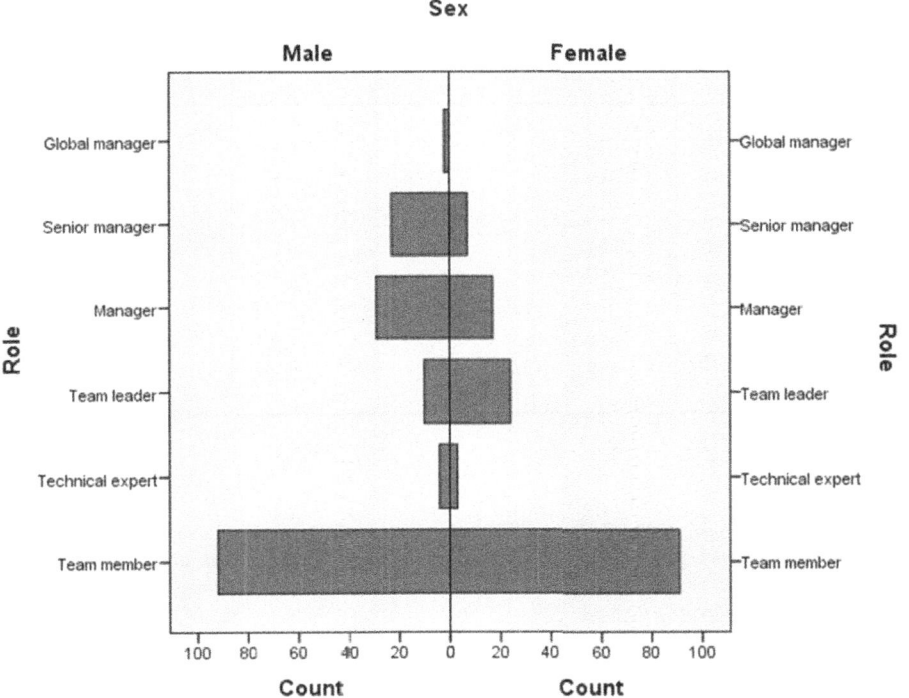

Fig. 2. Population pyramid

4.2 Career Anchors in the SSC - Schein's Theory Revisited

Throughout the qualitative data there were suggestions that lifestyle, general managerial, security/stability (employability and organisational) and global working anchors were important. SG1 explained how in her work in the SSC she enjoys aspects of global working most:

Table 5. Current location * Sex Crosstabulation

Count		Sex		Total
		Male	Female	
Current location	India	119	27	146
	Malaysia	8	41	49
	Philippines	7	14	21
	Poland	4	14	18
	United Kingdom	30	55	85
Total		168	151	319

Table 6. Original and revised anchors - Prevalence and descriptive statistics

	N	Minimum	Maximum	Mean	Std. Deviation	Skewness		Kurtosis	
	Statistic	Statistic	Statistic	Statistic	Statistic	Statistic	Std. Error	Statistic	Std. Error
Employability security/stability	319	1.0	5.0	4.119	.6833	-1.233	.137	3.499	.272
Lifestyle	319	1.0	5.0	3.932	.6107	-.551	.137	.793	.272
Security/stability	319	1.0	5.0	3.907	.6163	-.874	.137	1.664	.272
Technical/functional	319	1.0	5.0	3.789	.5189	-.597	.137	2.493	.272
Pure challenge	319	1.0	5.0	3.761	.6356	-.611	.137	1.118	.272
Global working	319	1.0	5.0	3.587	.7020	-.506	.137	.174	.272
Autonomy/independence	319	1.0	5.0	3.523	.7183	-.302	.137	-.016	.272
Service/dedication to a cause	319	1.0	5.0	3.503	.6968	-.220	.137	-.218	.272
Organisational security/stability	319	1.0	5.0	3.268	.8371	-.249	.137	-.128	.272
Entrepreneurial creativity	319	1.0	5.0	3.244	.7922	-.006	.137	-.389	.272
General managerial competence	319	1.0	5.0	3.220	.6927	-.143	.137	-.263	.272
Valid N (listwise)	319								

SG1: *Mostly it's been that kind of cross cultural experience and the travelling with this role and with previous roles. And that's been really kind of satisfying. So I think the whole kind of realising that you're part of a global organisation, a worldwide organisation, having the chance to communicate with people all over the world is probably the biggest attraction in that respect.*

Table 6 shows the prevalence of Schein's original anchors revised to include new concepts of career anchors that have been previously theorised in the literature [4, 27].

A newly proposed anchor, employability security/stability [4] was the most prevalent anchor for the sample, reinforcing that skills and training helped these individuals navigate their careers. This was followed by the needs based anchors: lifestyle and security/stability [14, 15]. The prevalence of needs based anchors (over talents or value based) may suggest that the moderation of career anchors by elements outside of vocation such as social and family contexts has increased [24, 50]. This is reinforced by some of the multiple regression output which found that neither professional nor shared services work explained variance in career anchors within this sample.

Based on vocational aspects, Schein hypothesised that finance professionals would be anchored by technical/functional competence [15] (ranked fourth most prevalent in this research), however findings from the present research indicates that needs based anchors are assigned higher value within the SSC context. The interviews confirmed the flat structures of SSC [42] and this may be a factor in individuals being more concerned with developing or consolidating skills that improve their employability security before considering upwards progression, transcending the importance of a standard professional knowledge base. To date, this appears to be the first study that empirically explores the existence of an 'employability anchor'. This research shows support for the notion and perhaps justifies further study and refinement in this area.

Less prevalent anchors (organisational security/stability, entrepreneurial creativity and general managerial competence) begin to highlight some discrepancies between the qualitative data here and Schein's anchors. The interviews found that many individuals were using the organisation to navigate and understand their careers; either they wished to progress vertically in the organisation (echoing features of an organisational career [1]) or they were using the resources of the organisation to enable them to progress in terms of newer boundaryless concepts of careers through personal development [51].

The general managerial competence anchor was the lowest ranked by respondents which is somewhat surprising in light of the themes emerging in the interview data which suggested the contrary. Of course, we cannot generalise these findings and expect them to translate to a much broader spectrum of professionals at varying stages of their careers, but it could be possible that Schein's 'general managerial' anchor [14] does not truly reflect the nuances of management in the SSC for finance workers. Substantial covariance between the global working and general managerial competence anchor (found in preliminary correlational analysis) may imply that individuals are understanding management in terms of the contemporary workplace which is why they may not fully relate to a management anchor defined in the 1970s.

Whilst the traditional theory allowed the researcher to understand some of the more prevalent anchors in terms of understanding individual values and self-perceptions, it also highlighted some flaws in applying a dated (although robust) theory of career orientations to a contemporary context. It appears that there is justification for challenging the underlying assumptions of career anchors (in line with a problematization approach; [52, 53]); exploratory factor analysis was employed to provide an in depth investigation into the issues highlighted.

4.3 Career Anchors in the 21st Century?

The final output from the factor analysis suggested that a framework of six new career anchors exist for our sample of contemporary finance professionals working within the SSC (see Table 7).

This exploratory analysis has found that constructs that were considered independent by Schein [14, 15] are actually explaining career orientations in the SSC in combination with one another, creating blended anchors that capture themes with more relevance to finance professionals within the shared services context. A descriptive approach was taken in labelling the factors (Table 8); these sought to provide a

Table 7. Pattern matrix

	Component					
	1	2	3	4	5	6
Pure challenge (item 5)	.685					
Pure challenge (item 4)	.665					
Pure challenge (item 3)	.652					
Pure challenge (item 2)	.640					
Pure challenge (item 1)	.560					
Service/dedication to a cause (item 2)	.538					
Entrepreneurial creativity (item 3)	.461					
Technical/functional competence (item 5)	.435					
Technical/functional competence (item 1)		.672				
Employability security/stability (item 1)		.645				
Technical/functional competence (item 2)		.627				
General managerial competence (item 1)		.561				
Global working (item 1)		.452		.417		
Employability security/stability (item 2)		.441				
Security/stability (item 3)			.827			
Security/stability (item 4)			.814			
Security/stability (item 5)			.769			
Security/stability (item 2)			.610			
Lifestyle (item 3)			.535			
Security/stability (item 1)			.514			
General managerial competence (item 3)				.722		
General managerial competence (item 5)				.585		
General managerial competence (item 4)				.573		
General managerial competence (item 2)				.544		
Global working (item 4)				.519		
Global working (item 2)				.506		
Global working (item 5)				.450		
Lifestyle (item 4)				-.416		
Entrepreneurial creativity (item 1)					-.808	
Entrepreneurial creativity (item 5)					-.804	
Entrepreneurial creativity (item 2)					-.770	
Entrepreneurial creativity (item 4)					-.748	
Service/dedication to a cause (item 4)					-.527	
Service/dedication to a cause (item 1)					-.444	
Service/dedication to a cause (item 3)	.412				-.418	
Autonomy/independence (item 4)						.671
Autonomy/independence (item 2)						.663

(*Continued*)

Table 7. (*Continued*)

	Component					
	1	2	3	4	5	6
Autonomy/independence (item 5)						.625
Autonomy/independence (item 3)						.584
Lifestyle (item 2)						.511
Autonomy/independence (item 1)		.434				.445
Lifestyle (item 5)						.420

Extraction Method: Principal Component Analysis.
Rotation Method: Oblimin with Kaiser Normalization.
a. Rotation converged in 23 iterations.

Table 8. Overview of new factor labels

Component number	Factor label assigned	Abbreviation
1	Organisational challenge	OC
2	Skills security/employability	SSE
3	Security/stability	SEC
4	Global managerial competence	GMC
5	Entrepreneurship and social engagement	ENS
6	Flexibility/freedom	FLX

heuristic function whereby each factor is theoretically suggestive and could potentially invoke further research [54]. These interpretations will be coloured by the understanding of the researcher, in this case influences on thinking were informed by the literature and the qualitative data stages in this work [55].

Before discussing the interpretation of factors, it is important to note the limitations of the research as executed here. Firstly, we cannot assume that all major dimensions of a factor have been represented by the variables tested [55]. There may be a number of other factors that are influencing career anchors here but are not captured by the research tools. However, the flexible, abductive nature of this research [56] and immersion into the deep qualitative data has shown an attempt to logically mitigate the risk of overlooking facets that may contribute to the prevalent career anchors for finance professionals working in the SSC. Second, interpretation of exploratory factor analysis only provides a hypothesis; unless these factors are tested with new and independent data, their existence cannot be completely confirmed [57]. The angle of the whole thesis is exploratory; the purpose of interpretation was to isolate the constructs that may have a purpose in building future theory suited to new ways of working for finance professions in a contemporary context.

4.4 Key Differences Between 'Traditional' and 'New' Anchors

The six factors identified in this research differ from those that currently exist in the literature [4, 14, 15, 22, 27, 28]. Although different, these new anchors do resonate with characteristics of those previously defined but appear to be characterised by their context which will be addressed below with references to relevant literature.

Table 9 presents an overview of the six most prevalent 'traditional' anchors (which incorporated some new ideas in the form of three proposed anchors):

Table 9. Original and revised anchors and newly proposed – prevalent anchors for this sample

Prevalence	Original and revised anchors	Newly proposed anchors
1st	Employability security/stability [4]	Skills security/employability (SSE)
2nd	Lifestyle [15]	Security/stability (SEC)
3rd	Security/stability [14]	Organisational challenge (OC)
4th	Technical/functional [14]	Flexibility/freedom (FLX)
5th	Pure challenge [15]	Global managerial competence (GMC)
6th	Global working [27]	Entrepreneurship and social engagement (ENS)

In line with the findings from Schein's original theory, the new anchors also reflect a preference for needs based anchors; the precise make up of skills security/employability (and its differences with employability) will be detailed later on however, we can assume that this anchor will be impacted by the needs of individuals. What is interesting to note is that lifestyle has not been defined as a separate anchor by the exploratory factor analysis (adverse to the findings of Hardin, Stocks and Graves [58] who found this to be the most prevalent anchor for US certified accountants working in public accounting, private industry and governmental accounting work). A potential reason for this is that items previously associated with the lifestyle anchor are occurring within three of the other anchors. These items appear to make sense in terms of where they fit in the newly proposed anchors but also suggest that lifestyle is an underlying driving force in career orientations in general, rather than a separate value or need. In many ways this lends support to Feldman and Bolino's [24] claim that career anchors are complementary and do not exist independently; here lifestyle is incorporated into other anchors which blends values, needs and talents together encouraging a more holistic view of career orientations.

> *SG7: I suppose the enjoyment of progressing in doing something challenging whilst maintaining that good work life balance. I don't think I'd ever enjoy a role that was solely work. I just wish I had more time. So I think I'd like to have a decent balance between work and outside work.*

This view demonstrates how work and lifestyle are not necessarily separable for finance workers in the SSC. SG7 talks about progression, challenging work and lifestyle together. Furthermore, the popularity of virtual roles at Oilco's UK centre highlights how work and career needs are shaped by lifestyle anchor related requirements.

The absence of a technical/functional competence anchor in the newly proposed model does not imply that it is redundant in this case. Characteristics of this anchor contribute to two of the new anchors in combination with items representing other values and self-perceptions. In part, the researcher can explain this with regards to the new professional environment which sees individuals embedded within organisational contexts [34] and often performing roles surrounding the strategy of an organisation rather than focused on their technical abilities [36]. The researcher does not believe that the absence of a pure technical/functional competence anchor suggests the deterioration of professional knowledge [32], rather that this knowledge exists mutually with other competences. It is still important, but perhaps the useful application of professional knowledge in the SSC environment requires the extended skills discussed earlier in this chapter (e.g. collaboration). The new anchors reflect the reciprocal relationship between the professional and their working environment [59]. The amalgamation between items representing different original anchors that has occurred does not reflect a jumbled version of a revised model of Schein's career anchors [14, 15]. When studied in detail, it is clear that these facets of career orientations are interacting demonstrating how finance professionals understand their values and self-perceptions in a contemporary context. This will now be discussed in detail in order of the dominant anchors from the sample.

4.5 Newly Proposed Anchors in the SSC

Skills Security/Stability. The concept of a skills security/employability (SSE) anchor existing for finance professionals in the SSC really draws together the findings surrounding the previous research questions regarding skills development as a strategy for navigating careers. The anchor was formed of items associated with Schein's original anchors of technical/functional and general managerial competence [14], employability [4, 22] and global working [27, 28].

In examining these items, holistically the anchor suggests that individuals are looking to build skills to secure their future employment. The items that form the anchor also provide more detail on what kind of skills these involve which were predominantly founded on talent based anchor items linked to technical and managerial competence. However, the interpretation of these two traditional anchors differs when we examine them in light of other items which contribute to this anchor such as employability security/stability and global working. The influence of items relating to employability security/stability [4] reinforce that professionals are building a relevant skill set to develop their careers in the SSC [41].

In terms of the contribution of global working items to this anchor, it may be that individuals are aware of their role in highly globally integrated organisation (as reflected by the interviews) and that this experience of cross-cultural working extends upon their technical and basic skill sets [41]. Moreover, it could be that the dialogue of 'cultural differences' is becoming redundant in a globally connected playing field levelled by common ERP systems and internal company processes.

Whilst a globalised working environment is not the most significant contributor to SSE, it does highlight how an awareness of global working is a point of reference for finance professionals in the SSC. Overall the anchor is resonant with the themes from the interviews whereby finance professionals were tending to seek vertical progression into management; this was founded on their technical knowledge but enabled by their adaptability in building 'soft' and 'business' skills that were relevant to managing teams. Moreover, finance professionals were aware of the need to build on these skills and develop personally.

Security/Stability. Security/stability (SEC) exists in n the same way that Schein originally suggested [14] but with the addition of an item representing lifestyle [15]. SEC is based on the needs of the individual in guiding their career decisions but in this context, it is also influenced by a value based item, namely lifestyle. Balancing personal, family, and career requirements could play a part in forming job security for individuals; for instance, individuals may not feel secure in a job if it does not coincide with their values surrounding lifestyle as the work may be unsustainable. Statistically, the internal consistency for the SEC anchor was high (Cronbach's $\alpha = .804$) implying that this item is measuring the same construct and therefore lifestyle can play a part in security. This is summarised by SG11:

> *SG11: Yes we work a bit of overtime but nothing too excessive, and I think if we were doing anything excessive then I think Oilco would step in and say this is unsustainable. We should be doing something to ensure that staff don't need to work these type of hours and that applies to me as much as anyone else. Oilco expects managers to manage it, so that staff aren't put under undue amount of stress.*

This quotation also questions perspectives on work life balance. Schein's original career anchor theory was based on the views of 44 male graduates from a university in the US [13]. However, the sample in this research is quite evenly distributed in terms of gender and also encompassed a number of cultures. This raises questions about both the impact of gender and culture on the understanding of work life balance. Research on 'work-life balance' has generally been dominated by North American and North European perspectives [60]. These perspectives showed an increase in working ways which accommodated both work and personal needs; for example alternate working (such as flexible schedules and part time work) has increased over time [61]. Furthermore the demographic shift in the shape of the workforce may have impacted this; women entering the workforce grew from the 1960's as did research on 'working mothers' [62]. This alludes to the potential differences between the current research's sample compared with Schein's original sample. These individual difference effects to do with gender and roles were highlighted by Mainiero and Sullivan's kaleidoscope theory primary care-giving females and their career trajectories [63].

The exploratory factor analysis has not found a split in the SEC anchor that has been posited in earlier literature [44, 64]. However, the findings surrounding this anchor do suggest that SEC was potentially oversimplified by Schein and is impacted by broader, related factors such as lifestyle.

The findings shed some light on the relationships between career anchors [24]. They claimed that a technical/functional competence anchor could be complementary to the SEC anchor if the individual has a desire for their working practices to remain unchanged. The current research extends upon the idea of complementary anchors and implies an increased blending of anchors as needs and values interact in the SSC (as demonstrated by SG11's quote). There is a strong indication that some of Schein's original anchors are still relevant in contemporary settings; however they exist differently to his original theory, exhibiting more similarities to alternative research [24].

A final point on SEC that is worth considering is the redundancy of the organisational security items proposed in this research. The items were formed on the basis that security may encompass more than one dimension [44] and the shift of professional work into organisational settings [36]. The anchor sought to explore if organisational security was relevant for these individuals given their context, however the items did not reflect the values and self-perceptions for these professionals. The SEC anchor explains a general level of security that is not associated to setting. However, the SSE anchor is much more reflective of context and suggests more of a boundaryless orientation [2] and individual approach to careers. Understandings of careers and how they are navigated has been characterised by organisational facets throughout the interviews. However, the quantitative data clarifies that this is not necessarily related to how the individuals perceive their security thus, one might ask, where does the organisational side of careers for professionals in the SSCs exist in terms of career anchors?

Organisational Challenge. SSE showed how finance professionals were anchored by a need to build relevant skills for their working context; organisational challenge (OC) focused more on the talents and abilities of these individuals to overcome challenges. Whilst this anchor is largely based on [15] original concept of pure challenge, the researcher believes that this is coloured by other factors that relate these challenges to the organisation. The reasoning behind this lies with the other factors contributing to the anchor, the output from the interviews and suggestions from the literature.

All five pure challenge items which occur within this anchor are supplemented by items traditionally associated with service/dedication to a cause, entrepreneurial creativity and technical/functional competence. The service/dedication to a cause item appears to have been interpreted on the basis of serving others with talents; because this particular item does not refer to humanity or society specifically (as the remainder of service/dedication to a cause items do), it may translate to a pure challenge here given its focus on skills. In fact, both the remaining items anchored in entrepreneurial creativity and technical/functional competence draw upon the application of skills (or talent) in order to overcome challenges. In some ways service/dedication to a cause, in this particular case, can be related to how individuals feel empowered by supporting others (perhaps reiterated by the reliance on informal mentoring in upwards progression within SSCs, as described in the qualitative findings).

So why has this been interpreted by the researcher as an organisational challenge? The interpretation of this factor has been influenced by the knowledge of the researcher [55] which is founded upon the findings from qualitative data, previous literature and theory. Firstly, the interviews found that 'pure challenge' existed for individuals in terms of obstacles to do with their work within the organisation.

The point to note here is that individuals associated challenge with specific characteristics of SSC work such as cultural challenges and the stimulating work associated with developing the centre (for senior staff). Pure challenge was the second most prevalent anchor for accountants working in private industry (which differed to the preferences for those in public and governmental accounting in the US) [58]. This supports the notion that a job setting can implicate the way in which individuals are anchored; in this case, it is the understanding of the underlying concept of pure challenge that differs. The present research suggests that Schein's original notion of pure challenge may be too broad for individuals to identify with in the SSC setting. In this way, OC incorporates items from other anchors that, once again, have a skills focus to form an anchor that finance professionals can identify with.

In terms of pre-existing literature, there are similarities to be drawn between the OC anchor and Derr's career orientation of 'getting high' [65]. According to this theory, individuals are driven by excitement, action and engagement in their work and tended to be creative and entrepreneurial types (supported by the form of this OC anchor) which also emphasises a holistic approach to career orientations.

Flexibility/Freedom. This anchor (FLX) combines the need based items from original autonomy/independence and lifestyle anchors [14, 15]. Attitudes reflected though the merging of these items appears to be centred upon the way in which individuals manage their workload, rather than a preference for autonomous working.

Schein's description of a dominant autonomy/independence anchor characterises individuals who would not give up the opportunity to define their own work. He states that individuals anchored in this way would opt for self-employment or highly autonomous work which allows flexibility [16]. The researcher believes that the formation of the FLX anchor in this work has a stronger emphasis on the notion of flexibility based on both the mix of items and qualitative data.

Two lifestyle items contributed to this anchor; these items shared a common theme of integrating work into lifestyle in order to minimise interference with personal and family concerns. In this way, it demonstrates the way in which individuals wish to balance their work and life through the organisation and management of their work; demonstrating how autonomy/independence and lifestyle can moderate one another.

This is similar to Schein's lifestyle anchor [14, 15] which is 'the integration of career and family issues' [16, p. 13] which is not specifically related to a career. However, FLX connects to the navigation of a career because it takes into the account the way in which individuals desire to work in order to achieve this balance. Whereas the autonomy/independence anchor is solely focused on the way of working and only suggests a preference as a reason for this rather than taking into account broader societal factors such as a family life.

This supports Feldman and Bolino's hypothesis that anchors can be complementary with individuals influenced by more than one anchor [24] (contrary to Schein's view). Feldman and Bolino proposed that anchors exist in an octagonal model instead of independently. Their hypothesis is broadly based on Holland's personal preference orientation scales [17] whereby individual categorisation represents a mix of preferences represented by a three letter code; i.e. conventional, realistic and investigative (CRI). Understanding careers in this way acknowledges the relationship and interaction between orientation types rather than considering them exclusive of other wider factors that could expand their original meanings (similar to Super's life space theory [18]). In this way, FLX could also represent two of Derr's orientations whereby individuals are 'getting free' for the purpose of 'getting balanced' [65].

Global Managerial Competence. The fourth most prevalent anchor also reflects how elements of career anchors need to be considered in view of other dimensions; however, this time, traditional anchors are blending with new ideas reflecting the work and values of finance professionals in the SSC. Global managerial competence (GMC) reflects influences from Schein's general managerial competence [14] and items from a proposed anchor of global working and also includes a lifestyle item.

The work of the SSC spans physical borders; therefore, more senior positions that are associated with general management in this context will tend to entail a higher level of global responsibility. Only one of the global working items alludes to physical mobility as a part of global work. We have seen how senior managers are required to have a level of physical mobility in their roles but how those in lower level positions are still able to work globally without the travel based element echoing the 'martini workers' in Rothwell, Herbert and Seal that are able to work 'any time, any place, anywhere' and now seemingly, from any location [8].

It is in this way that GMC differs to Lazarova, Cerdin and Liao's internationalism anchor [28]. Whilst this was suitable for their highly mobile sample of French expatriates, it doesn't quite explain the global nuances of SSC work. GMC is more concentrated on the type of work accountants are engaging with in the SSC, and the integrated nature of centres across borders.

GMC gives the impression that a preference for this anchor comes with a disclaimer; the inclusion of an item related to lifestyle shows that individuals also want to balance the demands of their professional and personal life before taking on a managerial position. This reinforces that lifestyle considerations are also guiding the preference for GMC.

Entrepreneurship and Social Engagement. The fifth most prevalent anchor has been interpreted as entrepreneurship and social engagement (ENS). It captures a mix of entrepreneurial creativity and service/dedication to a cause items from Schein's original inventory [14, 15].

This interpretation was based on the items that contributed to this anchor; the qualitative data did not provide information surrounding these themes. It appears that some individuals are wishing to start their own enterprise (based on talent) which would contribute to the welfare of society (based on their values). The last service/dedication to a cause item highlights the role of skills in attaining these goals. This existence of an anchor like this was totally unpredicted prior to data collection and analysis; however, the researcher can draw on information regarding Oilco's corporate social responsibility in attempt to explain the emergence of this anchor.

It was reported that 45.8 % of survey respondents were currently located in India. The reason for this large proportion was due to the Chennai centre being the second largest for Oilco (with 2,100 employees) and because they employed many professionals that were suitable for the purposes of the survey. Their website (as an organisational cultural artefact; [66]) describes a number of corporate social responsibility activities that are specific to India. These include community development projects, promotion of education, road safety and helping those with disabilities in the country. As part of this, workers are able to volunteer for roles on these projects. Oilco interacts with a number of Non-Government Organisations (NGOs) in India to complete their work and this could potentially influence or explain the existence of the ENS anchor.

The influence of national culture was also considered using Hofstede's cultural dimensions [67] with an expectation that high levels of collectivism[2] could explain this anchor. However, the scores for India did not reflect high collectivism, nor did the score for other Asian countries within the sample. These countries also did not reflect feminine societies whereby the dominant values in society would be caring for others and quality of life.

In summary, the ENS anchor shows how flexible research approaches, such as problematization [52, 53], can produce unexpected findings. Although unpredicted, this anchor shows how Schein's original anchors [14, 15] can combine to create something new and relevant to workers in specific contemporary contexts. Moreover, the identification of this anchor raises a number of other questions; for example, to what extent does organisational and national culture impact career anchors? This was considered beyond the scope of the current study. Of course, changes in cultures will mean a difference in values among the sample, however the nature of professional finance work is standardised across Oilco's centres; the focus of this research was on work and careers as an overall picture rather than focusing in on certain cultures and the differences between them.

5 Conclusions and Suggestions for Further Research

The previous section hopes to demonstrate the connectedness between professional work, environment and career orientations and how this is relevant in terms of career anchor theory. In this way, the research promotes a holistic view of career orientations that does not constrain thinking and investigation into assumptions associated with previous research.

The new career anchors suggest that individuals place high value on developing their skills to sustain their employability [4, 22]. This may be in response to a

---

[2] Collectivism can broadly be defined as acting within a larger framework for the greater good of one's society [67].

realisation surrounding the skills gap for professional workers in the SSC [8], as well as the requirement for professionals to adapt their skills for organisational contexts [41]. Whilst skills development appears to be an individual approach to career management it is evident that the role of the organisation is still important in facilitating this development. However this isn't to the extent of the 'organisational man' [9] rather it is reminiscent of a new organisational career which takes a more balanced approached to careers that are managed both individually and with the resources of organisations [7].

Although general managerial competence, as an original anchor, seemed prevalent from the interviews; the initial study of traditional anchors did not support this and the findings from new anchors showed that it existed in a different way to Schein's original framework [14]. Instead, the construct of this anchor seemed increasingly centred on globalised work (which was proposed as a new and separate anchor, but loaded with others) which had already been suggest in the literature [27, 28]. In this case, 'international' anchors did not need to be centred on the physical mobility of individuals; rather, in this case, it is about being part of a global operation.

It has been suggested that anchors could exist together and complement one another [24]. The findings from this research support their hypothesis in a way. Instead, some anchors (with FLX as a prime example) merged two original anchors into a new, blended anchor. This showed how concepts could complement each other but more importantly showed the potential relationships that exist between orientations of careers. We cannot assume that an individual is guided by a single value, motivation or competence [17, 18]. Rather, researchers should adopt an increasingly holistic approach to fully comprehend a broad range of factors that can influence career orientations [50]. This research has followed this perspective and has subsequently provided a number of contributions to the fields of professional work, SSCs and understanding career orientations in new contexts.

In sum, the use of a traditional theory, such as Schein's career anchors, can aid in understanding the values and self-perceptions of professional workers in the SSC. The structure of the theory and some of the original anchors provide a secure foundation for contemporary empirical investigations into new career anchors [28]. Application of the theory here, and the exploratory nature of this work, has shown that anchors do exist but differently to how Schein first proposed. This work serves as a foundation into understanding careers in the SSC and shows that there is value in challenging traditional ways of understanding constructs in new contexts.

In terms of practical implications, an updated version of career anchors for contemporary working contexts could serve as a more suitable self-help tool for individual career management for finance professionals in SSCs in the spirit of Schein's original intentions for the theory [14]. It could also be employed by organisations for job matching to identify opportunities that are congruent with individual anchors that are based around employees' competences (such as GMC). Overall the findings of this research suggest that anchors are specific to environment and that there is further opportunity to refine new anchors to better suit new working contexts.

Acknowledgments. The project was supported by the Economic and Social Research Council (ESRC), the Chartered Institute of Management Accountants (CIMA) General Charitable Trust and the School of Business and Economics, Loughborough University.

References

1. Weber, M.: The Theory of Economic and Social Organization. Translated by A. M. Henderson & Talcott Parsons. The Free Press, NY (1947)
2. Arthur, M.B., Rousseau, D.M. (eds.): The Boundaryless Career. New Employment Principle for a New Organizational Era. Oxford University Press (1996)
3. Inkson, K., Gunz, H., Ganesh, S., Roper, J.: Boundaryless careers: Bringing back boundaries. Organ. Stud. **33**(3), 323–340 (2012)
4. Baruch, Y.: Transforming careers: from linear to multidirectional career paths: organizational and individual perspectives. Career Dev. Int. **9**(1), 58–73 (2004)
5. Hall, D.T.: Long live the career. In: Hall, D.T. (ed.) The Career is Dead-Long Live the Career, pp. 1–12. Jossey-Bass, San Francisco (1996)
6. Lyons, S.T., Schweitzer, L., Ng, E.S.W.: How have careers changed? an investigation of changing career patterns across four generations. J. Manag. Psychol. **30**(1), 8–21 (2015)
7. Clarke, M.: The organizational career: not dead but in need of redefinition. Int. J. Hum. Resour. Manage. **24**(4), 684–730 (2013)
8. Rothwell, A.T., Herbert, I.P., Seal, W.: Shared service centers and professional employability. J. Vocat. Behav. **79**(1), 241–252 (2011)
9. Whyte, W.: The Organization Man. Simon and Schuster, New York (1956)
10. Lips-Wiersma, M., Hall, D.T.: Organizational career development is not dead: a case study on managing the new career during organizational change. J. Organ. Behav. **28**(6), 771–792 (2007)
11. Granrose, C.S., Baccili, P.A.: Do psychological contracts include boundaryless or protean careers? Career Dev. Int. **11**(2), 163–182 (2006)
12. Schein, E.H.: The individual, the organization and the career: a conceptual scheme. J. Appl. Behav. Sci. **7**(4), 401–426 (1971)
13. Schein, E.H.: Career anchors and career paths: A panel study of Management school graduates. May, Technical report No.1, Sloan School of Management (1974). http://dspace.mit.edu/bitstream/handle/1721.1/1878/SWP-0707-02815445.pdf. Accessed 30 July 2011
14. Schein, E.H.: Career Anchors: Discovering your Rent Values. University Associate Inc., San Diego (1978)
15. Schein, E.H.: Career Anchors: Trainer's Manual, revised edn. Alfred P. Sloan School of Management, MIT, Cambridge, MA (1990)
16. Schein, E.H.: Career Anchors, 3rd edn. Pfeiffer (2006)
17. Holland, J.L.: Making Vocational Choices: A Theory of Careers. Prentice Hall (1973)
18. Super, D.E.: A life-span, life-space approach to career development. J. Vocat. Behav. **16**(3), 282–298 (1980)
19. Gubler, M., Arnold, J., Coombs, C.: Organizational boundaries and beyond: a new look at the components of a boundaryless career orientation. Career Dev. Int. **19**(6), 641–667 (2014)
20. Danziger, N., Rachman-Moore, D., Valency R.: The construct validity of Schein's career anchors orientation inventory. Career Dev. Int. **13**(1), 7–19 (1986). Derr, C.B.: Five definitions of career success: implications for relationships. Applied (2008)
21. Ituma, A., Simpson, R.: Moving beyond Schein's typology: Individual career anchors in the context of Nigeria. Pers. Rev. **36**(6), 978–995 (2007)
22. Marshall, V., Bonner, D.: Career anchors and the effects of downsizing: Implications for generations and cultures at work. a preliminary investigation. J. Eur. Ind. Training **27**, 281–291 (2003)
23. Yarnall, J.: Career anchors: results of an organisational study in the UK. Career Dev. Int. **3**(2), 56–61 (1998)

24. Feldman, D., Bolino, M.: Careers within careers: reconceptualizing the nature of career anchors and their consequences. Hum. Resour. Manag. Rev. **6**(2), 89–112 (1996)
25. CGMA. Chartered Global Management Accountant (2015). About CGMA. http://www.cgma.org/AboutCGMA/Pages/default.aspx. Accessed 15 Jan 2015
26. Smedley, T.: New accountants seek happy balance. The Financial Times, 28 January 2015. http://www.ft.com. Accessed 14 April 2015
27. Suutari, V., Taka, M.: Career anchors of managers with global careers. J. Manag. Dev. **23**, 833–847 (2004)
28. Lazarova, M., Cerdin, J., Liao, Y.: The internationalism career anchor: a validation study. Int. Stud. Manag. Organ. **44**(2), 9–33 (2014)
29. Larson, M.: The Rise of Professionalism: A Sociological Analysis. University of California Express, Berkeley (1977)
30. Covert, E.C.: Is nursing a profession? Am. J. Nurs. **18**(2), 107–109 (1917)
31. Abbott, A.: The System of Professions: An Essay on the Division of Expert Labour. University of Chicago Press, Chicago (1988)
32. Haug, M.: Deprofessionalization: An alternative hypothesis for the future. Sociol. Rev. Monogr. **20**, 195–211 (1973)
33. Oppenheimer, M.: Proletarianization of the professional. In: Halmos, P. (ed.) Professionalization and Social Change, pp. 219–227. University of Keele, Keele, England (1973)
34. Faulconbridge, J., Muzio, D.: Organizational professionalism in globalising law firms. Work Employ Soc. **22**(1), 7–25 (2008)
35. Greenwood, R., Suddaby, R., Hinings, C.R.: Theorizing change: The role of professional associations in the transformation of institutionalized fields. Acad. Manag. J. **45**(1), 58–80 (2002)
36. Suddaby, R., Viale, T.: Professionals and field-level change: Institutional work and the professional project. Curr. Sociol. **59**(4), 423–442 (2011)
37. Muzio, D., Faulconbridge, J.: The global professional service firm: 'One firm' models versus (Italian) distant institutionalized practices. Organ. Stud. **34**(7), 397–925 (2013)
38. Herbert, I.P., Seal, W.B.: Shared services as a new organisational form: Some implications for management accounting. Br. Acc. Rev. **44**(2), 83–97 (2012)
39. Schulman, D.S., Dunleavy, J.R., Harmer, M.J., Lusk, J.S.: Shared services. Adding Value to the Business Unit. Wiley & Sons (1999)
40. Quinn, B.E., Cooke, R.S., Kris, A.: Shared Services: Mining for Corporate Gold. Financial Times, Harlow (2000)
41. Mohamed, E.K.A., Lashine, S.H.: Accounting knowledge and skills and the challenges of a global business environment. Manag. Financ. **29**(7), 3–16 (2003)
42. Farndale, E., Paauwe, J., Hoeksema, L.: In-sourcing HR: shared service centres in the Netherlands. Int. J. Hum. Resour. Manage. **20**(3), 544–561 (2009)
43. Sekaran, U.: Research Methods for Business: A Skill-Building Approach John Wiley & Sons, Inc. (2000)
44. Petroni, A.: Strategic career development for R&D staff: a field research. Team Perform. Manag. **6**, 52–61 (2000)
45. Accenture. Shared services location strategy: Asia Pacific perspectives (2015). https://www.accenture.com/us-en/insight-shared-services-location-strategy-asia-pacific-perspectives.aspx. Accessed 6 June 2015
46. Sinkovics, R.R., Alfoldi, E.A.: Progressive focusing and trustworthiness in qualitative research: The enabling role of computer-assisted qualitative data analysis software (CAQDAS). Manag. Int. Rev. **52**(6), 817–845 (2012)
47. Weiler, A.: Information-seeking behaviour in generation Y students: Motivation, critical thinking, and learning theory. J. Acad. Librarianship **31**(1), 46–53 (2004)

48. Nimon, S.: Generation Y and Higher Education: The Other Y2K. J. Inst. Res. **13**(1), 24–41 (2007)
49. Williams, A., Coupland, J., Folwell, A., Sparks, L.: Talking about generation X: defining them as they define themselves. J. Lang. Soc. Psychol. **16**(3), 251–277 (1997)
50. Rodrigues, R., Guest, D., Budjanovcanin, A.: From anchors to orientations: towards a contemporary theory of career preferences. J. Vocat. Behav. **83**(2), 142–152 (2013)
51. Pemberton, P., Herriot, C.: New Deals: Revolution in Managerial Careers. John Wiley and Sons (1995)
52. Locke, K., Golden-Biddle, K.: Constructing opportunities for contribution: structuring intertextual coherence and "problematizing" in organizational studies. Acad. Manag. J. **40**(5), 1023–1062 (1997)
53. Alvesson, M., Sandberg, J.: Generating research questions through problematization. Acad. Manag. Rev. **36**(2), 247–271 (2011)
54. Rummel, R.J.: Applied Factor Analysis. Northwestern University Press (1970)
55. Comrey, A.L., Lee, H.B.: A first course in factor analysis, 2nd edn. Erlbaum (1992)
56. Blaikie, N.: Approaches to social enquiry. Polity, Cambridge (1993)
57. Mulaik, S.A.: Blurring distinctions between component analysis and common factor analysis. Multivar. Behav. Res. **25**(1), 53–59 (1990)
58. Hardin, J.R., Stocks, M.H., Graves, O.F.: The effect of match or mismatch between the career anchors and the job set tings of CPAs: An empirical analysis. Adv. Account. **18**, 119–148 (2001)
59. Muzio, D., Brock, D.M., Suddaby, R.: Professions and institutional change: towards an institutionalist sociology of the professions. J. Manage. Stud. **50**(5), 699–721 (2013)
60. Guest, D.E.: Perspectives on the study of work-life balance. Soc. Sci. Inf. **41**(2), 255–279 (2002)
61. Presser, H.B.: Job, family and gender: determinants of nonstandard schedules among employed Americans in 1991. Demography **32**, 577–595 (1995)
62. Lewis, S., Cooper, C.: The work–family research agenda in changing contexts. J. Occup. Health Psychol. **4**(4), 382–393 (1999)
63. Mainiero, L.A., Sullivan, S.E.: Kaleidoscope careers: An alternative explanation of the "opt-out" revolution. Acad. Manag. Executive **19**(1), 106–123 (2005)
64. Igbaria, M., Greenhaus, J.H., Parasuraman, S.: Career orientations of MIS employees: an empirical analysis. MIS Q. **15**(2), 151–169 (1991)
65. Derr, C.B.: Five definitions of career success: implications for relationships. Appl. Psychol. **35**(3), 415–435 (1986)
66. Schein, E.H.: Organizational Culture and Leadership: A Dynamic View. Jossey-Bass (1992)
67. Hofstede, G.: Culture's consequences: International Differences in Work-Related Values. SAGE (1980)

An Examination of the Relationship Between Organizational Culture Determinants and Retained Organizations Growth Stages

Albert Plugge[✉], Christiaan Kooijman, and Marijn Janssen

Faculty of Technology, Policy and Management, Delft University of Technology,
Delft, The Netherlands
a.g.plugge@tudelft.nl

Abstract. Empirical research on the maturity of retained IT organizations has remained scarce. IS literature shows that studies do not investigate the effect of organizational culture determinants on the relationship with the growth stage of an retained organization. The aim of this paper is to examine the relationship between organizational culture determinants and retained organizations stages of growth. Data from three case studies was collected and the Social Exchange Theory is used to understand the degree of interaction between the staff of retained organizations. Our analysis identified that culture determinants form a predictable pattern with the growth stage of a retained organization. Specifically, the culture determinants Management and Focus fit with their assumed growth stage in all three case studies. This might indicate that both determinants are interrelated as executive management of a firm has to develop a clear focus to achieve their IT mission and goals. Moreover, from an individual level, the results show that the degree of social interaction between staff is influenced by the perception of IT in the organization.

Keywords: Retained organization · Organizational culture · Social exchange theory · Case study

1 Introduction

In an effort to deal with increased competition firms have developed various business strategies to cater for competition [1]. Literature shows that outsourcing can be seen as a valuable business strategy to adapt to market demands [2, 3]. Joha [4] argues that in case of outsourcing firms establish an intermediary function or liaison between their business units and IT vendors, also labelled as the retained organization. A firm's retained organization fulfills an essential role in creating coherence in bundling business need while managing vendors delivery of IT services. As a retained organization is influenced by their organizational structure [5] different growth stages or maturity levels can be identified. Gottschalk and Solli-Sæther [6] argue that growth stages are based on the 'assumption of predictable patterns (conceptualized in terms of stages) that exist in the growth of organizations…, and the diffusion of information technology, p 280'.

Literature reveal that organizational culture determinants are affected by social interactions in organizational settings [7], which is related to a retained organizations growth stage. Examples include job attitudes [8] and technology practices [9]. As an effect, organizational culture determinants, such as organizational structure, communication, and leadership [10] should be aligned with the growth stage of an organization. Misalignment between a firm's growth stage and dominant organizational culture determinants may deteriorate the performance of a firm. To identify the growth stage of an organization Nelson and Burns [11] defined a framework ranging from ranging from reactive, responsive, proactive, and high performing. This high-performance framework is based on the assumption that a firm's organizational culture determinants affects their performance. However, studies on firms' organizational culture [12–14] have some important shortcomings. First, the main stream of research focuses on firms' corporate function while the relationship with their IT organization or in case of outsourcing, a firm's retained organization is limited. Second, research on the relationship between organizational culture and Information Technology (IT) is only related to software process improvements [15] and maturity models like CMMi and Cobit [16, 17]. Instead in this research we will study the relationship between the assumed organization culture dimensions and the growth stage of an retained organization from an employee's individual perspective.

Staff as a part of a firm's retained organization are considered to be a key element in shaping the organizational culture determinants. This is related to the *Social Exchange Theory* (SET) which is based on the assumption that there are differences in the actors that are involved in a firm's relationships [18]. Literature shows that IT mission and objectives might be subject to various cultural interpretations of staff who are involved [19]. However, the influence of organizational culture determinants on firms' retained organization related growth stages is yet unclear. Although previous organizational culture studies on IS/IT shed some light on their effects Leidner and Kayworth [20] argue that 'there is very little research devoted to examining the role of organizational culture determinants in the process of IT planning, p. 369'. In addition, Gottschalk and Solli-Sæther [6] state that 'work related to stages of growth has to a large extent been conceptual, p 279'. Research on how organizational culture determinants affects retained organizations growth stages is still scarce. Therefore, the objective of this paper is to empirically examine the relationship between organizational culture determinants and retained organizations stages of growth.

This paper is organized as follows. First, based on literature we introduce the core constructs (e.g. growth stages, organizational culture determinants, and social interaction) of our study in more detail. Next, we explain the research approach followed by the findings of the case analysis. Subsequently, we discuss the implications followed by the research conclusions, limitations and recommendations for further research.

2 Literature Background and Introduction Core Constructs

Our research focused on the relationship between organizational culture determinants and retained organizations growth stage. The basic assumption is that a specific growth stage requires an accessory set of culture determinants that ideally should fit.

2.1 Retained Organization and Growth Stages

Retained organizations focus on strategic and tactical tasks such as planning, service portfolio management, architecture, and relationship management. In fulfilling their role a retained organization emphasizes managing business demands rather than delivery IT services. Literature [21, 22] reveal that a firm's retained organization provide tasks that previously belong to the IT department, which were not outsourced to the market. Kern and Willcocks [23] stated that the main goal of a retained organization is to mitigate risks and achieve productive and efficient IT operations. Today clients' retained organization and supporting capabilities are perceived to be critical to ensure that it can exploit business advantages over time [24]. Although literature shows various definitions for the term retained organization, such as 'residual IT organization' [25], 'sustaining organization' [26], and 'lean and dynamic group' [22] a clear definition is lacking. In view of our research objective we define a retained organization as 'a firm's IT management function that is responsible to determine an IT mission, objective and plans that are aligned with the firm's business departments while managing the delivery of IT services by external vendors' [adapted from Reich and Benbasat, 27, p. 56].

Literature show that scholars have studied firms' objectives to improve their organizational performance [28–30]. As the performance of an organization is affected by the staff's behavior and quality we may assume that the stage of growth or maturity of retained organizations may differ. Literature shows that stages-of-growth models have been used in IT management research [31]. Gottschalk and Solli-Sæther [32] argue that the concept of stages of growth also received some skepticism as previous studies neglected the relationship between the firm's staff. Kazanjian and Drazin [33] state that organizations do not necessarily demonstrate change by means of a linear sequence of stages, but rather that observed configurations of problems, strategies, structures, and processes will determine a firm's progress. Burn [34] argues that an important feature of stage models and their manifestations is to identify transition points that can be used to improve the quality of organizations. Notably, a firm's organizational culture has an effect on individual behavior of an organization [10] and consequently on the growth stage of a retained organization.

2.2 Organizational Culture

Organizational culture is an ambiguous concept that has been defined and interpreted in multiple studies [7, 14, 35]. Hofstede et al. [14] operating definition of culture is 'the collective programming of the mind that distinguishes the members of one group or category from other' [36 p. 5]. Scholars studied the concept of organizational culture from various perspectives, such as a value based approach [10], technology transfer practices [9], firm performance [12], and linkages between culture and IS/IT [20]. Grover [37] studied the planning culture of executive management in IS organizations and found that structured planning facilitates the importance of strategic systems investments. Another study conducted by Kanungo [38] revealed that innovative type cultures are most closely associated with firms having a delineable IT strategy. Leidner and Kayworth [20], who conducted an extensive literature review on organizational culture, found evidence for the influence of organizational culture determinants on IT management and strategy.

Nelson and Burns [11, 39] developed a vision to program an organization to achieve a state of high performance based on the assumption that a firm's organizational culture affects their performance. The authors define four frames of growth stages, ranging from reactive, responsive, proactive, and high performing (see Table 1). The reactive frame describes an organization in which ad hoc decisions are made while limited collaboration and distrust between team members prevail. Next, the responsive frame describes an organization where team members are able to handle their work effectively, focusing on achieving near-time goals by following organizational rules. Subsequently, the proactive frame characterizes an organization that is able to anticipate and handle difficult situations, and applies shared vision and values. Finally, the high performance frame describes an organization that is based on a high level of synergy among team members and where the staff is capable of going beyond expectations, applying a creative and innovative approach. In this research we use the culture determinants of [11] to evaluate their effect on stages of growth. A description of the culture determinants is provided in Appendix B.

Table 1. Organizational culture determinants

Culture determinants	Reactive stage	Responsive stage	Pro-active stage	High performing stage
Planning	Justification	Activities	Strategy	Evolution
Communication	Force feed	Feed back	Feed forward	Feed through
Change mode	Punitive	Adaptive	Planned	Programmed
Structure	Fragmented	Hierarchical	Matrix	Networks
Management	Who's to blame	Coordination	Alignment	Navigation
Focus	Diffused	Output	Result	Excellence
Motivation	Avoid plan	Rewards	Contribution	Accomplishment
Development	Survive	Cohesion	Attunement	Transformation
Perspective	Self	Team	Organization	Culture
Time frame	Past	Present	Future	Flow
Leadership style	Enforcing	Coaching	Purposing	Empowering

2.3 Social Interactions

From an exchange perspective social interactions trade social costs and benefits by means of normative rules and agreements [40]. This is related to the view of Social Exchange Theory (SET). A general assumption of SET, which is developed by various scholars [41–43], is that there are differences in actors involved within a firm's relationships [18]. Firms' staff, for instance, can form various relationships, ranging from internal co-workers [44] to external vendors [45]. As individuals return received benefits, they are likely to be helpful to internal or external partners with whom they have positive social exchange relationships [46]. Therefore, rules of exchange are based on 'normative definition of the situation that is formed among or is adapted by the participants in an exchange relation' [45, p. 351].

Thus, norms of exchange form guidelines to facilitate the exchange process between firms. Key exchange rules or control mechanisms are used to govern people's social behavior [40, 47]. The exchange rule generalized reciprocity is recognized as a norm for collaboration [40]. Das and Teng [47] describe generalized reciprocity as 'a group-based exchange relationship in which actors expect quid pro quo exchanges within the group, but not necessarily with any specific actor'. An important tenet of SET is that relationships change over time, influencing the degree of trust, which results in mutual commitments [18]. When establishing trust, Anderson and Narus [48] suggest that the collaborative actions of firms will result in outcomes that exceed expectations compared to a situation in which they are focused on their own best interests. Thus, relationships based on trust should be more flexible regarding decision-making than those that are not.

Social sanctions, which are related to mutual monitoring between actors, can be seen as a behavioral control mechanism to facilitate conflict resolution. A lack of continuous monitoring of behavior, however, may influence the reputation of other actors involved. Sanctions may result in excluding an actor from interactions within a sourcing arrangement. As actors in a sourcing arrangement are more aware of their position and reputation related to other actors, they are expected to contribute to exchange information. The objectives of actors involved may be contradictory which might hinder the exchange of information and services. Das and Teng [47] argue that a common culture forms a prerequisite for behavioral control in an inter-firm relationship. Moreover, Ekeh [49] states that a cooperative form of a common culture is valuable as it facilitates both generalized reciprocity and social sanction.

3 Research Approach

3.1 Overall Approach

When focusing on the retained organization, the unit of analysis in this research addresses organizational cultural determinants and their relationship with retained organizations growth stage. The unit of observation is the individual employee of the retained organization who is engaged in IT planning activities. Given the relative newness of our study, we opted for a qualitative research method. Analyzing a small number of case studies is an appropriate qualitative research method as such revelatory cases [50] may provide rich insight. Our qualitative method thus yielded an exploratory, case-study-based research [50], which is one of the most common qualitative method used in the field of Information Systems [51]. As we intend to study various types of growth stages related to retained organizations, we opted to apply the high performance framework of Nelson and Burns [11]. Our basic assumption is that retained organizations have experience with organizing and executing IT tasks at least to some degree. Hence, we excluded the reactive growth stage as described by Nelson and Burns [11] in our research. We selected three case studies, each representing a different growth stage that reflects the HPP framework (e.g. responsive, proactive, high performance). A short description of the case studies including their background is provided in Appendix A. We used two main criteria to select appropriate case studies, namely: (A) criticality of IT differentiation in the industry, and (B) the role of IT management. Both criteria are based on the findings from Peppard et al. [52] and Willcocks et al. [53] that the growth stage of the IT organization and the corresponding role of IT management are ideally aligned with the criticality of IT for differentiation in the industry. These criteria are consistent with research from Luftman [54] that classifies the role of IT in the three different growth stages.

3.2 Data Collection and Data Analysis

Data was gathered between August 2014 and March 2015, and drew on various sources. These ranged from desk research, and a survey, to a series of semi-structured interviews, both formal face-to-face and informal telephone interviews. Regarding desk research, information was gathered from internal publications, web sites, organizational charts, and meeting structures. In addition, field notes were recorded during informal meetings, which provided relevant background information to the influence of organizational culture determinants on retained organizations' growth stages. By using multiple data sources we are able to increase the reliability of the data [55]. In total 16 in-depth interviews were conducted with various staff members, including business and IT executives, business information managers, IT team leads, controllers, and experts positioned across the firms. In this way we apply a cross-section within the organizations to gain a richer insight in the effects of organizational culture determinants and to contribute to creating construct validity. Each interviewee was asked to fill out a survey. The survey, which was based on the culture determinants of Nelson and Burns [11], consisted of the three growth stages and related culture determinants. Moreover, considering the need for clarity, and preventing the terminology from being interpreted differently, a glossary of definitions was included (see Appendix B). As the interviews were confidential, we anonymized the companies. All interviews with participants, which were held in the Dutch language, were conducted by one of the authors of this paper. A semi-structured interview protocol was designed to gather data regarding the interpersonal interaction, culture determinants and retained organization. The different hierarchical levels of the interviewed staff members prevent potential limitations of the evolving phenomenon from arising. Interviews varied from 60 min to 120 min in duration while some interviews were replicated for clarification purposes.

The results of the case studies were written down in a case study report and sent to the participants to be validated. Interview data of the staff members was stored in a case study data base. We applied numerous data analysis iterations to create an overview of the firms under study. First, we analyzed the interviews with regard to our core constructs (e.g. interpersonal interaction, culture determinants and retained organization). As a next step statements (i.e. codes) were grouped into the construct categories. Next, we studied the influence of organizational culture determinants on growth stages, which provided us with a more holistic view on the mutual relationships and effect within the context of an retained organization. This step was conducted by multiple researchers. During the second stage of data analysis, we focused on the differences and similarities of organizational cultural determinants of the selected case studies and their related growth stages. The findings of the data analysis were categorized and stored into the case study data base. We will discuss each element hereafter.

4 Findings from the Case Studies

As our aim is to contribute to deeper insights in the relationship between organizational culture determinants and retained organizations growth stages, this section describes the findings of the three case studies. The description of the findings focuses on the differences between culture determinants (see Table 1) and their assumed growth stage.

Culture determinant Planning. When addressing the determinant *Planning* the second case study revealed that the client's business departments consciously invite representatives of the retained organization to co-develop strategic business plans. Business executives have the opinion that IT has become a strategic asset which may become a differentiator in the market. In contrast, strategic IT planning is conducted with limited business participation. An explanation for this finding is a strong focus of the retained organization on modernizing of the IT landscape, such as applications and terminal automation systems. As the existing IT function can be considered as complex, the retained organization is struggling to manage multiple IT projects, which are partially interdependent. Hence, additional coordination is required to manage the modernization initiative. However, from a planning perspective we find an unbalance between business and IT when aligning mutual activities and tasks.

> 'The IT planning decision-making process is quite complex as managers typically strive to achieve consensus among key stakeholders, which slows down the process. This is strengthened by the internal hierarchy in the company by which key decisions about modernization initiatives are pending. We consider the retained organization to be in a vacuum as a conscious strategic direction is missing. We focus on daily issues and activities, rather than focusing on executing a strategic plan.' (Source: Information manager, second case study).

Culture determinant Communication. As a consequence of the replacement of IT applications we observed that the client in the second case study is mainly focusing on internal communication within the retained organization and towards external vendors. Interviewees stated that IT staff mainly focuses on day-to-day operations with regard to IT modernization initiatives and, as a result, neglect communication with business representatives. Interestingly, on a management level we find that the executive management of the IT organization is improving the communication with business representatives to encourage collaboration and improve planning as part of IT planning activities. This finding creates a tension between an IT push at an operational level and an IT pull at a management level. Thus, the determinant *Communication* is perceived at a lower growth stage.

> 'At C-level we do recognize a close alignment between business executives and senior IT managers. At tactical and operational level the relationship between the users in the organization and the retained organization can best be characterized at an arms-length type of relationship which hinders the level of communication.' (Source: COO, second case study).

Culture determinant Change mode. With regard to the third case study our analysis of the *Change mode* shows that the client under study aims to achieve a state of excellence that contributes to maintaining their position as a high-performance organization. We find that the client proactively adapts to changes in the field of IT and are planned upfront, such as transforming applications, and the development of digitization initiatives. Within the context of IT planning these initiatives take place in close collaboration with business and IT representatives. However, our research identified that the organization as a whole is not able to deal with agility as a form of routine. Although the client encourages staff to apply their creativity to initiate new ideas, not all staff are able to do so as some focus on exploiting assets instead of developing new ones. This finding might be an explanation why the *Change mode* is indicated as Planned.

> 'Our ideal culture would be an adhocracy type of culture where agility and creativity flourish best. However, the internal pressure to deliver commercially viable solutions based on a short time-to-market requires a careful plan where we invest and innovate'. (Source VP of Development third case study).

Culture determinant Structure. According to the third case study the findings on the culture determinant *Structure* demonstrated that the client is not capable yet to achieve the high-performance status of Network. An explanation can be found in the existing capabilities of IT staff as well as in the complexity of the IT function. We find that the coordination of multiple local vendors by the retained organization requires additional management attention as the provisioning of various applications are dependent of multiple vendors. Next, existing sourcing capabilities need to be strengthened, for instance: governance, collaboration and organizational design. These capabilities can be seen as a prerequisite for profound coordination. In addition, the retained organization focuses on solving operational issues that require continuous alignment with individuals vendors. In doing so, they are unable to govern and collaborate with vendors to achieve a high-performing ecosystem and focus on achieving common goals.

> 'The unit within our retained organization that is responsible for developing critical customer facing applications has just entered its third stage of development. The first stage focused on the introduction of a global innovation platform followed by development of this platform in terms of products and solutions, as well as its geographical reach. The third stage provides a company-wide innovation platform that supports all business divisions. Getting everyone on board was seen as a necessary hurdle before the unit could be organized more loosely as a network organization. (Source VP of Development, third case study).

Culture determinant Motivation. Analyzing the third case study we find that the determinant *Motivation* is considered at a lower growth stage as expected as the results relate to the position of Contribution. Interviews revealed that Motivation is related to staff behavior and mindset. Importantly, our findings indicate that IT staff, which were originally part of local IT departments, became part of the centralized retained organization during the past year. As a result, the IT staff increased from 150 up to 300 staff. However, IT staff that were originally part of local IT departments had to change their mindset, shifting from a focus on their contribution to being proud of their accomplishments. As these IT staff are geographically dispersed it may take some time to change.

> 'We experienced that the combination of growth and centralization while changing the organizational culture at the same time is hard to achieve. For instance, changing the structure in terms of allocating staff to a team is quite a change, however, changing staff tasks at the same time is even more difficult to achieve. In the end it's about changing behavior.' (Source VP of Development, third case study).

<u>Culture determinant Development.</u> Interestingly, our findings in the second case study indicate that the determinant *Development* is perceived as transformational. This finding can be explained by a strong focus of the retained organization on technology as the existing IT landscape is transformed and modernized into a state-of-the art IT environment. The client under study allocated establishing a dedicated technology innovation team to the retained organization, with an own mandate to develop initiatives and which may act independent of existing processes. Interviewees postulated that the focus of the retained organization is on continuing transformation and renewal.

> 'During the past years a lot of effort was spend on implementing successful Lean processes and principles within our Global IT Service Center. We try to learn from every challenge and continuously adapt to the changing business demands. Dealing with continuous improvements is a central theme in Lean. This may explain the more transformational way in which we organize development.' (Source: Global IT Service Center manager, second case study).

<u>Culture determinant Perspective.</u> Interestingly, the findings of the first case study showed that the outcome of the determinant *Perspective* was indicated at an organizational level, which is related to the proactive growth stage. We observed that during the past three years the client was involved in various Mergers and Acquisitions. Consequently, the IT function of the various companies had to be integrated to support business processes. The retained organization of our client under study took the initiative to start the integration process and IT management had the opinion that in the near future IT might be a differentiator to increase the firm's market share. Interviews revealed that IT managers focus on the organization as a whole rather than on team level.

> 'We believe that the first step towards pro-activity lies in the fact that IT management and staff must increase their customer orientation. In all our decisions the added value to the business instead of technical considerations should prevail.'(Source: Manager Program & Project management, first case study)

<u>Culture determinant Time Frame</u> Regarding the culture determinant *Time Frame* the first case study demonstrate that IT annual planning cycles are discussed between business and the retained organization biannually. Although business and IT departments mainly focus on their own activities, and show a limited personal interaction between staff, planning IT tasks is consciously aligned to ensure the support of business processes. As a result of the various M&A projects the impact of IT integration require mutual alignment regularly. Hence, *Time Frame* is perceived as a proactive task.

> *'Our staff are typically very task oriented. We are extremely good in doing what has to be done. As a result of the recent mergers the retained organization was challenged to plan and act ahead as the integration process of the new acquired companies' IT infrastructures took a long time. Moreover, the IT integration projects had to be completed directly after the merger was approved. This increased our ability to plan complex portfolios of IT investment and infrastructure projects.' (Source: CIO, first case study).*

The modernization of the IT function as sketched in the second case study demonstrates that the project-oriented approach as applied by the retained organization is focused on present problems that need to be solved immediately. From a *Time Frame* perspective this finding is related to the responsive growth stage. Our findings on *Time Frame* are consistent with the determinants *Planning* which is also perceived at a lower growth stage. Based on our analysis we find both *Planning* and *Time Frame* are interrelated as a main focus on IT activities correspond with solving operational IT issues in the present situation.

> *'In practice we spend a lot of time in the retained organization in dealing with daily issues and activities, rather than focusing on executing a strategic plan.' (Source: Enterprise architect, second case study).*

When addressing the third case study we found that within the context of IT planning plans are set up annually and discussed at a central level. This finding is related to the proactive growth stage. We found evidence that the client's goal is to develop a high resolution vision of future services which encourages IT staff to be creative, initiate innovation projects, and mutually develop services with business participation. This finding is consistent with the aim of the client to become a full high-performance organization.

> *'The retained organization's mission is to provide highly accountable industry-leading IT services for infrastructure and back-office systems, and collaborative technology leadership across the firm' (Source CEO, third case study).*

<u>Culture determinant Leadership style.</u> Our observations of the first case study shows that as a result of the client's recent M&A initiatives the firm shifted from a single disciplinary role (e.g. dredging) into multidisciplinary roles (e.g. dredging, offshore, energy and maritime market). According to the interview with the CIO, in the near future IT will be perceived as a strategic asset that may influence the position of the client in the market. When addressing the culture determinant *Leadership style* we found that the IT executive management focuses on the empowerment of both IT staff and business representatives to stimulate innovation. This reflects the empowering position in the high-performance growth stage. This approach requires intense collaboration with stakeholders across the firm and outsourcing vendors. This finding is consistent with our findings as described to *Time Frame* as currently the planning of IT tasks is consciously aligned with business departments.

> *'Our corporate culture bears strong elements of a power culture. That's why we see empowerment as a key-success factor for the IT organization's future success. We noticed that the delegation of responsibilities was often problematic in practice. Senior managers had a tendency to interfere in the decision-making process at operational level, which resulted in a lack of trust and confidence on both sides. It seems as if the leadership had skipped the goal of having 'shared*

purposes' as a prerequisite for delegation without close monitoring.'(Source: manager Program and project management, first case study.

The findings of the case studies, which show the relationship between the culture determinants and assumed growth stage, are summarized in Table 2. The results of the research are reflected by the black dots (case study A), grey dots (case study B), and white dots (case study C). Table 2 shows that elements of all three cases are in more than one stage. Although case study A, which is identified by the black dots, was primarily in the responsive stage it has two elements in the pro-active stage and one in the high-performing stage. Case study B, illustrated by the grey dots, is predominantly in the pro-active stage but some elements are in lower stages and one element is in a higher stage. The final case study C, which is reflected by the white dots, is mainly in the high-performing stage, however, 4 out of 11 elements are in a lower stage. Although the cases show that culture determinants form a predictable pattern with the assumed growth stage it is also shown that a case study might reflect to more than one stage. Not all of the culture determinants might show the characteristics of that particular stage. The results are discussed in Sect. 5.

Table 2. Overview of culture determinants per case study

Culture determinants	Responsive stage (Case study A)	Pro-active stage (Case study B)	High performing stage (Case study C)
Management	Coordination	Alignment	Navigation
Focus	Output	Result	Excellence
Planning	Activities	Strategy	Evolution
Communication	Feed back	Feed forward	Feed through
Change mode	Adaptive	Planned	Programmed
Structure	Hierarchical	Matrix	Networks
Motivation	Rewards	Contribution	Accomplishment
Development	Cohesion	Attunement	Transformation
Perspective	Team	Organization	Culture
Time frame	Present	Future	Flow
Leadership style	Coaching	Purposing	Empowering

5 Discussion

As empirical research on retained organizations growth stages remains scarce, the objective of this paper is to empirically examine the relationship between organizational culture determinants and retained organizations stages of growth.

Three cases were studied using interviews and a survey administered by employees of clients. The results provided evidence that culture determinants form a predictable pattern with the assumed growth stage. The results from our analysis show that the culture determinants *Management* and *Focus* fit with their assumed growth stage in all three case studies. This might indicate that both determinants are interrelated as executive management of a firm has to develop a clear focus to achieve their IT mission and goals. The social interaction between retained organizations staff affects the relationship between culture and growth stages as identified by examples of the degree of collaboration between staff. The way in which IT is positioned within the organization also affects the degree of collaboration between IT staff in aligning tasks. The more IT is positioned as a strategic asset, the more social interactions between staff members are required. As a consequence, the level of trust between staff members will increase that is a prerequisite to exchange essential information. Next, we will elaborate on the findings related to the studied growth stages.

Responsive stage. Our analysis reveals that culture determinants related to the client in the first case study in majority fits with the responsive growth stage. The determinants *Perspective, Time Frame* and *Leadership*, however, differ positively as they are related to the proactive and high-performance growth stage respectively. From a historical view, the client is acting in an industry (e.g. dredging) where IT is perceived as a cost driver, rather than a strategic asset. However, endogenous developments (e.g. M&A strategy) changes the client's perspective on IT, which shifts in focus from cost efficiency towards a market differentiator. This might be an explanation for our finding of the determinant *Leadership* that reflects the shift to the high-performing growth stage. Our findings show that the interaction between staff to align mutual IT related tasks is limited. The client's retained organizational structure can be described as hierarchal. The IT teams are strictly separated, each focusing on delivering their own output. This might explain why the cultural determinant *Management* indicates coordination rather than alignment.

Our analysis shows that retained organizations management have the opinion that IT will become more important and IT tasks within the retained organization should be aligned. However, we found that IT staff are focusing on executing their own tasks rather than on collaboration. As a result, tensions between staff of different teams influenced their behavior negatively. In turn, the degree of social interaction and trust between staff decreased. Applying a SET lens, social sanctions are related to the continuous monitoring of behavior, which can be seen as a behavioral control mechanism to deal with conflict resolution. Based on our analysis we found that retained organizations staff did not focus on collaboration between teams to share information and knowledge. Moreover, we did not find evidence that mechanisms were implemented to continuously monitor the behavior of staff. We argue that the client has to develop and implement monitoring mechanisms to encourage the exchange of information and knowledge.

Proactive stage. When addressing the second case study we identified that seven out of eleven culture determinants fit with the assumed growth stage, which provides evidence for a predictable pattern. Importantly, we found that staff of various IT teams collaborated and contributed to developing strategic IT plans. Based on our analysis we found a deviation of the determinants *Development* and *Time frame* with regard to their assumed growth stage. From a *Development* perspective we found that IT staff is motivated to transform and modernize the IT function that appeals to their technical skills and capabilities. As a result the culture determinant *Development is* related to the high-performing stage. In an opposite direction the determinant *Time frame* deviates from the proactive stage negatively. Interviews reveal that IT staff pay less attention to solving operational IT issues which cause performance issues, affecting the business.

We found evidence for social interaction between staff of various IT teams as shown by the determinants *Management, Focus* and *Motivation*. Due to the interaction of management as well as staff between teams in the retained organization, the degree of trust increased. However, the findings about the determinants *Planning* and *Communication* show a lack with regard to the proactive stage and correspond to the responsive stage. An explanation might be found in the dominant attention of IT staff for content related topics such as transforming IT applications and infrastructure, which reflects their technical skills. Consequently, they spend limited time on planning and communication in aligning mutual tasks. Our analysis shows that management and IT staff invested in building relationships during the past years, which resulted in sharing insights in developing strategic IT plans. Strengthening the social interaction between staff over time corresponds to the SET exchange rule of generalized reciprocity [18] which is recognized as a norm for collaboration [40]. Our findings demonstrate that the degree of trust between IT staff increased through indirect reciprocal processes. This is consistent with Das and Teng [47] who argue that actors in a group receive benefits from a specific actor and subsequently pay back the favor to another actor.

High-performing stage. The findings of the third case study provide evidence for a predictable pattern as seven out of eleven determinants fit with the assumed high-performing growth stage. Although the client's IT strategy focuses on excellence, four determinants are indicated at the proactive stage, namely: *Change mode, Structure, Motivation* and *Time frame*. Interviewees state that the matrix type of organizational structure is perceived as highly complex as multiple IT teams, which are geographically dispersed, have to align tasks between staff intensively. We found that the client under study is struggling to change the culture determinants *Change mode* and *Structure* specifically to cater for exogenous developments taking multiple existing IT vendors into account. We argue that strengthening those determinants may encourage the implementation of an ecosystem network. In addition, interviews show that the client's *Leadership style* is based on empowerment as IT staff is encouraged to initiate innovations and support business growth. Subsequently, the degree of social interaction increased as a result of the collaboration between staff.

Interviews revealed that creating shared IT goals increased the degree of social interaction between staff. Our analysis demonstrates that the highly collaborative mode between staff resulted in an iterative form of communication approach to determine the IT planning. In turn, we found that the degree of trust between staff increased as their personal contribution to collaboration was rewarded. Social exchange literature suggests that shared values require current knowledge about one's partner to the exchange by means of an existing exchange process. Sharing common values involves communication as well as an understanding of the goals and values of the partner. The case study showed evidence for the existence of a common culture that was supported by the determinants *Management* and *Communication*. Nord [56] argues that in generalized social exchanges, a common culture is important to establish sustainable exchange relationships between actors. It should be noted that firms that invest in building a common culture are more comfortable with indirect reciprocity [49]. When applying shared values less attention is required for coordination or in our case study on aligning IT tasks between staff in the retained organization.

6 Conclusions and Limitations

The relationship between organizational culture determinants and retained organizations from an individual perspective is an ill-researched concept in sourcing literature. The aim of this research was to empirically examine the relationship between organizational culture determinants and retained organizations stages of growth. Given the scarce attention for retained organizations this discussion has sought to assist both researchers and practitioners. With regard to science the case studies shed some light on the under-researched topic of retained organizations and some first indications of the influences of social interactions. The culture determinants *Management* and *Focus* fit with their assumed growth stage in all three case studies. This might indicate that both determinants are interrelated as executive management of a firm has to develop a clear focus to achieve their IT mission and goals. Moreover, the results show that the degree of social interaction between staff is influenced by the perception of IT in the organization (e.g. IT as cost driver or strategic asset). Although the cases show that culture determinants form a predictable pattern with the assumed growth stage it also shown that a case study might be in more than one stage. Not all of the determinants might show the characteristics of that particular stage.

Our research also aims to contribute to practitioners as they become aware of the impact of culture determinants in a specific growth stage of the retained organization. As reflected in the first case study, culture determinants such as *Planning*, *Management*, *Focus* and *Motivation* invoke strategic, alignment and collaboration skills which influences behavior as more social interaction is required between staff. We argue that clients have to consider whether their organizational structure encourages social interaction between staff. In a response type of growth stage IT is organized in a more hierarchal way and operates on arms-lengths. However, as the boundaries between departments in high-performing organizations are blurred, a more network type of organization is used. Thus, to achieve effectiveness the type of management has to be consistent with the type of organizational structure used.

Limitations and suggestions for further research. Although our study provides important implications for retained organizations, we are aware that our exploratory case study approach shares several limitations associated with this study. First, this study was limited to Information Technology outsourcing. Culture determinants that impact the outsourcing of other functions such as Human Resources, Finance and Accounting, Research and Development, could have another effect when compared to the IT function. Secondly, the degree in which IT tasks are outsourced (e.g. limited scope, extended scope) may influence the boundaries of the retained IT organization and subsequently, the way culture determinants effect the retained organization's growth stage. Examples include *Change mode*, *Structure*, and *Motivation* as a retained organization is dependent on its vendors. Finally, although the research is based on three case studies, the generalizability of the results is limited. The case studies identify, however, multiple avenues that require a more rigorous validation of our findings. We hypothesize that culture determinants may vary per industry, and therefore have another effect on clients retained organization. Our results suggest that monitoring culture values regularly is a prerequisite for clients to assess if their intended growth stage is still valid. Further research may provide insights if clients are willing and able to strengthen culture determinants that are underexposed related to their intended growth stage.

Appendix A: Background to Case Studies

Case Study 1: Represents a Reactive Stage of Growth

The client under study is a leading global services provider operating in dredging, maritime infrastructure and the maritime services sectors. The company develops innovative all-round solutions to provide major infrastructural projects in the maritime, coastal and delta regions of the world. The company comprises 11,000 staff and is operational in 75 countries across six continents. The retained organization is strongly centralized and hierarchically structured into functional teams: IT infrastructure; application management team, service desk and project management. The size of the retained IT organization is a staff of 90 persons, largely centralized in their headquarters. Information Technology is on the tipping point to become a strategic asset. The retained function operates largely independently and it is directly funded from the Board. It manages its own budgets and investment projects. The majority of IT tasks are coordinated and executed in-house. External vendors are almost exclusively used for hiring specialized skills and/or capacity. The client's vision is to outsource specialized services gradually.

Case Study 2: Represents a Proactive Stage of Growth

The client under study is the world largest independent provider of bulk storage and handling capacity of liquid chemicals, gasses and oil products. It operates in 28 countries spread around the globe along the major shipping routes and is comprised of approximately 6,000 staff. The client is acting in a very dynamic and competitive market and their ambition is to excel in a strongly rooted culture of safety, flawless execution, and operational excellence. Information Systems play an essential role and is perceived as a strategic asset and used to develop innovative IT solutions that contribute to the efficiency of terminal operation. The retained organization, which consists of 150 staff, is set-up as a federated matrix type of organization. Divisional IT teams are responsible for both information management and management of local applications. Management of IT infrastructure and companywide type of applications are organized on a central level.

Case Study 3: Represents a High Performing Stage of Growth

The client under study provides professional publishing services based on information services and decision support systems globally. The client provides services in over 150 counties and is comprised of 19,000 staff. The client's executive management focuses on acting as a high-performance organization in which they emphasize a customer focus, embrace innovation, clear accountability and integrity, value creation and teamwork. The retained organization, which consists of 300 staff, is based on a federated structure and organize IT tasks in a matrix type of organization. In order to create a competitive advantage in the market the client decided to focus on innovation and develop applications in-house. In addition, the client outsourced their IT infrastructure management and coordinates the delivery of a range of in-house services, namely: data centers, networks and corporate applications.

Appendix B: Organizational Culture Determinants

Planning. In a responsive organization the central theme in the planning process is the planning of *activities* of tasks to be done (operational planning). In the proactive organization the planning cycle is targeted around defining long-term results and *strategies* to achieving them. In the high-performing organization the management's time sense allows them to plan a continuing *evolution* of the organization towards an even more promising future.

Communication. In a responsive organization managers and staff feel free to provide *feedback* on information, tasks and achievements. In the next level of maturity communication is focused on the future and how the future goals can be achieved (*feed forward*). In a high-performance organization leaders make sure that information is *fed through* all parts of the network. Successes are communicated to unleash new energy and drive the organization towards excellence.

Change mode. In the responsive organization management keeps team efforts coordinated and responsive (*adaptive*) to changing needs and conditions. Staff in the organization work as cohesive teams, able to adapt as they identify problems. In the proactive organization changes are *planned* upfront and changes are used by leaders as a method to keep the organization clearly focused on its purpose. In the high-performing state the agility of the organization is *'programmed'* in the organization's culture and values and by satisfying the conditions for energy, creativity and innovation to be able to excel.

Structure. In responsive (*hierarchical*) organizations the distribution of power is according to a hierarchical organization structure. In proactive organizations authority is distributed along two or more dimensions (*matrix*). People may have multiple reporting lines. In high-performing organizations the IT organization shares power with other stakeholders (e.g. third parties in the *network*).

Management. In a responsive organization management is setting goals and focuses on the *coordination* of tasks that need to be done to achieve these goals. In a proactive organizations management ensures the *alignment* and integration of sub-organization objectives within the greater whole. In high-performing organizations leaders focus on strategic *navigation* of the total organization, also the parts that do not fall under their direct formal power (e.g. networks and partners).

Focus. In a responsive organization the successful completion of tasks and delivery of related *output* is seen as the prime purpose of the organization. In the proactive organization the focus is on *results* recognized and valued by its customers. Not so much the output is the target but the resulting outcome. Ultimately (high-performing) the focus can shift to achieving high standards of *excellence* by identifying new potentials, seeking out new avenues of opportunities and activating human spirit.

Motivation. In a responsive organization people are motivated by positive feedback and increased pay, based on merit (*rewards*). In the proactive organization staff are motivated by the opportunity to make a *contribution* toward achieving a future they value. Finally in the high-performing organization leaders create a work environment that energizes the staff, who are proud of their *accomplishments*.

Development. In responsive organizations staff work in *cohesive* teams, with a strong 'we' focus. Development takes place by the participation of all members in defining new and higher goals and better plans of action. In the proactive state the organization develops by raising the awareness of larger perspective of the organization and the *attunement* of goals and plans of action accordingly. In the high-performing state the focus on development is on continuing *transformat*ion and renewal.

Perspective. In a responsive organization leaders and members take a *team* perspective rather than a self-centered one, which results in team members reaching out for each other. In later stages Perspective extends to the entire *organization*. The interest of the staff in the entire organization comes first. Ultimately leaders include the organizational culture into their frame of reference. They build a strong corporate *culture* that give members a strong and proud heritage to maintain and reinforce.

Time Frame. The responsive organization is characterized by a strong focus on *present* problems that need immediate solving. In the proactive organization the *future* focused time frames are built around, for instance, annual planning cycles. When in state of *'flow'* leaders are able to build on rich legacies, proud traditions as valued roots of the organization's past and sustain and communicate a high-resolution vision of the future they want to create (high performing).

Leadership style. In a responsive organization leaders *coach* their followers on the path of organizational growth. They adapt their leadership style to fit the maturity of their subordinates. To reach the proactive state leaders must adopt a value-based leadership style. They focus on developing their followers' potential and satisfying their needs. The leaders in high-performing organizations follow a holistic view where they not only lead their own organization but the entire environment with which their organization interacts. They push power down to *empower* their followers so that they gain the freedom and energy to seek creativity and innovation.

References

1. Volberda, H.W.: Toward the flexible form: how to remain vital in hypercompetitive environments. Org. Sci. **7**(4), 359–374 (1996)
2. Lacity, M.C., Khan, S.A., Willcocks, L.P.: A review of the IT outsourcing literature: insights for practice. J. Strat. Inf. Syst. **18**(3), 130–146 (2009)
3. Teece, D.: Business models, business strategy and innovation. L. Range Plan. **43**, 172–194 (2010)
4. Joha, A.: The retained organization after IT outsourcing: The design of its organizational structure, Unpublished Master Thesis, Delft Univ. of Tech. (2003)
5. Weill, P., Ross, J.: IT Governance: How Top Performers Manage IT Decision Rights for Superior Results. Harvard Business School Press, Boston (2004)
6. Gottschalk, P., Solli-Sæther, H.: The modeling process for stage models. J. Org. Comp. Elect. Com. **20**(3), 279–293 (2010)
7. Nadler, D., Tushman, M.: Strategic Organization Design. Scott Foresman and Company, Glenview (1988)
8. Birnbaum, D., Sommers, M.J.: The influence of occupational image subculture on job attitudes, job performance, and the job attitude-job performance relationship. Hum. Rel. **39**(7), 661–672 (1986)
9. Hussain, S.: Technology transfer models across culture: Brunei-Japan joint ventures. Int. J. Social Econ. **25**(6–8), 1189–1198 (1988)
10. Cameron, K.S., Quinn, R.E.: Diagnosing and Changing Organizational Culture. Jossey-Bass, San Francisco (2006)
11. Nelson, L., Burns, F.L.: High performance programming: a framework for transforming organizations. In: Adams, J.D. (ed.) Book Section Transforming Work. 2nd edn. Miles River Press, Alexandria (2005)
12. Gordon, G.G., DiTomaso, N.: Predicting corporate performance form organizational culture. J. Mgt. Stud. **29**(6), 783–798 (1992)
13. Schein, E.H.: Organizational Culture and Leadership. Jossey-Bass, San-Francisco (2006)
14. Hofstede, G., Hofstede, G.J., Minkov, M.: Cultures and Organizations, 3rd edn. McGraw-Hill, London (2010)
15. Dybå, T.: An empirical investigation of the key factors for success in software process improvement. IEEE Trans. S. Eng. **31**(5), 410–424 (2005)
16. Ngwenyama, O., Nielsen, P.A.: Competing values in software process improvement: an assumption analysis of CMM from an organizational culture perspective. IEEE Trans. Eng. Mgt. **50**(1), 101–111 (2003)
17. Müller, S.D., Axel, N.P.: Competing values in software process improvement a study of cultural profiles. Inf. Tech. P. **26**(2), 146–171 (2013)
18. Cropanzano, R., Michell, M.S.: Social exchange theory: an interdisciplinary review. J. Mgt. **31**(6), 874–900 (2005)
19. Scholz, C.: The symbolic value of computerized information systems, in symbols and artifacts: views of the corporate landscape. Gagliardi, P. (ed.), pp. 233–254. Aldine de Gruyter, New York (1990)

20. Leidner, D.A., Kayworth, T.: A review of culture in information systems research: toward a theory of information technology culture conflict. MIS Q. **30**(2), 357–399 (2006)
21. Cullen, S., Seddon, P.B., Willcocks, L.P.: Managing outsourcing: the lifecycle imperative. MIS Q. Exec. **4**(1), 229–246 (2005)
22. Gewald, H., Helbig, K.: A governance model for managing outsourcing partnerships: a view from practice. In: Proceeding of 39th Hawaii International Conference on System Sciences (2006)
23. Kern, T., Willcocks, L.P.: The Relationship Advantage. Information Technologies. Sourcing and Management, Oxford University Press, Oxford (2001)
24. Oshri, I., Kotlarski, J., Willcocks, L.P.: The Handbook of Global Outsourcing and Offshoring, 3rd edn. Palgrave Macmillan, London (2015)
25. Willcocks, L.P., Fitzgerald, G.: A Business Guide to Outsourcing Information Technology. Business Intelligence, London (1994)
26. Enlow, S., Ertel, D.: Achieving outsourcing success: effective relationship management. Compensation Benefits Rev. **38**(3), 50–55 (2006)
27. Reich, B.H., Benbasat, I.: Measuring the linkage between business and information technology objectives. MIS Q. **20**(1), 55–81 (1996)
28. Kasarda, J.D., Rondinelli, D.A.: Innovative infrastructure for agile manufacturers. Sl. Mgt. Rev. **39**(2), 73–82 (1998)
29. Pollitt, C.: The Essential Public Manager. Open University Press, Manchester (2003)
30. De Waal, A.: The characteristics of a high performance organization. Bus. Strategy Series **8**(3), 179–185 (2007)
31. Thompson, S.H.T., King, W.R. Integration between business planning and information systems planning: an evolutionary-contingency perspective. J. Mgt. Inf. Syst. **14**(1), 185–214 (1997)
32. Gottschalk, P., Solli-Sæther, H.: Maturity model for IT outsourcing relationships. Ind. Mgt. & Data Syst. **106**(2), 200–212 (2006)
33. Kazanjian, R.K., Drazin, R.: An Empirical Test of a Stage of Growth Progression Model. Mgt. Science **35**(12), 1489–1503 (1989)
34. Burn, J.M.: Information systems strategies and the management of organizational change - strategic alignment model. J. Inf. Tech. **8**(4), 205–216 (1993)
35. Pettigrew, A.M.: On studying organizational cultures author(s). Adm. Science Quart. **24**(4), 570–581 (1979)
36. Hofstede, G.H.: Cultures and Organizations: Software of the Mind. McGraw-Hill, London (1991)
37. Grover, V., Teng, J.T.C., Fiedler, K.D.: IS investment priorities in contemporary organizations. Com. ACM **41**, 40–48 (1998)
38. Kanungo, R.N.: Ethical values of transactional and transformational leaders. Can. J. Adm. Sci. **18**(4), 257–265 (2001)
39. Nelson, L., Burns, F.L: High performance programming: a framework for transforming organizations. In: Adams, J.D. (ed.) Transforming Work: A Collection of Organizational Transformation Readings. Miles River Press, Alexandria (1984)
40. DiDomenico, M.L., Tracey, P., Haugh, H.: The dialectic of social exchange: theorizing corporate social enterprise collaboration. Org. Stud. **30**(8), 887–907 (2009)
41. Homans, G.C.: Social Behavior: Its Elementary Forms. Hartcourt Brace, New York (1961)
42. Blau, P.M.: Exchange and Power in Social Life. Wiley, New York (1964)
43. Emerson, R.M.: Social exchange theory. Amer. Rev. Soc. **2**, 335–362 (1962)
44. Flynn, F.J.: How much should i give and how often? The effects of generosity and frequency of favor exchange on social status and productivity. Acad. Mgt. J. **46**, 539–553 (2003)

45. Perrone, V., Zaheer, A., McEvity, B.: Free to be trusted? Organizational constraints on trust in boundary spanners. Org. Sci. **14**, 422–439 (2003)
46. Masterson, S.S., Lewis, K., Goldman, B.M., Taylor, M.S.: Integrating justice and social exchange: the differing effects of fair procedures and treatment on work relationships. Acad. Mgt. J. **43**(4), 738–748 (2000)
47. Das, T.K., Teng, B.S.: Alliance constellations: a social exchange perspective. Acad. Mgt Rev. **27**(3), 445–456 (2002)
48. Anderson, J., Narus, J.A.: A model of distributor firm and manufacturer firm working partnerships. J. Mark. **54**(1), 42–58 (1990)
49. Ekeh, P.P.: Social Exchange Theory: Two Traditions. Princeton University Press, New York (1974)
50. Yin, R.K.: Case Study Research. CA Sage Publications, Design and Methods. Thousand Oaks (2009)
51. Orlikowski, W.J., Iacono, C.S.: Research commentary: desperately seeking the "IT" in IT research: a call to theorizing the IT artefact. Inf. Syst. Res. **12**, 121–134 (2001)
52. Peppard, J., Edwards, C., Lambert, R.: Clarifying the ambiguous role of the CIO. MIS Q. Exec. **10**(1), 31–44 (2011)
53. Willcocks, L.P., Cullen, S., Graig, A.: The Outsourcing Enterprise: From Cost Management to Collaborative Innovation. Palgrave Macmillan, London (2011)
54. Luftman, J.: Assessing business-IT alignment maturity. In: Van Grembergen, W. (ed.) Strategies for Information Technology Governance. Idea Group Publishing, Hershey (2003)
55. Benbasat, I., Goldstein, D.K., Mead, M.: The case research strategy in studies of information systems. MIS. Q., 369–386 (1987)
56. Nord, W.R.: An Integrative approach to social conformity. Psych. Bul. **71**, 174–208 (1969)

The Clash of Cultures in Information Technology Outsourcing Relationships: An Institutional Logics Perspective

Nikolaus Schmidt[✉], Bastian Zöller, and Christoph Rosenkranz

University of Cologne, Albertus-Magnus-Platz, 50923 Cologne, Germany
{nikolaus.schmidt,
christoph.rosenkranz}@wiso.uni-koeln.de,
bastizoeller@googlemail.com

Abstract. The outsourcing of information technology (IT) to external vendors promises lower delivery cost while attaining higher delivery quality. Despite these positive prospects, many IT outsourcing (ITO) projects still fail. On key aspect for non-working ITO engagements are cultural differences between organizations, teams, and individuals. This study explores the concept of culture in the context of ITO relationships by identifying and explaining particular cultural differences in such relationships. Building upon data from focus group discussions, we identify specific cultural differences in ITO relationships on the level of national culture (macro), organizational culture (meso) as well as team and individual culture (micro). Based on this, we apply the institutional logics perspective as a theoretical lens to derive institutional logics in ITO relationships, which explain and reason the identified cultural differences. With our results, we shed light on the under-researched concept of culture in ITO based on a multi-level analysis approach.

Keywords: IT outsourcing relationships · Culture · Multi-level analysis · Institutional logics perspective

1 Introduction

Information technology outsourcing (ITO) is defined as the subcontracting of an organization's information technology-related tasks such as software development or system monitoring to an external vendor [1]. The partnering of client and vendor organizations in such ITO relationships is an important part of contemporary organizations' IT strategies [2, 3]. However, the failure rate for ITO projects is still surprisingly high [4, 5], and recent studies reveal that 60 % of client organizations involved in ITO are not able to meet their pre-defined targets [6].

From a research perspective, a comprehensive body of knowledge already exists for ITO in general [7–10]. By now IS researchers have, for example, defined decision and governance models [11], identified success factors [12, 13], and made recommendations on how to establish successful relationships [14, 15]. One especially prevailing issue is the effect of *cultural differences* between client and vendor organizations on the ITO client-vendor relationship quality [7, 16, 17]. In this context, prior studies identified a positive relationship between ITO project success and cultural compatibility on a macro (country or ethnic groups) as well as on a meso (organization) and micro level (team, individual). Nevertheless, these findings are mostly limited to one specific level and have there-fore not been generalized or investigated on a large scale. Consequently, recent IS research has called for investigating the effect of cultural differences between client and vendor in ITO relationships on a broader level [7, 8, 18–22]. This situation leads to the overarching question guiding our research: *What kind of cultural differences exist in ITO relationships and how can they be explained?*

Past research analysing cultural differences in the context of IS revealed that analysing culture is quite complex due to the lack of a clear definition of culture in general, the multi-dimensional "umbrella" character of culture as well as the lack of suitable frameworks to explain the various layers of culture in the context of IS in general and ITO in particular [23]. To cover this issue, our research applies the *institutional logics perspective* [24] as a theoretical lens, which enables the identification of cultural differences (ex-pressed through differences in institutional logics) between the different groups (institutions) in an ITO relationship on multiple levels.

Our research project is exploratory in nature and builds upon data collected within four focus group discussions [25] with ITO experts from clients, vendors, and consultancy organizations. The discussions focused on (1) the identification of cultural differences in ITO relationships and (2) the development of corresponding institutional logics, which explain the cultural differences. Based on this approach, we were able to either identify or confirm 12 unique institutional logics in the context of ITO relationships, which together were able to explain a set of 14 cultural differences existing in such relationships. Furthermore, by applying the cultural framework of Leidner and Kayworth [23] within the context of our research, we categorized the identified cultural differences and institutional logics based on the macro-, meso- and micro-level of culture.

The remainder of the paper is structured as follows. The next section provides information on the theoretical background in terms of the concept of culture and the institutional logics perspective. Section 3 introduces the research design including a description of the data collection and analysis methods. Section 4 explains the results of our analysis with a specific focus on describing the newly identified institutional logics identified within our research project. Before concluding our work in Sect. 6, Sect. 5 summarizes the contributions of our study for both research and practice as well as provides insights on the limitations of our work.

2 Theoretical Background and Framework Definition

2.1 The Concept of Culture

The concept of culture is complex and hence difficult to define. For example, in their early work Kroeber and Kluckhohn [26] describe culture as "the historically differentiated and variable mass of customary ways of functioning of human societies". Building upon the work of Kroeber and Kluckhohn [26], Hofstede [27] defines the still widely accepted definition of culture as "the collective programming of the mind that distinguishes the members of one group or category of people from another". However, a challenge that lies in any analysis of culture in any kind of context is that there are several levels that provide different symbols and practices [23]. For example, to explain the behaviour of social actors, you have to keep in mind that there is an interaction of values from different levels of culture, for example, the culture of the organization that the individual is embedded in as well as the individual's own culture based on formal education and upbringing [28]. Therefore, a cultural analysis should always consider these different levels of culture [23].

By building upon the work of Leidner and Kayworth [23], our study conceptualizes culture in ITO based on four different levels of analysis: (1) *national culture* on the macro level, (2) *organizational culture* on the meso level, and (3) *team culture* as well as (4) *individual culture* on the micro level of analysis. A very popular approach towards national culture is given by Hofstede [27]. He describes culture as differences in values in the four dimensions of power distance, uncertainty avoidance, individualism-collectivism and masculinity-femininity [27]. Most of the approaches analysing national culture try to identify values, which appear in every country, but in varying extents [23]. On the lower meso level of analysis is the culture of organizations. The objective of research on organizational culture is the identification of dominant values that influence organizational behaviour in order to distinguish organizations [23]. But similar to national culture, differing concepts and approaches towards organizational culture exist. Researchers are divided about, for example, if organizations have "uniform, homogenous values or, instead, various local cultures, each with their own distinctive values" [29]. Team culture and individual culture are separated on the micro level [23]. Based on the definition of organizational culture from Schein [30] and the corresponding work of Karahanna et al. [31], groups and teams also develop a distinct group or team culture through own rituals, norms, and symbols.

In the light of ITO research, there are several studies that evaluate the concept of culture on various levels. For example, the study of Avison and Banks [32] investigates how national culture-induced differences in communication affect offshore software development teams [32]. Another recent study evaluated how differences in the client's and vendor's national culture affect ITO success and how these cultural differences could be mitigated within such relationships [33]. From an organizational culture perspective, the study of Rai et al. [34] identified, based on a longitudinal field study of 155 offshore IS projects, a relationship between cultural differences at the organizational and team level and ITO project success. In terms of team culture-related research in ITO, there are studies available that evaluated, for example, the positive influence of collaborative team culture ("one team approach") on project performance [35]. In the context of research evaluating culture in ITO relationships on an individual level, there are limited sources available and there are several calls for future research [23]. For example, a recent study evaluated how individual project members in global ITO projects cope with culture-specific behaviour and how the project members' cultural intelligence enables the emergence of negotiated culture [36].

To sum up, due to its "umbrella" character, culture is a difficult concept to analyse, both in general and within the context of ITO in particular. Especially research focussing on a multi-level analysis of culture is still rare and a preceding gap in our knowledge on ITO [23, 36, 37].

2.2 The Institutional Logics Perspective

To enable a multi-level analysis of culture in the context of ITO, our study applies the institutional logics perspective (ILP) as a theoretical lens. The ILP originates from institutional theory and describes organizational forms, managerial practices, and individual actions through institutional logics (IL) [38–40]. An institutional logic is generally defined as a "socially constructed, historical pattern of cultural symbols and material practices, including assumptions, values, and beliefs, by which individuals and organizations provide meaning to their daily activity, organize time and space, and reproduce their lives and experiences" [24]. The ILP approach presumes that individual actors or organizations are part of an inter-institutional system. Within this system, the actors are surrounded by so called institutional orders, which operate on multiple levels of analysis. These institutional orders mainly shape the behaviour of an actor in the system through symbols, practices, and organizing. For example, the orders of family, state, market or profession are instances of institutional orders. Each of these institutional orders comprises an own institutional logic that determines its organizing principles and provides the actors with a sense of self [41].

We chose ILP as our theoretical lens due to the fact that it is closely tied to culture, and is generally considered as a "new way of looking at culture" [24]. Specifically, ILP reflects normative and symbolic elements of culture for the analysis of organizational or individual behaviour [24]. ILP presumes that institutional logics operate on multiple levels of analysis [24], and these levels generally match the four cultural levels (national culture, organizational culture, team culture and individual culture), which are the baseline for analysing and categorizing cultural differences. The identification of institutional logics that are embedded on these different cultural levels could provide both, a suitable reasoning and categorization of cultural differences in the context of ITO client-vendor relationship, as well as information about what influences the behaviour and the relations between organizational and individual actors in ITO relationships.

Building on ILP, our study adopts the framework of institutional logics proposed by Berente and Yoo [42]. In particular, Berente and Yoo [42] suggest four dimensions to describe institutional logics, which we adopt for the identification of institutional logics within our work. A brief description of the four dimensions, the guiding question in regards to the dimension, and an example based on Berente and Yoo [42] are given in Table 1.

Based on the explanations of the concept of culture and the introduction into ILP as our theoretical lens, Fig. 1 summarizes our research framework, which we used as a sanitizing guideline for our research design and data analysis.

Table 1. Dimensions of an institutional logic (based on Berente and Yoo [42]).

Dimension	Guiding Questions	Example (based on "Logic of Project Management Professionalism", Berente and Yoo [42])
Principle	What is the guiding principle behind the institutional logic? What are the goals behind the institutional logic?	Deliver space and aeronautics project results
Assumption	What are the assumptions about cause and effect of the institutional logic? How can the principles of the institutional logic be achieved?	Project results through tracking and communicating project progress
Identity	What are the identities of people when they draw on these logics? Why do people act like they do based on the particular institutional logic?	Track and communicate unpredictable activity
Domain	At what time and place (*when*) is the institutional logic applied? Where does the institutional logic exist in particular?	Financial as well as other domains associated with projects

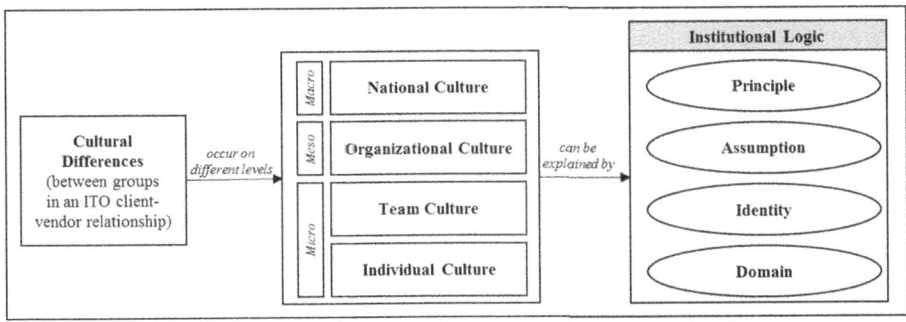

Fig. 1. Research Framework.

3 Research Design

3.1 Research Method Overview

Building upon the type of our research question ("what") and our research framework, our study followed a qualitative, exploratory research design based on focus group discussions. We chose a qualitative design because (1) studies taking into account the multi-dimensional analysis of culture in both IS in general and ITO in particular are still limited [23] as well as (2) this study is, to the best of our knowledge, the first study which applies the ILP in the context of ITO. A qualitative research approach is best suited to "help researchers under-stand people and the social and cultural contexts within which they live" [43], which relates to the overall goal of our research project.

We used focus group discussions for data collection because focus groups allow the gathering of knowledge on complex problems within a short timeframe [25]. A focus group combines instruments such as interviews and group discussions [44], and especially enables the interaction between experts on the chosen problem, which leads to a deeper understanding as well as the gathering of in-depth knowledge on the problem [25].

We planned and executed our focus groups based on a three step approach [45] including (1) conception, (2) execution, and (3) analysis.

3.2 Data Collection and Analysis

Conception Phase. Within this phase, we defined the underlying problem for the focus group discussions (*cultural differences in ITO client-vendor relationships*), prepared the code of practice, and selected the study participants in terms of organizations and employees. To allow a broad spectre of experience and knowledge, we chose the participating organizations based on role (client, vendor, consultant), branch, size (number of employees and yearly turnover), and experience with ITO. We used direct mailings addressed to the organization's head of IT as well as personal contacts to ensure the organizations' collaboration. Based on an initial set of 23 contacted organizations, we identified 4 organizations who met our selection criteria and agreed to participate in our research project. In terms of focus group participants, we wanted to ensure a preferably diverse set of participants, and therefore asked the organizations to identify participants from different backgrounds in terms of position and experience (overall and ITO). Based on the input from the organizations, 16 employees of the 4 organizations attended our focus groups. An overview about the organizations including branch, size, experience in ITO, and role is provided in Table 2. An overview about the participants within the focus groups is provided in the appendix of this paper.

Table 2. Overview of participating organizations.

ID	Branch	Size		ITO EXP	Role
		EMP	TO		
A	Telecommunications/IT	11–50	<2	100	Vendor
B	Retail	>250	>50	25	Client
C	Telecommunications/IT	11–50	<2	>20	Vendor
D	Various	11–50	≤10	>150	Consultancy

Legend: *ID:* ID of the company for further reference; *Branch:* Branch of the organization; *EMP:* Number of Employees; *TO:* Yearly turnover in Mio. EUR; *ITO EXP*: ITO experience of the company based on number of executed ITO projects; *Role:* Role of the organizations within ITO projects (client, vendor, consultant); *n/a*: In cases of N/A the company decided to provide no information (e.g. due to confidentiality reasons).

Execution Phase. We organized one focus group per participating organization. Due to the organizations' requirements in terms of confidentiality, cross-organizational focus groups were not possible. The focus group discussions took place in April and May 2015 and lasted about two hours each. The spoken language was German. One of the focus group discussions took place at the university, three focus group discussions were organized within the participating organizations' headquarters. All focus groups were attended by two researchers to ensure suitable documentation and moderation capabilities. In addition to detailed write-ups, the researchers video-recorded and transcribed all focus groups. In addition, we provided three brief questionnaires to the participants focussing on information in regards to the organization, the participant's background, and past ITO projects. All focus groups followed a detailed code-of-practice based on the guidelines of Schulz et al. [45] and Liamputtong [25], including the identification of the cultural differences in ITO relationships based on two to four current or past ITO projects.

Analysis Phase. The data analysis started after conducting all four focus group discussions and built on written transcripts of the video files recorded during the focus group discussions, the written documentation of the focus groups, as well as the visualized results developed during the focus group discussions (e.g., flipchart writings). As a first step of our data analysis, we identified and categorized the cultural differences between the different groups in an ITO relationship based on the interview transcripts. In the second step, we applied the framework of Berente and Yoo [42] (see Sect. 2.2) to identify and describe institutional logics that could explain the specific cultural differences. Within this step, we particularly tried to match the identified cultural difference to an already existing institutional logic. In case we were not able to find a previously identified institutional logic suitably explaining the cultural difference, we developed an explaining institutional logic based on the four dimensions for institutional logics from Berente and Yoo [42].

4 Analysis and Results

Our data analysis resulted in a consolidated list of categorized cultural differences in ITO relationships as well as the corresponding institutional logic, which explains the reason behind the particular cultural difference. In total, we identified 14 cultural differences within the different cultural levels. We were able to match these cultural differences to 12 explaining institutional logics. Out of these 12 institutional logics, 7 were already identified in past research and hence confirmed in the context of ITO relationships based on our research. 5 institutional logics explaining 7 cultural differences were newly developed based on the data derived from the focus group discussions. Table 3 provides an overview of the identified cultural differences, the level of the cultural difference according to the multi-level framework on culture from Leidner and Kayworth [23], and the corresponding institutional logic explaining and reasoning the identified cultural difference. In case the particular institutional logic was already identified and described within past research, corresponding references are provided.

Table 3. Overview of identified cultural differences and corresponding institutional logics.

ID	Cultural Difference	Level of Culture				Corresponding Institutional Logics	Key References
		N	O	T	I		
(A) Cultural Differences on the Organizational Level							
A.1	**Solution-Orientation** (joint vs. pressured)		X			Private-Side Logic vs. Public-Side Logic	Beck, Gregory [46], Currie and Guah [47], Marschollek and Beck [48]
A.2	**Inter-organizational Collaboration** (trust-based vs. contract-based)		X			Private-Side Logic vs. Public-Side Logic	Beck, Gregory [46], Currie and Guah [47], Marschollek and Beck [48]
A.3	**Organizational Attitude** (protection vs. trial & error)		X			Private-Side Logic vs. Public-Side Logic	Beck, Gregory [46], Currie and Guah [47], Marschollek and Beck [48]
A.4	**Organizational Behavior** (hierarchical vs. flat)		X			*Logic of the Enterprise* vs. *Entrepreneurial Logic*	*new*/Berente, Hansen [49]
A.5	**Negotiation Style** (direct vs. mandated)		X			*Logic of the Enterprise* vs. *Entrepreneurial Logic*	*new*/Berente, Hansen [49]
A.6	**Management Style** (strong vs. weak)		X			*Logic of the Enterprise* vs. *Entrepreneurial Logic*	*new*/Berente, Hansen [49]
A.7	**Degree of Standardization** (high vs. low)		X			*Logic of the Enterprise* vs. *Entrepreneurial Logic*	*new*/Berente, Hansen [49]
A.8	**Organizational Strategy** (short- vs. long-term)		X			Logic of Managerial Rationalism vs. Logic of Organizational Persistence	Berente and Yoo [42]
(B) Cultural Differences on the Team Level							
B.1	**Working Motivation** (protective vs. up-stepping)			X		Logic of Managerial Rationalism vs. Logic of Organizational Persistence	Berente and Yoo [42]
B.2	**Working Attitude** (autonomy vs. heteronomy)			X		Logic of Instruction Dependency vs. Logic of Self-Regulation	Currie and Guah [47]
B.3	**Risk-Orientation** (averse vs. affine)			X		*Logic of Proactivity* vs. *Logic of Reactivity*	*new*

(Continued)

Table 3. (Continued)

ID	Cultural Difference	Level of Culture				Corresponding Institutional Logics	Key References
		N	O	T	I		
(C) Cultural Differences on the Individual Level							
C.1	**Commitment Intensity** (low vs. high)				X	*Full-Time Project Employee Logic vs. Part-Time Project Employee Logic*	new
(D) Cultural Differences appearing on Different Levels							
D.1	**Project Dedication** (high vs. low)	X	X	X	X	Consulting Profession Logic vs. Logic of Organizational Persistence	Berente, Hansen [49]/ Berente and Yoo [42]
D.2	**Problem-Solving Attitude** (proactive vs. reactive)	X	X	X		*Logic of Proactivity vs. Logic of Reactivity*	new

Legend: *ID:* Identification number; *Cultural Difference Description:* Short Description of the identified Cultural Difference including the two extremes (in brackets); *Level of Culture:* Level of Culture the difference has been categorized as by the focus group participants (N = National, O = Organization, T = Team, I = Individual); *Corresponding Institutional Logics:* The institutional logics that give meaning to the identified cultural differences (non-italic: existing IL in literature; *italic:* derived from collected data); *Reference:* Reference to the literature in case of already existing IL.

Due to space restrictions, we are not able to provide detailed descriptions and explanations for all identified cultural differences and the corresponding institutional logics. Hence, the remainder of this section includes details on interesting findings as well as examples in terms of matchings between cultural differences and corresponding institutional logics.

Organizational Level. On the *organizational level*, we identified 8 cultural differences, which are explained by 6 corresponding institutional logics. One of these institutional logics ("logic of the enterprise") was developed by the authors based on the findings from the focus group discussions.

The cultural differences on the organization level generally evolved around the overarching attributes and mindsets of the client and vendor organizations engaged in an ITO client-vendor relationship. In general, most of the identified cultural differences on the organizational level (*solution-oriented attitude (A.1), inter-organizational collaboration (A.2), working attitude (A.3)* and *organizational strategy (A.8)*) can be thoroughly explained by the previously identified private- and public-side institutional logic [46–48] as well as the Logic of Managerial Rationalism and the Logic of Organizational Persistence [42]. Additionally, the focus group discussions revealed further cultural differences (*organizational structure (A.4), negotiation style (A.5), management style (A.6),* and *degree of standardization (A.7)*), which cannot be fully explained by already existing institutional logics. For example, one participant described cultural differences in terms of negotiation style based on the client's and vendor's company size and type, which seriously affect the length of negotiations within ITO relationships:

> *"There is always a difference [in the negotiation style] based on the company size. A small company does not have its own legal department. In case of negotiations, they engage an independent lawyer. In such cases, the lawyer is often not directly involved in the negotiations and you negotiate directly with the management of the company. This makes negotiation different from negotiations with a large provider. In this case, you negotiate with the vendor's own lawyer, who gets the mandate by the board. After the negotiation, he needs to discuss the changes with his management."* (adopted from Focus Group 4, translated from German)

Another participant from the same focus group discussion explained cultural differences concerning the management style based on the involved organization's size, separating large enterprises from small ownerled, organizations:

> *"In smaller organizations [...] the management function is more involved in the project. This is leading to faster processes and results. On the other hand, in bigger organizations, there is less involvement from the management. In this case, departments act independently, which is allowed."* (adopted from Focus Group 4, translated from German)

Building upon the participants' explanations of the cultural differences, we identified the institutional "logic of the enterprise" and the "entrepreneurial logic" as a suitable explanation for the identified cultural differences. Within many ITO relationships, large enterprises outsource software development or maintenance tasks to smaller software development startups, for example, the development and maintenance of mobile applications. The enterprises on the client side hereby follow the principle of standardization (e.g., by implementing hierarchies and distinct delegations). In contrast, smaller software development startups follow the entrepreneurial institutional logic [49], which allows for "leanness, informality, bricolage, and adaptability associated with entrepreneurial scripts for practice" [49]. A description of the newly identified "logic of the enterprise" based on the framework of Berente and Yoo [42] is provided in Table 4 below.

Table 4. Logic of the enterprise – description.

Inst. logic dimension	Characterization of the logic of the enterprise	Representative quotations
Principle	Focus on Standardization	*"The larger the organization, the higher the degree of standardization"* (Focus Group 4)
Assumption	Standardization through hierarchies, distinct delegation and overarching rulesets	*"There are always hierarchies [in enterprises]. For example, there is someone who has a general overview, and another one responsible for the details."* (Focus Group 3)

(*Continued*)

Table 4. (*Continued*)

Inst. logic dimension	Characterization of the logic of the enterprise	Representative quotations
		"Within negotiations, the lawyer is delegated by the management. After the negotiations, he needs to clarify all changes with the management" (Focus Group 4)
Identity	A Standardized, hierarchical structure with distinct delegations implies a certain degree of inflexibility and the definition of independent departments and centres	*"An issue within the ongoing ITO client-vendor relationship is the degree of inflexibility"* (Focus Group 4) *"Within large organizations [...] the different departments work independently, which is accepted by the management"* (Focus Group 4)
Domain	Large, multi-national organizations involved in ITO relationships	*"In general, you could say we are a multi-national organization from a structural point of view"* (Focus Group 2)

Team Level. On the team level, we identified three cultural differences, which can be explained by six corresponding institutional logics. The cultural differences of *working motivation (B.1)* and *working attitude (B.2)* hereby explain differences in the type of motivation by the different teams involved in an ITO relationship (e.g., team member level vs. management level). Our research hence confirms the existence of the already identified logics of "managerial rationalism" and "organizational persistence" [42] in the context of ITO. These logics describe different mindsets of management and employees in largescale IT projects, for example, based on the job role (e.g., project managers and software developers).

In addition, our study revealed the cultural difference of *risk-orientation (B.3)* as important when managing interorganizational teams within an ITO relationship. Different participants mentioned that, especially in large-scale organizations, there are always teams involved in ITO relationships, which are either risk-averse (e.g., the legal department) or risk-affine (e.g., the client's IT management).

> *"Within a large organization, the legal department is generally interested in minimizing the risk potential, this includes the minimization of all risks"* (adopted from Focus Group 4, translated from German)

> *"The IT management generally says, I need this and the cost and risk are not important"* (adopted from Focus Group 3, translated from German)

This cultural differences goes hand in hand with the cultural difference concerning the *problem-solving attitude (D.2)*, which we identified on different cultural levels (national culture/organizational culture/team culture). We identified differences in the problem-solving attitude based on differences in the national culture of the resources (e.g., India vs. Germany), the organizational culture (private vs. public organization), and the team culture (team members vs. management). For example, one participant explained the more reactive problem-solving attitude of software developers from India compared to German software developers:

> *"They have a different culture when it comes to problems. They won't come to you directly and say, that they are either overstrained or that the timeframe is not sufficient."* (adopted from Focus Group 2, translated from German)

In summary, these two cultural differences (B.3; D.2) can be explained by the newly defined, general institutional *logics of proactivity and reactivity*. We identified that organizations and teams engaged in ITO relationships act either proactive or reactive based on their overarching mindset and beliefs, which are derived from their cultural backgrounds. The details of the two institutional logics are described in Tables 5 and 6.

Table 5. Logic of proactivity – description.

Inst. logic dimension	Characterization of the logic of proactivity	Representative quotations
Principle	Appreciating change	*"When working with private organizations [...], you always get direct feedback [on problems]"* (Focus Group 4)
Assumption	Appreciating change through proactive management, risk-affinity, trust and general ITO affinity	*"Within our ITO relationship, the underlying product allows the [clients] management function to directly manage and control the operational ranks of the organization."* (Focus Group 1) *"The client's IT management within our ITO relationship just provide a general frame and afterwards trust us to deliver within this frame"* (Focus Group 2) *"The idea of outsourcing is accepted within the [client's] management"* (Focus Group 2)
Identity	A behaviour which appreciates change implies a certain degree of management skills, trust towards the vendor organization, ITO experience and service orientation	*"Even if [the client's IT management] needs to report the status to his management on a weekly basis, he leaves us alone. It's like 'you provided me with a plan for two weeks, so just do it'"* (Focus Group 2)

(Continued)

Table 5. (*Continued*)

Inst. logic dimension	Characterization of the logic of proactivity	Representative quotations
		"On the [client's] management level, you find people who are similar to yourself, who have experience and a certain level of education". (Focus Group 1) *(FG1)* "The client [management] in the ITO relationship needs to be service oriented" (Focus Group 4)
Domain	Client top management function (within private organizations); Client IT management function;	No specific quotation, reasoning for domain based on context

Table 6. Logic of reactivity – description.

Inst. logic dimension	Characterization of the logic of reactivity	Representative quotations
Principle	Minimizing change	"When you are working with departments on the client's side, I think their overarching goal is to change as less as possible" *(FG4)*
Assumption	Minimizing change through reactive and risk-obverse behaviour, prevention activities and passivity	"Teams or employees who seek topics like data security or legal issues to prevent the engagement." *(FG1)* "The legal department's main focus is the minimization of all risks associated to the ITO engagement." *(FG4)*
Identity	Focussed on minimizing change due to inexperience, passivity and inflexibility	"Internal teams [from the client] are often working on one topic or one product and they don't really know what else is going on. Hence there is not that much experience [...] and when it comes to change, this is an issue" *(FG3)*
Domain	Client teams or individual employees from lower ranks engaged in ITO relationships; Client legal department; Vendor employees from particular cultural backgrounds (e.g. India)	"When ITO engagements and corresponding decisions are blocked, it originates nearly always from hierarchically low ranks within the [client] organization" *(FG1)* "Software developers from India have a different culture when it comes to problems" *(FG2)*

Individual Level. On the *individual level* we identified one cultural difference, which is explained by two institutional logics. The cultural difference arose from the intensity of the commitment for the ITO relationship based on the participant's individual cultural background. We especially identified differences in the ITO relationship commitment between client employees fully staffed to the project on the one hand and project employees, for example, freelancers or client subject matter experts, who are not fully staffed to the project, on the other hand:

> "We have employees, who are traditionally, permanently hired [internal]. They have a completely different focus. They want to have a secure job. [...]. The freelancer generally has a contract for the specific project. He/She is already looking for a follow-up project as soon as he started on our project." (adopted from Focus Group 2, translated from German)

Building upon the data from our focus group discussions, we defined the *fulltime project employee logic* and the *parttime project employee logic* as suitable logics for explaining the particular cultural difference of ITO relationship commitment. Hereby, the most vivid difference between individuals acting based on either the internal employee logic and the external employee logic is the security-focus versus the shortterm focus of the individual's behaviour and actions. A detailed description of the institutional logics is provided in Tables 7 and 8.

Table 7. Internal project employee logic – description.

Inst. Logic Dimension	Characterization of the full-time project employee logic	Representative quotations
Principle	(Job) security focus; high, long-term commitment	"We have employees, who are traditionally, permanently hired [internal]. They have a completely different focus. They want to have a secure job" (Focus Group 2)
Assumption	Individual's focus on job security through risk-averse, slow-moving behaviour and working within known boundaries	"Especially when there are difficult topics like the transfer of employees to the external provider. In this case, you won't get the acceptance of the internal employees [technical staff]" (Focus Group 4) "It looks like that the internal teams are working slower when it comes to deadlines" (Focus Group 2)
Identity	Focus on job-security due to fear, inexperience and partially autistic behaviour on the one hand and a high degree of technical know-how	"He [the particular employee]is driven by fear" (FG1) "I think all [internal] IT guys are autistic by nature" (Focus Group 4)

(Continued)

Table 7. (*Continued*)

Inst. Logic Dimension	Characterization of the full-time project employee logic	Representative quotations
		"I think our internal IT has a higher degree of technical know-how compared to the vendor" (Focus Group 2)
Domain	Internal employees from the client's side (e.g. software developers)	No specific quotation, reasoning for domain based on context

Table 8. External project employee logic – description.

Inst. Logic Dimension	Characterization of the part-time project employee logic	Representative quotations
Principle	Short-term focus/low commitment	"The freelancer generally has a contract for the specific project. He/She is already looking for a follow-up project as soon as he started on our project." (Focus Group 2) "He [the expert] is not committed to the project" (Focus Group 3)
Assumption	Short-term focus as well as low commitment due to the overarching agreement (e.g. contract) for the individual as well as the opposing responsibilities (e.g. line-work vs. project-work)	"In case an SME is not available anymore and his successor is not interested in the project, then he de-prioritizes the project work" (Focus Group 3) "When you ask [the SME], you never get a response, because he is also involved in his line-work. And with the project he is not really engaged" (Focus Group 3)
Identity	Short-term focus and low commitment is leading to passive working behaviour and limited availability	"For some resources it is not relevant to speak up on Tuesday that there is something wrong with the requirement and that they need to correct this. Because in this case they need to correct this and then there will be no deliverable on Friday" (Focus Group 2) "The experts are not really available, because they are involved in several projects" (Focus Group 3)

(*Continued*)

Table 8. (*Continued*)

Inst. Logic Dimension	Characterization of the part-time project employee logic	Representative quotations
Domain	Freelancers engaged by the client to support the ITO engagement; Subject Matter Experts involved in the ITO engagement based on a part-time contract	No specific quotation, reasoning for domain based on context (see especially principle quotations)

5 Discussion

Based on our research question and our exploratory research design, the major outcome of our study is the identification and explanation of cultural differences in ITO relationships. Explicitly, we identified and confirmed overarching institutional logics for explaining particular cultural differences between individuals, teams, and organizations involved in ITO relationships. Based on this result, our study contributed to IS research in general and ITO-related research in particular by several means:

First, by providing further insights into the concept of culture in ITO-related research, we allow for a more detailed explanation. As described in Sects. 1 and 2, past research evaluating culture in the context of ITO focused mostly on one or two particular levels, for example, national culture [50] or organizational and individual culture [34]. Research using multi-level approaches to analyse the concept of culture in the context of ITO relationships is limited. Our research particularly contributes to this gap in our knowledge by applying the multi-level cultural framework of Leidner and Kayworth [23]. We were able to identify 14 cultural differences vivid in ITO relationships on different levels. Hereby it is important to note that we identified particular cultural differences on the organizational level (e.g., different types of *interorganizational collaboration (A.2)*), the team level (differences in *risk-attitudes (B.3)*) and the individual level (differences in the *ITO engagement commitment (B.1)*). Furthermore, we identified two cultural differences, which occurred on different cultural levels (e.g., different *problem-solving attitudes (D.2)*). Based on this result, our research indicates that cultural differences can occur on different levels simultaneously within an ITO relationship, and that future research is required to evaluate these cultural differences and their interactions on a larger scale. Furthermore, our results indicate, that cultural differences occur, to a large extent, on the organizational level. Hence, we suggest for future research to evaluate the organizational level to understand the relationship between cultural differences on this level and ITO success in detail.

Second, by applying the ILP for explaining the identified cultural differences within ITO relationships, we offer a novel perspective on culture in ITO. As described in Sect. 2.1, the concept of culture is generally difficult to describe and explain due to its "umbrella" character. We used ILP for explaining and reasoning particular cultural differences within the context of ITO. Specifically, by applying the categorical framework of Berente and Yoo [42], we were able to confirm, enhance, as well as define new institutional logics, which shape and form the interaction of organizations, teams, and individuals within ITO relationships. Our research, on the one hand, confirmed and enhanced several logics, already mentioned in the context of IS by previous research (see Table 3). Furthermore, we developed 5 previously unknown logics in the context of ITO. This result of our exploratory research could be used as a baseline for both validating the existence of the particular institutional logics in different types of ITO relationships (e.g., onsite IT infrastructure maintenance vs. offshore software development projects) as well as evaluating the effect of these logics (and the corresponding cultural differences) on the quality of the ITO relationship and the overall ITO project success.

As regards to limitations of our study, *first*, we need to take into account the limitations of focus group discussions as a data collection method in qualitative, exploratory research. Although focus group discussions allow the gathering of knowledge on complex problems within a short timeframe [25], we cannot argue for generalizability and comprehensiveness based on purely qualitative data collection. We tried to cover this limitation by choosing a diverse set of organizations for our focus groups including clients, vendors and consultants with experience in ITO relationships. Nevertheless, we would strongly recommend other researchers to continue this research endeavour by applying, for example, methods like case study research and surveys to further evaluate the concept of culture in the context of ITO based on a multi-level approach.

Second, we need to recognize our limited set of organizations involved in our data collection. Although we tried to cover different aspects of an ITO relationship by involving client, vendor and consultancy organizations into our focus group discussions, all these organizations and the discussed projects focussed on relationships between clients in Germany and vendors in India. To get a more diverse view of culture in the context of ITO relationships, especially in terms of differences on the national culture level, we would strongly recommend future research evaluating culture in ITO relationships based on a more diverse set of organizations and ITO projects, for example, comparing projects with vendor organizations in India, South America and Eastern Europe.

6 Conclusion

For the very first time, our study applied ILP as a theoretical lens to evaluate the concept of culture in the context of ITO. By confirming, enhancing, as well as identifying new institutional logics, explaining particular institutional logics in the context of ITO, we enhanced our understanding of culture in ITO. Our exploratory research is usable as a suitable starting point for an indepth, multi-level evaluation of culture in ITO relationships, which is currently a gap in our knowledge on information technology outsourcing relationships. Further studies on how cultural differences, as espoused by different institutional logics, affect client-vendor relationships and ITO success will offer valuable insights.

Appendix: Overview of Focus Group Participants

ID	Position & Role	Working Experience	ITO Projects	Project Lead	Project Figures		
					TM	DUR	VEN
1	Software Developer	8	n.i.	n.i.	n.i.	n.i.	n.i.
2	CEO & Founder	11	50	40	5–15	6–24	1–3
3	CEO & Founder	10	40	30	5–15	6–24	1–3
4	Software Architect	20	6	5	5–15	3–24	1–2
5	Head of Business Intelligence and Product Development	10	>10	2	15–20	9–30	1–3
6	Software Developer	13	20	8	2–5	6–50	1
7	Software Architect	19	20	10	2–5	6–50	1
8	CEO & Founder	25	50	50	30–100	6–12	2–14
9	Managing Director	29	>53	26	2–50	3–36	2–10
10	Senior Consultant	18	15	0	10–15	13–24	10–20
11	Principal Consultant	15	42	40	5–27	9–18	10–20
12	Senior Consultant	7	3	0	20–50	17–30	5–8
13	Senior Consultant	6	2	0		3–12	1
14	Senior Consultant	5	8	4	3–5	6–12	2–3
15	Senior Consultant	>20	6	2	5–20	3–9	1–12
16	Senior Consultant	22	4	2	8–12	17–24	6–7

Legend: *Position & Role:* Description of the research participant's level, organization (V = Vendor; C = Client) and role; *Working Experience:* Research participant's working experience in years; *ITO projects:* Number of ITO projects, the research participant was assigned to (overall); *Project Lead:* Number of ITO projects, the research participant was assigned to (as project lead); *Project Figures:* TM = no. of team members/DUR = Duration (in month)/ VEN = number of involved vendors (all project figures listed as min to max (e.g. TM = 1–20 > min. 1 team member/max. 20 team members)

n.i. = no information provided due to personal reasons.

References

1. Jin Kim, H., Shin, B., Lee, H.: The mediating role of psychological contract breach in IS outsourcing: interfirm governance perspective. Eur. J. Inf. Syst. **22**(5), 529–547 (2013)
2. Hall, J.A., Liedtka, S.L.: Financial performance, CEO compensation, and large-scale information technology outsourcing decisions. J. Manage. Inf. Syst. **22**(1), 193–221 (2005)
3. Seddon, P.B., Cullen, S., Willcocks, L.P.: Does Domberger's theory of 'The Contracting Organization' explain why organizations outsource IT and the levels of satisfaction achieved? Eur. J. Inf. Syst. **16**(3), 237–253 (2007)
4. Kern, T., Willcocks, L.: Exploring relationships in information technology outsourcing: the interaction approach. Eur. J. Inf. Syst. **11**(1), 3–19 (2002)
5. Poston, R.S., Simon, J.C., Jain, R.: Client communication practices in managing relationships with offshore vendors of software testing services. Commun. Assoc. Inf. Syst. **27**(1) 2010
6. Horvath, IT Outsourcing Satisfaction Survey 2014 (2014)
7. Blaskovich, J., Mintchik, N.: Information technology outsourcing: a taxonomy of prior studies and directions for future research. J. Inf. Syst. **25**(1), 1–36 (2011)
8. Dibbern, J., et al.: Information systems outsourcing: a survey and analysis of the literature. ACM SIGMIS Database **35**(4), 6–102 (2004)
9. Lacity, M.C., et al.: A review of the IT outsourcing empirical literature and future research directions. J. Inf. Technol. **25**(4). 395–433 (2010)
10. Lacity, M.C., Willcocks, L.P., Khan, S.: Beyond transaction cost economics: towards an endogenous theory of information technology outsourcing. J. Strateg. Inf. Syst. **20**(2), 139–157 (2011)
11. Kaiser, J., Buxmann, P.: Organizational design of IT supplier relationship management: a multiple case study of five client companies. J. Inf. Technol. **27**(1), 57–73 (2012)
12. Aron, R., Clemons, E.K., Reddi, S.: Just right outsourcing: understanding and managing risk. J. Manage. Inf. Syst. **22**(2), 37–55 (2005)
13. Lee, J.-N., Miranda, S.M., Kim, Y.-M.: IT outsourcing strategies: universalistic, contingency, and configurational explanations of success. Inf. Syst. Res. **15**(2), 110–131 (2004)
14. Kern, T., Willcocks, L.: Exploring information technology outsourcing relationships: theory and practice. J. Strateg. Inf. Syst. **9**(4), 321–350 (2000)
15. Lee, J.-N., Kim, Y.-G.: Effect of partnership quality on IS outsourcing success: conceptual framework and empirical validation. J. Manage. inf. syst., p. 29–61 (1999)
16. Blaskovich, J., Mintchik, N.: Accounting executives and IT outsourcing recommendations: an experimental study of the effect of CIO skills and institutional isomorphism. J. Inf. Technol. **26**(2), 139–152 (2011)
17. Dibbern, J., Winkler, J., Heinzl, A.: Explaining variations in client extra costs between software projects offshored to India. MIS Q. **32**(2), 333–366 (2008)
18. Dibbern, J., Chin, W.W., Heinzl, A.: Systemic determinants of the information systems outsourcing decision: a comparative study of German and United States Firms. J. Assoc. Inf. Syst. **13**(6), 466–497 (2012)
19. Gupta, A., et al.: Use of collaborative technologies and knowledge sharing in co-located and distributed teams: towards the 24-h knowledge factory. J. Strateg. Inf. Syst. **18**(3), 147–161 (2009)
20. Nicholson, B., Aman, A.: Managing attrition in offshore finance and accounting outsourcing. Strateg. Outsourcing Int. J. **5**(3). 232–247 (2012)
21. Pannirselvam, G.P., Madupalli, R.: Antecedents of project success: the perception of vendor employees. Qual. Manage. J. **18**(3), 7–20 (2011)

22. Rustagi, S., King, W.R., Kirsch, L.J.: Predictors of formal control usage in IT outsourcing partnerships. Inf. Syst. Res. **19**(2), pp. 126–143, 240–241 (2008)
23. Leidner, D.E., Kayworth, T.: Review: a review of culture in information systems research: toward a theory of information technology culture conflict. MIS Q. **30**(2), 357–399 (2006)
24. Thornton, P.H., Ocasio, W., Lounsbury, M.: The Institutional Logics Perspective: A New Approach To Culture, Structure, and Process. Oxford University Press, Oxford (2012)
25. Liamputtong, P.: Focus Group Methodology: Principle and Practice. Sage, Los Angeles (2011)
26. Kroeber, A.L., Kluckhohn, C.: Culture: a critical review of concepts and definitions. Papers. Peabody Museum of Archaeology & Ethnology, Harvard University (1952)
27. Hofstede, G.: National cultures in four dimensions: a research-based theory of cultural differences among nations. Int. Stud. Manage. Organ., pp. 46–74 (1983)
28. Chang, Y.-W., et al.: Knowledge sharing intention in the United States and China: a cross-cultural study. Eur. J. Inf. Syst. **24**(3), 262–277 (2014)
29. Alavi, M., Kayworth, T.R., Leidner, D.E.: An empirical examination of the influence of organizational culture on knowledge management practices. J. Manage. Inf. Syst. **22**(3), 191–224 (2005)
30. Schein, E.H.: Organizational Culture and Leadership. The Jossey-Bass Business & Management Series. Jossey-Bass, San Francisco (2010)
31. Karahanna, E., Evaristo, J.R., Srite, M.: Levels of Culture and Individual Behavior: An Investigative Perspective. Journal of Global Information Management (JGIM) **13**(2), 1–20 (2005)
32. Avison, D., Banks, P.: Cross-cultural (mis)communication in IS offshoring: understanding through conversation analysis. J. Inf. Technol. **23**(4), 249–268 (2008)
33. Winkler, J.K., Dibbern, J., Heinzl, A.: The impact of cultural differences in offshore outsourcing–case study results from German-Indian application development projects. Inf. Syst. Frontiers **10**(2), 243–258 (2008)
34. Rai, A., Maruping, L.M., Venkatesh, V.: Offshore information systems project success: the role of social embeddedness and cultural characteristics. MIS Q. **33**(3), 617–647 (2009)
35. Gopal, A., Gosain, S.: The role of organizational controls and boundary spanning in software development outsourcing: implications for project performance. Inf. Syst. Res. **21**(4), pp. 960–982, 1002 (2010)
36. Gregory, R., Prifling, M., Beck, R.: The role of cultural intelligence for the emergence of negotiated culture in IT offshore outsourcing projects. Inf. Technol. People **22**(3), 223–241 (2009)
37. Leidner, D.E.: Globalization, culture, and information: towards global knowledge transparency. J. Strateg. Inf. Syst. **19**(2), 69–77 (2010)
38. Greenwood, R., et al.: The multiplicity of institutional logics and the heterogeneity of organizational responses. Organ. Sci. **21**(2), 521–539 (2010)
39. Mola, L., Carugati, A.: Escaping 'localisms' in IT sourcing: tracing changes in institutional logics in an Italian firm. Eur. J. Inf. Syst. **21**(4), 388–403 (2012)
40. Vasudeva, G., Alexander, E.A., Jones, S.L.: Institutional logics and interorganizational learning in technological arenas: evidence from standard-setting organizations in the mobile handset industry. In: Organization Science (2014)
41. Thornton, P.H., Ocasio, W.: Institutional Logics. In: The Sage Handbook of Organizational Institutionalism, vol. 840, pp. 99–128 (2008)
42. Berente, N., Yoo, Y.: Institutional contradictions and loose coupling: postimplementation of NASA's enterprise information system. Inf. Syst. Res. **23**(2), 376–396 (2012)
43. Myers, M.D., Avison, D.: Qualitative research in information systems. Manage. Inf. Syst. Q. **21**, 241–242 (1997)

44. Dürrenberger, G., Behringer, J.: die Fokusgruppe in Theorie und Anwendung. Akad. für Technikfolgenabschätzung in Baden-Württemberg (1999)
45. Schulz, M., Mack, B., Renn, O. (eds.) Fokusgruppen in der empirischen Sozialwissenschaft: Von der Konzeption bis zur Auswertung. Springer, Germany (2012)
46. Beck, R., Gregory, R.W., Marschollek, O.: The interplay of institutional logics in it public private partnerships. SIGMIS Database **46**(1), 24–38 (2015)
47. Currie, W.L., Guah, M.W.: Conflicting institutional logics: a national programme for IT in the organisational field of healthcare. J. Inf. Technol. **22**(3), 235–247 (2007)
48. Marschollek, D.-K.F.O., Beck, R.: Alignment of divergent organizational cultures in it public-private partnerships. Bus. Inf. Syst. Eng. **4**(3), 153–162 (2012)
49. Berente, N., Hansen, S.W., Rosenkranz, C.: Rule Formation and Change in Information Systems Development: How Institutional Logics Shape ISD Practices and Processes (2014)
50. Khan, S.U., Azeem, M.I.: Intercultural challenges in offshore software development outsourcing relationships: an exploratory study using a systematic literature review. IET Software **8**(4), 161–173 (2014)

Outsourcing and Innovation: A Comparative Study of Italy and the UK

Giovanni Vaia[1] and Ilan Oshri[2(✉)]

[1] Ca' Foscari University, Venice, Italy
[2] Loughborough Research Centre for Global Sourcing and Services, Loughborough, UK
i.oshri@lboro.ac.uk

Abstract. Italy is known for bringing to the world some of the greatest inventions and arts. Indeed, creativity and innovation are not strange phrases in many Italian sectors such as fashion, automotive and leather. But challenges to achieve innovation in the Italian service outsourcing sector still lay ahead. Recent reports have highlighted the complexity involved in fostering collaborative innovation between a client firm and a supplier, often resolving is unsatisfactory results. Hence, in this report, we seek to unveil whether the long innovative tradition plays a role in its local service outsourcing industry. A study of 150 British and Italian Service Outsourcing executives was carried out to examine their comparative innovation performance and the mechanisms that support innovation in each country. The results show that Italian client firms reported more satisfaction with the quality, frequency and impact of innovation delivered by suppliers than their British counterparts. The main differences between the Italian and British cases that may explain our results were (i) Italian client firms' strategic intent has been revolving around the objective to increase the pace of innovation within the firm while their British counterparts have been focusing on cost reduction, (ii) Italian client firms have mainly been using outcome base pricing model while British client firms have mainly been using fixed-price model and (iii) Italian client firms have been using advisory firms to a far more extent than their British counterparts. We conclude by offering a practical framework to achieve innovation through outsourcing.

Keywords: IT outsourcing · Innovation · Relational and contractual governance · Survey

1 Trends in Outsourcing

Recent years have witnessed an unprecedented growth of the outsourcing industry. By the end of 2014, the market has exceeded US$700 billion. Recent estimates predict that the market will see 4.8% compound annual growth through the end of 2018. Interestingly, in 2014 growth in Europe has exceeded growth in the US for the first time ever. Further, nearly 120 offshore locations are now competing for IT outsourcing and business process services around the globe. As firms become more savvy consumers of outsourcing services, they apply various sourcing models varying from multi-supplier sourcing arrangements to the setting up of offshore captive centres where skills are available at the right cost.

There is now strong evidence that client firms have been focusing on getting value adding services from their third party supplier in addition to cost savings. In the quest for value adding services, client firms need to develop a systematic approach of working together with their third party suppliers to ensure the delivery of innovative solutions as part of their outsourcing engagements.

2 Innovation in Outsourcing: Background

In management terms, innovation can take the form of a new product or service offered to clients or a new process through which an organisation develops products or delivers services. Innovation can also be anything that is state-of-the-art and also anything which is new to the organization. Innovation does not come easy, whether as an in-house process or through external partners. When in-house, inertia forces often obstruct attempts to innovate and break away from old ways. And when sought through relationships with partners, innovative efforts face additional challenges, for example having to agree and monitor how each party contributes to the partnership as well as benefits from the value created.

The outsourcing context poses additional challenges to achieving innovation between a client firm and a supplier. One of the main reasons often cited by CIOs for failing to achieve innovation in outsourcing is the difficulty to find the sweet spot between the collaborative attitude and the transactional approach, both needed in joint innovation projects. Further, client firms struggle to use pricing models that motivate the supplier to engage in high risk innovation projects while safeguarding the parties' benefits.

So how can companies achieve innovation through outsourcing engagements? In this study, we answer this question by comparing innovation performance of Italian and British client firms.

3 About This Research

This research was conducted by Prof. Ilan Oshri, Director of the Research Centre for Global Sourcing and Services at Loughborough University, Prof. Giovanni Vaia (Ca' Foscari University, Venice, Italy) and Engineering, an Italian firm.

The results of this study are based on a cross-industry survey carried out in 2015 with 150 client firms in Italy (75 firms) and the UK (75 firms) at the executive level who were directly involved in achieving innovation through outsourcing.

Forty five (45%) percent of Italian executives interviewed for this study work in firms that employ less than 1000 employees from various sectors such as manufacturing (25%), retail (25%), finance (9%) and public sector (12%). Fifty three (53%) percent of them work in the information technology department within the business with 34% of them having more than 5 years outsourcing experience.

Seventy one (71%) of British executives in this study work in firms that employ more than 1000 employees, representing similar spread of sectors such as manufacturing (23%), retail (23%), finance (16%) and public sector (13%). Fifty-three (53%) percent of them work in the IT area and 55% of them have more than 5 years experience.

4 The Nature of Innovation: UK and Italy

Innovation comes in various forms and may have differing levels of impact. Some innovations are at the functional level while others are strategic. Innovations can be incremental, gradually affecting the business while other initiatives can be transformative, radically changing the way business is conducted in a short time. Traditionally, suppliers have been viewed as mainly capable of improving operations with little involvement in strategic challenges faced by their clients. Our results confirm this observation with respondents from the UK (85%) and Italy (88%) reporting that innovation achieved was mainly operational with the most common example cited as moving a system (e.g. email or procurement) to the Cloud. The few examples at the strategic level of innovation reported in this study were 'the development of a customer-focused platform to manage customer relationship' (Italy) and '[supplier] tailored a low-level solution for the Asian markets' (UK). Our results suggest that there is little difference in how innovation is perceived in the Italian and British outsourcing sector. It is also evident that the adoption of Cloud Services by many organisations is perceived as an innovation initiative, though the focus is still on the technological solution rather than the impact on the business.

4.1 Achieved Benefits from Innovation: UK and Italy

Innovation can deliver various benefits to the client firm. Strategic innovation is expected to positively affect the way the client firm competes and penetrates new markets while operational innovation is likely to reduce operating costs and improve efficiencies. Our study reveals a significant difference in 6 areas of benefits from innovation between the Italian and British outsourcing sector.

Cost Saving Benefits. Sixty seven (67%) percent of Italian executives reported that they strongly agree or agree with the statement that innovation contributed to a decrease in running costs compared with only 41% of the British executives (see Fig. 1). These results may suggest the following: (i) innovation in Italy delivers a reduction in running costs more broadly than in the UK, and/or (ii) Italian executives are more content with the level of costs reduction deliver through innovative solutions by their suppliers than their British counterparts.

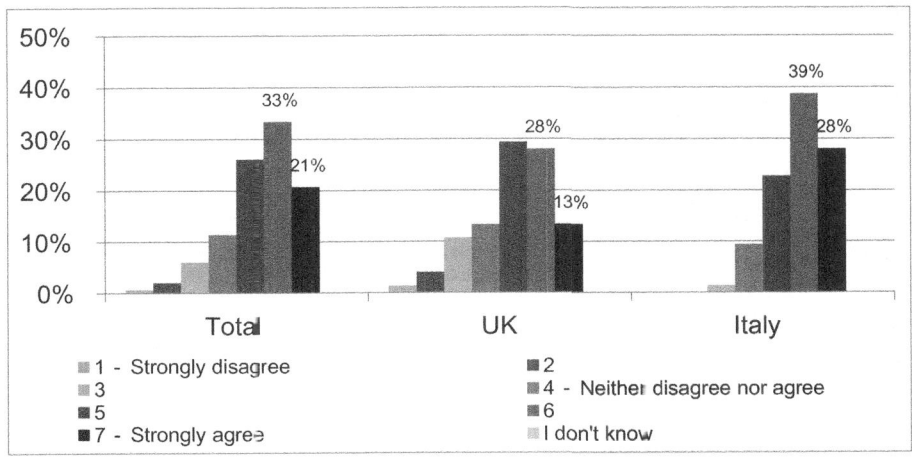

Fig. 1. The innovation contributed to a decrease in our running costs

Improve Service Offering. Seventy two (72%) percent of Italian executives reported that they either agree or strongly agree with the statement that innovation delivered by suppliers improved their service offering compared with only 49% of British executives. These results suggest that (i) innovation delivered in Italy is achieving a broader strategic impact on the business than in the UK and that (ii) Italian executives are more satisfied than British executives with the impact on service offering achieved by their suppliers through innovation (Fig. 2).

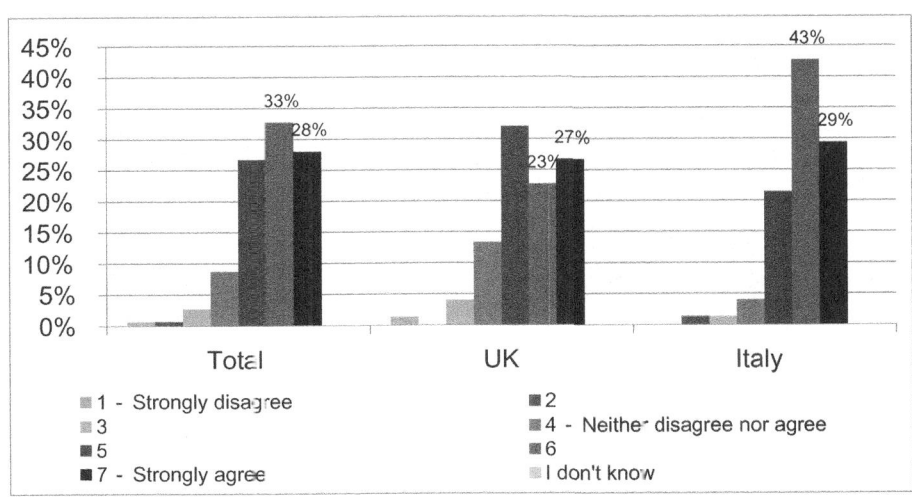

Fig. 2. The innovation improved our service/product offering

Process Transformation Effect. Seventy three (73%) of Italian executives reported that they agree or strongly agree with the statement that innovation has led to transformation in processes compared with only 54% of their British counterparts. The results suggest that innovation in the Italian outsourcing sector delivers process transformation more broadly than in the UK and that Italian executive report satisfaction with the transformation delivered by their suppliers (Fig. 3).

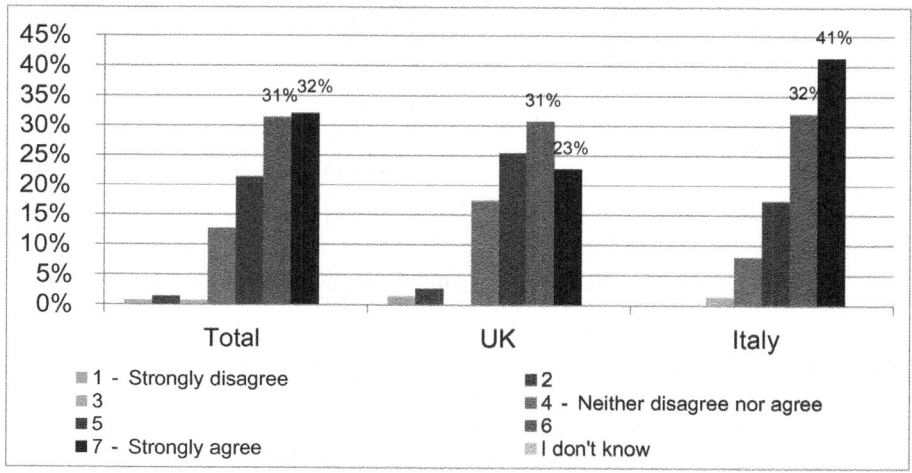

Fig. 3. Innovation led to beneficial transformations in our processes

Number of Innovation Solutions Delivered by Supplier. Another indicator of innovation performance is the number of actual innovative solutions delivered by suppliers. An increase in solutions delivered by suppliers can be seen as a healthy indicator while a decrease in numbers may suggest that the parties have lost interest in pursuing innovation.

In our study, 57% of Italian respondents indicated that the actual number of innovation solutions has either 'increased a lot' or 'significantly increased' compared with only 31% of their British counterparts (Fig. 4).

The Quality of Innovation Delivered. We have also examined comparative perceptions of the quality of innovation solutions delivered by supplier. Sixty five (65%) of Italian executives reported that the quality of innovation solutions delivered by supplier has either 'increased a lot' or 'significantly increased' as compared with only 36% of the British executives (Fig. 5).

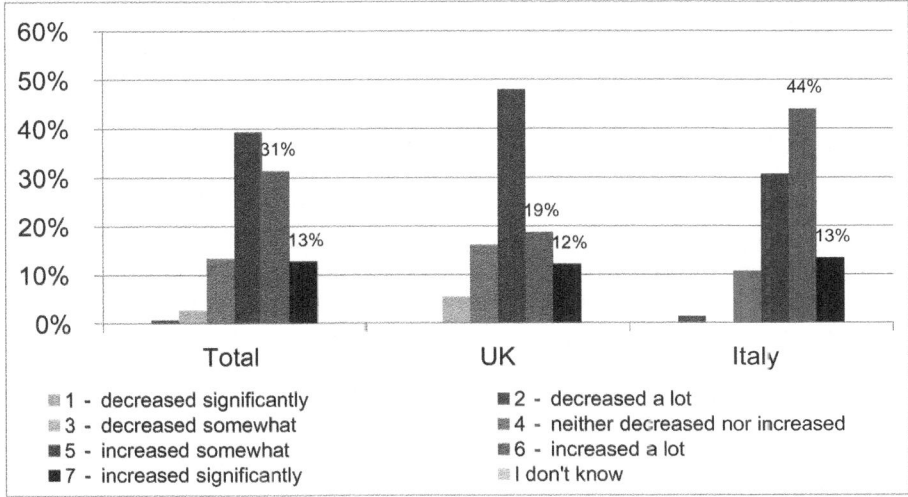

Fig. 4. The actual number of innovative solutions delivered by our third party suppliers has…

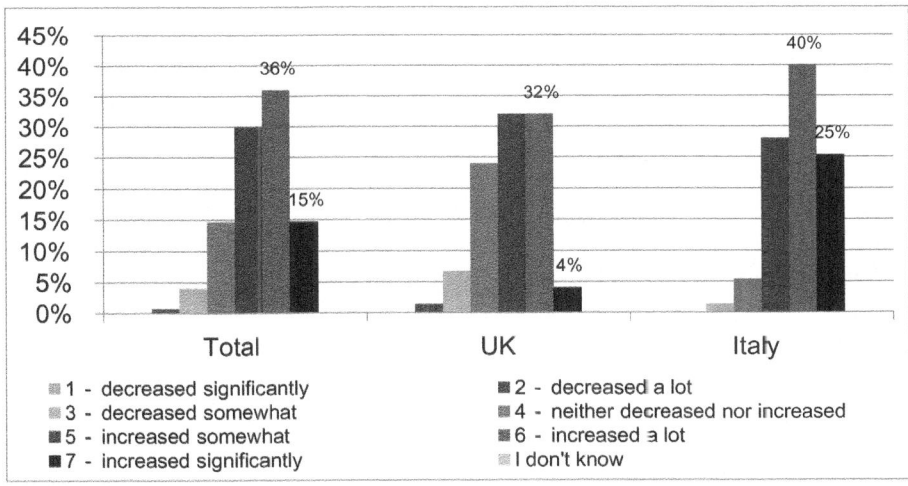

Fig. 5. The quality of innovations delivered through outsourcing has…

<u>Interval Between Innovation Solutions Delivered by Suppliers.</u> The rate that suppliers deliver innovative solutions is another health check of innovation performance in outsourcing engagements. Forty four (44%) of the Italian executives indicated that the frequency of delivering innovation solutions has either 'increased a lot' or 'significantly increased' as compared with only 19% of British respondents.

To sum, it is evident from the six areas of benefits examined here that Italian executives hold a much more positive view on their gains from innovation delivered by suppliers than their British counterparts. It is therefore intriguing to understand why

Italian executives either gain or believe that they gain more than their British counterparts in terms of the number and quality of innovative solutions delivered by their suppliers.

4.2 Differences and Similarities: The UK and Italy Outsourcing Sectors

We start investigating the sources of the differences in benefits from innovation by examining the characteristics of the outsourcing sectors in Italy and the UK.

We found three fundamental differences between the Italian and British outsourcing sector. First, the percentage of large firms (bigger than 1000 employees) participating in this study was higher in the UK (71%) than in Italy (55%). Indeed, the Italian economy is characterised by the relatively higher population of smaller firms as compared with most Western-European economies. The implications of this difference in terms of the firm size is that smaller firms are more likely to work with smaller suppliers thus more capable of maintaining close relationships with their suppliers that often lead to successful innovation.

Second, the strategic intent for outsourcing the functions in which innovation was sought in Italy and the UK is different. In Italy, the main reason for seeking innovation was to speed up the rate of innovation within the client firm (39%) while in the UK the main driver was to reduce costs (39%). Indeed, most studies have persistently showed that the vast majority of the client firms' drive to outsource is cost reduction. In this regard, the Italian case presents a new motivator in the outsourcing literature that is purely focusing on innovation as an outcome of the outsourcing engagement (Fig. 6).

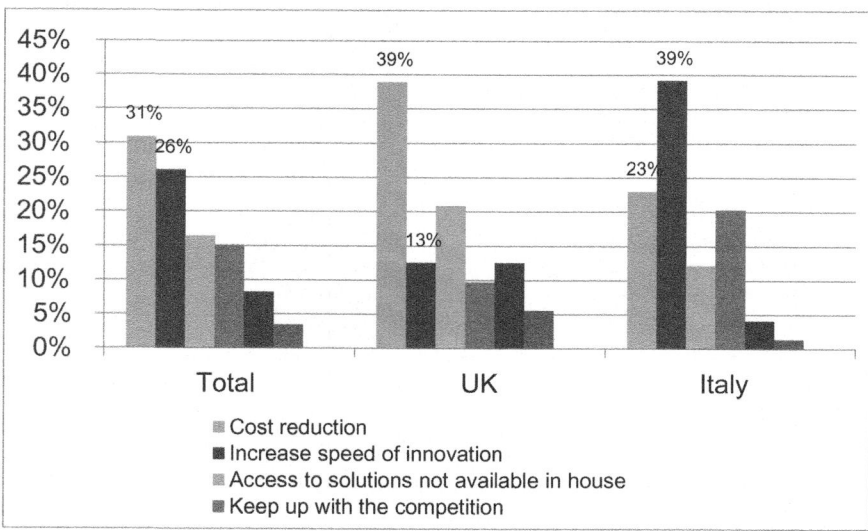

Fig. 6. What was your organisation's strategic intent behind outsourcing the areas for which innovation was important?

Last but not least, the vast majority of Italian client firms (65%) have used advisory firms to help them achieve innovation in their outsourcing engagements compared with only 39% of their British counterparts. This approach by Italian firms may have helped them use best practices and advance methodologies leading to high innovation performance (Fig. 7).

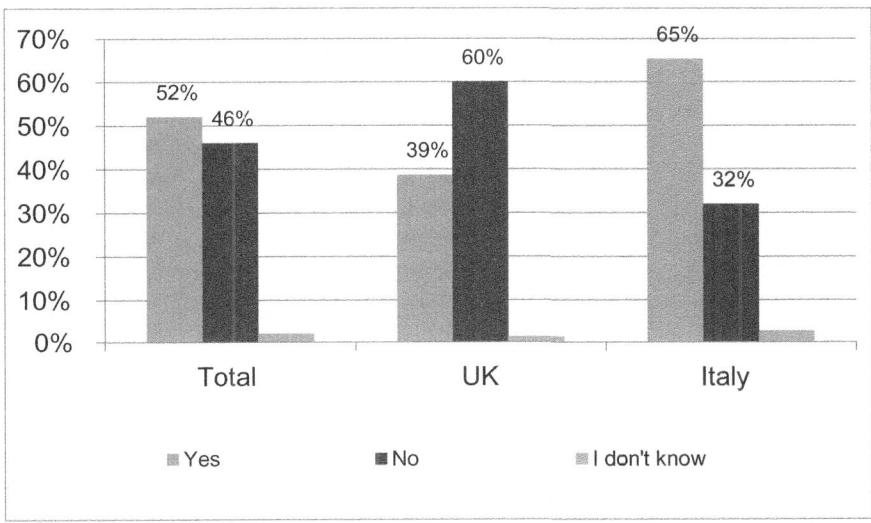

Fig. 7. Did your organisation use an advisory firm to help you get innovation from your third party suppliers?

Other parameters examined in this study did not show significant differences between Italian and British outsourcing sector. Respondents from the UK and Italy were predominately from the IT area within the organisation (see Fig. 8) with an average of 5 (Italy) or 7 (UK) years experience in outsourcing. Similarly, both Italian and British client

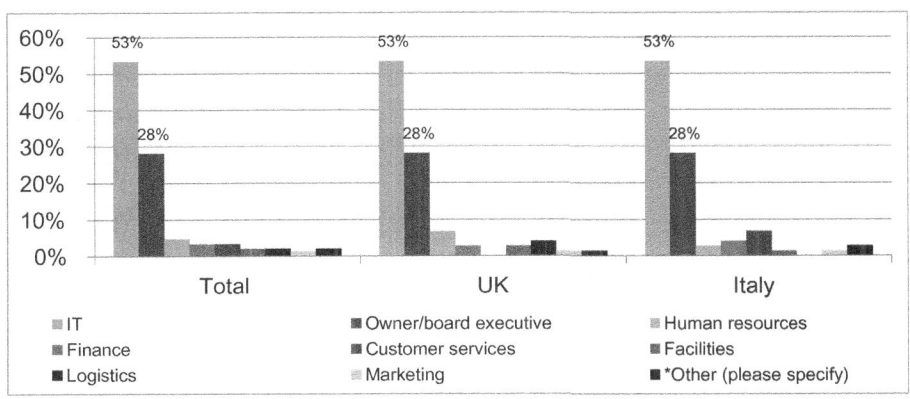

Fig. 8. Which area of your organisation do you work in?

firms have had 6 years of outsourcing experience on average. The distribution of functions outsourced by Italian and British firms is very similar with IT infrastructure as the most popular and legal as the least popular functions (see Fig. 8).

4.3 Pricing Models for Innovation: The UK and Italy

Selecting a pricing model that may facilitate innovation is imperative. The professional and academic literature has traditionally focused on two pricing models: fixed-price and time and materials. Recently, an outcome-based pricing model has been applied more frequently in outsourcing settings though it is still not as popular as the other two. The common assumption in the academic literature is that these pricing models can play different roles in supporting innovation. At the basis of this claim is the postulation that innovation bares some degree of uncertainty for the supplier. Therefore, a fixed price model, which presents little tolerance of uncertainty, is unlikely to support innovation. Time and materials may accommodate the supplier's risk mitigation strategy as the supplier can recover any investment made; however, the client might be exposed to on-going payments which may negatively affect the relationships with the supplier if the innovation is not well defined. Last but not least, an outcome-based model may reduce the client's risk and may serve the supplier's agenda to pursue well-defined innovation targets. As such, an outcome-based model may support innovation. Recently we reported that the combination of incentive-based clauses with either fixed-price or time and materials is also likely to promote innovation (Fig. 9).

Base: all respondents	Total	UK	Italy
IT infrastructure	71%	65%	77%
Application development	57%	57%	57%
Software testing	49%	49%	48%
Application maintenance	47%	49%	45%
Finance and accounting	35%	28%	43%
Data warehousing	32%	36%	28%
Procurement	29%	20%	37%
Human resource management	23%	17%	28%
Contact centres	23%	24%	21%
*Other (please specify)	2%	4%	0%
Base	150	75	75

Fig. 9. Which of these areas does your organisation currently outsource to third party suppliers?

In this study we observed a significant difference between the pricing model used by Italian and British firms in outsourcing engagements were innovation was sought. While fixed-price was the leading pricing model in the UK (45%), Italian firms have adopted an outcome-based pricing model (40%) (see Fig. 10). These results confirm our observation that outcome-based pricing models are more likely to result in higher degrees of innovation while fixed-price contracts are more challenging to deliver innovation. Our results also show incentive-based models such as gain-sharing or risk sharing are hardly used in the UK and Italy, though executives from both sectors hold the perception that such pricing models are likely to deliver innovation (total 60%) (see Fig. 11).

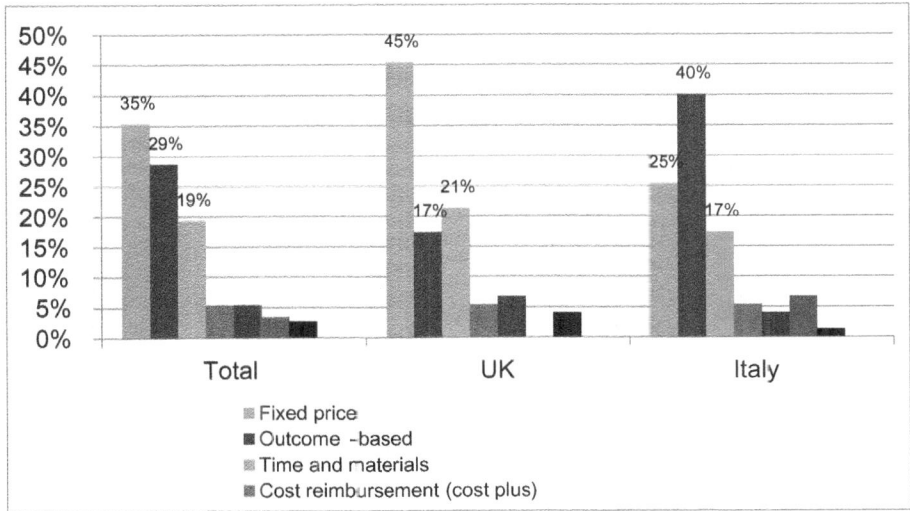

Fig. 10. What was the pricing model used in the project in which your organisation achieved or tried to achieve innovation?

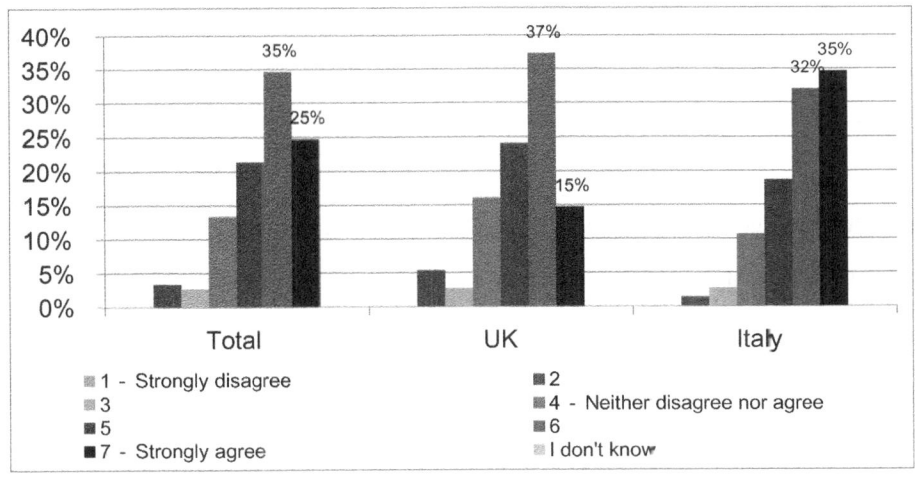

Fig. 11. A contract with gain-sharing clauses provides incentives for third party suppliers to deliver innovation in outsourcing engagements

4.4 The Content of the Contract and Innovation: The UK and Italy

While the pricing model signals whether innovation can be accommodated, there are elements captured in the contract that may inhibit or promote innovation. We have examined 5 aspects namely, mandatory targets, measures for innovation, flexibility about delivery scopes, penalty schemes, flexibility regarding service costs and service quality, and their effect on innovation according to the views hold by Italian and British executives. Our analysis shows that Italian executives supported penalty schemes (51% versus 40%), flexibility in terms of service costs (57% versus 43%) and preferred to focus on service quality rather than costs (64% versus 50%), which in their opinion led to innovation (Fig. 12).

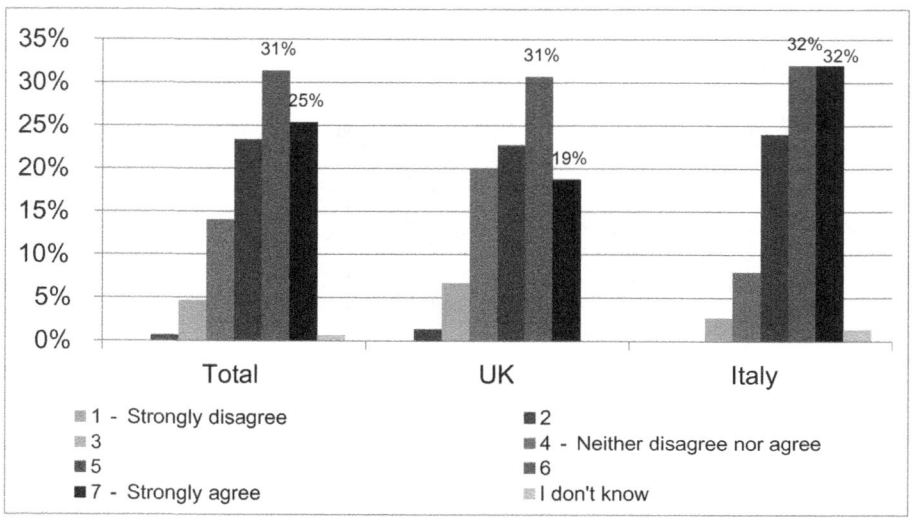

Fig. 12. In order to achieving innovation through outsourcing, the contractual agreement between the client and third party supplier needs to focus on service quality rather than costs.

4.5 Knowledge Exchange and Capabilities: The UK and Italy

Innovation is enabled by the innovator's ability to understand the challenge, apply knowledge to search and develop solutions, tap into resources and capabilities in order to implement a solution and measure the impact of the innovation. Firms that have outsourced functions may have lost specific domain knowledge that may hamper their innovation efforts. Therefore, it is imperative to understand the role that knowledge and capabilities play in supporting innovation in outsourcing.

In our study, 77% of the Italian executives agree or strongly agree that suppliers have had in-depth knowledge of the particular service where innovation was achieved as compared with 56% of their British counterparts. Similarly, 71% of Italian executives agree or strongly agree that suppliers understood processes relating to this particular service as compared with only 56% of the British executives. The most striking difference was found with regard to the statement that third party suppliers understood processes relating to this particular service, where 73% of the Italians strongly supported it compared with only 43% of the British respondents (Fig. 13).

Outsourcing and Innovation 129

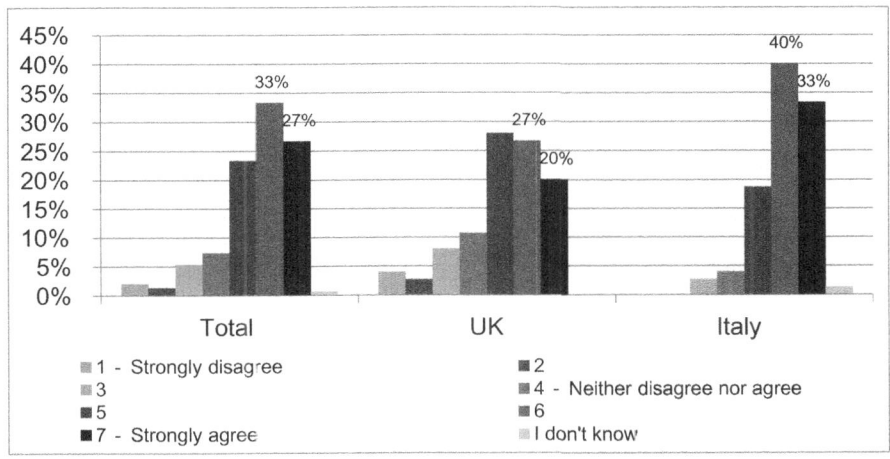

Fig. 13. How much you agree or disagree with the statement – third party supplier understood the strategic roadmap of this particular service.

While it is imperative for successful joint innovation projects that the supplier possesses domain and strategic knowledge about the client's systems and services, it is no less important that the client firm understands the supplier's capabilities and its strategic goal. In our study, 76% of Italian executives agree or strongly agree that they possessed sufficient understanding of the supplier's capabilities and understand the supplier's strategic goal for this particular service (75%) compared with 52% and 56% of the British respondents respectively (Fig. 14).

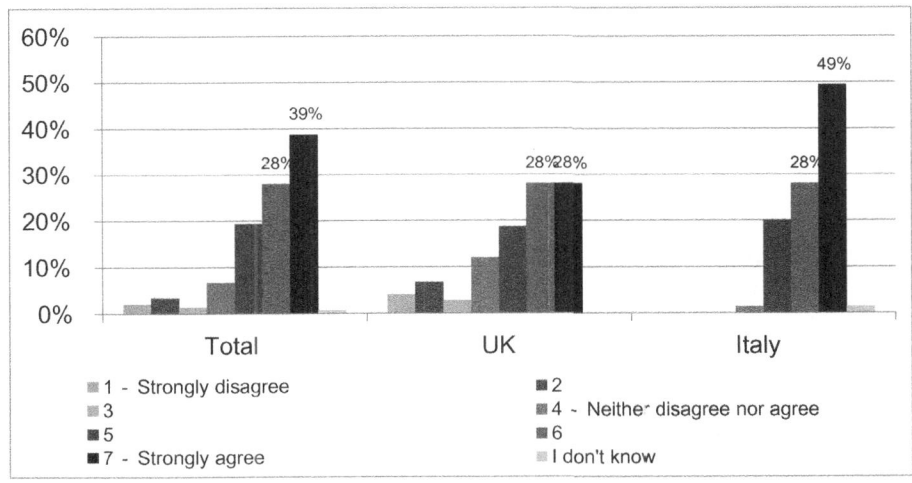

Fig. 14. We understood the supplier's strategic goal for this particular service

When examining the on-going trend towards exchanging knowledge between the client and supplier, we found that 61% of Italian executives hold to the view that suppliers' knowledge of their business challenge has either increased a lot or significantly increased in the last 5 years as compared with only 45% of their British counterparts. Further, 59% of Italian executives claim that their efforts to educate suppliers about business challenges has increased a lot or significantly increased as compared with only 33% of the British respondents. Last but not least, 64% of Italian respondents hold to the view that in the last 5 years their ability to assess suppliers' capabilities to innovation has increased a lot or significantly increased compared with only 33% of the British executives in this study (Fig. 15).

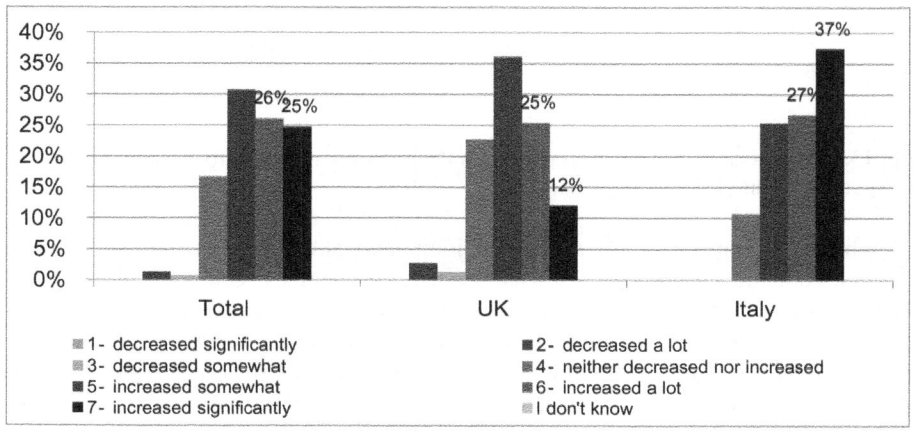

Fig. 15. My organisation's ability to assess the third party suppliers' capability to innovate has...

To sum, this study shows that the Italian outsourcing sector is expressing confidence in its ability to exchange knowledge between the client and supplier, educate the supplier about business challenges and develop tools to assess the supplier's ability to innovate. The British outsourcing sector holds a positive view on these matters; however, far more reserved about its ability to exchange knowledge with its suppliers.

4.6 The Relational Aspect: The UK and Italy

Close collaboration between client and supplier is imperative for innovation through outsourcing. It is not easy to develop a collaborative mode, as client firms often find it easier to resort to a transactional approach, in particular when cost reduction is the primary objective. A collaborative approach often means that the client and supplier need to align their goals and objectives, develop shared understanding and continue to motivate each other to pursue innovation. There has to be a high degree of trust and open communication between the parties as well as high commitment to implement innovative ideas.

Our results show that both Italian (59%) and British (57%) executives agree or strongly agree that their suppliers are part of the team that works on innovation and hold a similar view about the level of trust between the parties (63% of Italian and 61% of British). However, when examining the way they collaborate with their suppliers, certain differences have emerged between Italian and British executives.

Sixty four (64%) of Italian executives reported that they either agree or strongly agree that they and the supplier work as one team in developing innovative solutions compared with 55% of British respondents. Further, 52% of the Italian executives (compared with 37% of their British counterparts) reported that supplier employees involved in innovative work were (at least temporarily) located at our organisation's site. Co-location of employees is in particular critical for the joint development of innovative solutions, such as business solutions. Finally, 63% of Italian respondents expressed that they treated supplier employees as their employees compared with only 45% of their British counterparts (Fig. 16).

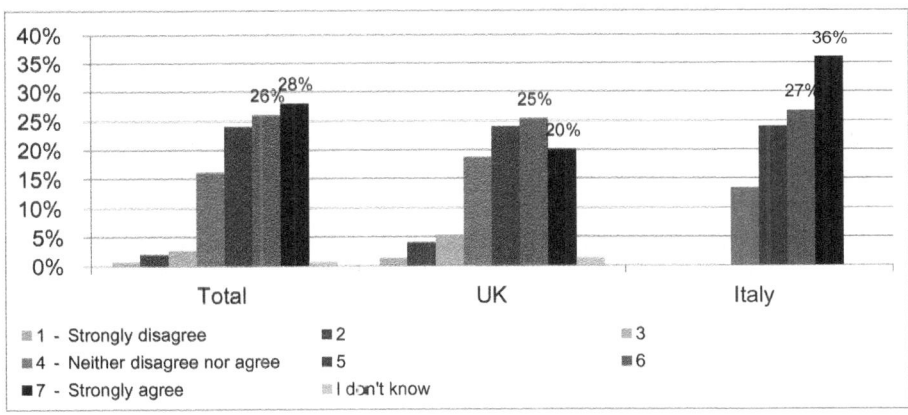

Fig. 16. We treated the key third party supplier employees like our own employees

4.7 Innovation Mechanisms: The UK and Italy

Respondents were asked to rank the mechanisms that led to innovation in their projects. Our results show that British and Italian executives are in agreement that 'clear innovation methodology' is the most important mechanism, followed by 'innovation champions' (2nd for British, 3rd for Italians), and 'value creation centres' (3rd for Italians and 3rd for British). Italian respondents ranked 'mandatory productivity targets' as second in importance, giving this mechanism higher weight in driving innovation in their projects (Fig. 17).

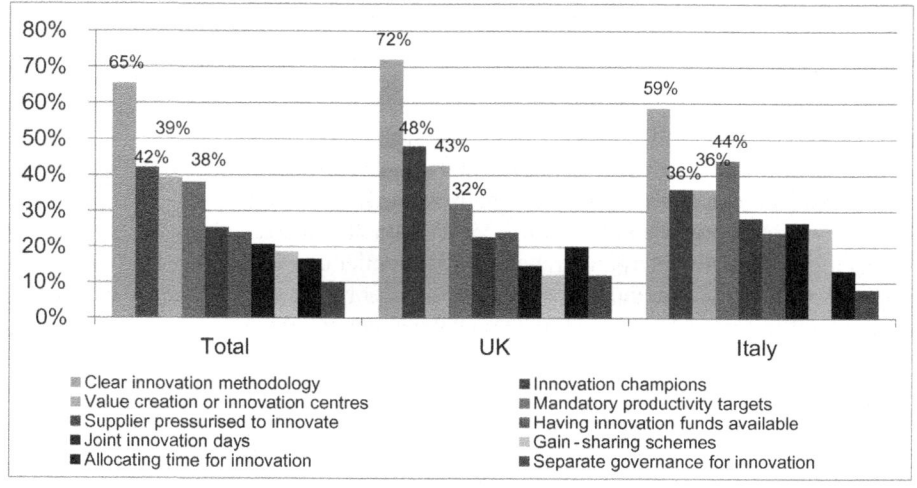

Fig. 17. The mechanisms leading to innovation

5 How to Achieve Innovation in Outsourcing: The Innovation Ladder

The data and analysis presented in this article offers a rare opportunity to examine why Italian client firms report higher levels of satisfaction with innovation delivered through outsourcing. At the heart of the analysis, we see an interaction between relational and contractual elements that create a far more accommodating collaborative platform for Italian client firms to motivate their suppliers to engage in higher risk innovative projects. Creating the conditions for innovation starts by having a strategic intent that is about improving innovation performance within the firm, as the Italian executives indicated, opposed to the cost reduction focus by British firms. However, client firms need to back-up their intentions with appropriate and relevant actions. Indeed, Italian executives reported higher commitment levels to pursue a relational approach through co-location and knowledge exchange tactics and a one-team approach as well as applied an outcome-based pricing model that is more likely to deliver innovative solutions. Further, though Italian firms were smaller in size, they reported a much more dependence on advisory than British firms, an approach that has led to higher degree of satisfaction from innovation delivered by their suppliers. Last but not least, Italian firms have persistently reported in this study that the quality of the service matters more than any other objective, a strong signal to suppliers that such a partnership is about searching for the best solution rather than the cheapest. Such an approach nurtures a culture of innovation within the client firm and its suppliers.

While our comparative analysis sheds some light about innovation in outsourcing, one pestering question remains: can client firms achieve innovation from suppliers in a systematic manner?

We developed a framework that we call The Innovation Ladder[1] (Fig. 18) to help client companies incorporate innovation in their outsourcing strategy. The emphasis in our approach, as opposed to some other studies we have seen, is that we believe that the innovation strategy should be integrated into the outsourcing strategy of the client firm. The Innovation Ladder is a full cycle approach from the beginning of the outsourcing relationship until the delivery of innovation. Yet, client firms can pick and choose some steps depending on the breadth of innovation sought and on the nature of the relationship they establish with their suppliers.

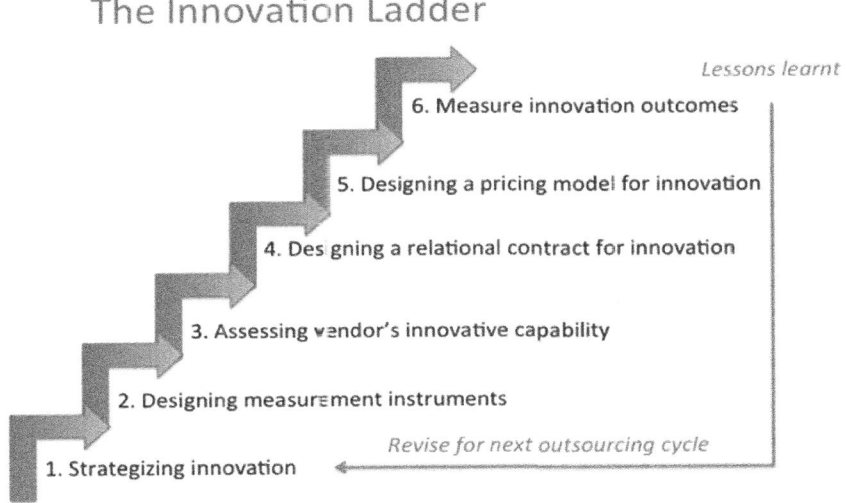

Fig. 18. the innovation ladder in outsourcing

Step 1: Strategizing innovation

Risk 1: Client and supplier do not define what innovation means to them

Method: A journey into innovation in outsourcing should start at the early stages of strategizing the outsourcing project. These early stages of the outsourcing life-cycle often involve the identification of objectives and the potential areas for improvement derived from the outsourcing engagement. At that point in time, it is imperative that executives will define what innovation means in the context of the outsourcing engagement.

In principle, executives should define three areas of improvements when strategizing innovation in outsourcing: information technology operational innovation, business process innovation and strategic innovation.

---

[1] Adapted from Oshri I., Kotlarsky J. and Willcocks L.P. (2015), The Handbook of Global Outsourcing and Offshoring, Palgrave.

IT operational innovation is when the supplier introduces technology changes not impacting firm-specific business processes. Business process innovation is about changes in the way the business operates in some important way and strategic innovation focus on transforming business performance or enabling the firm to enter new markets.

By bringing together these three aspects of innovation in outsourcing during the early stages of the planning, clearly defining each area, the client firm will be able to devise an approach to realizing the innovation potential from each setting. Below we describe in depth each of the following steps.

Step 2: Designing measurement instruments

Risk 2: Client's strategic intent to achieve innovation is not outlined and communicated to the supplier.

Method: As a second step, client firms need to develop a framework within which innovation will be pursued. Within this framework, client firms should outline specific areas of innovations expected in the outsourcing engagement. These innovations should be labelled as IT operation innovation, business process innovation and strategic innovation and the strategic intent behind each area should be clearly outlined. Client firms should also develop the measurement instrument per each area of innovation (e.g., % of cost reduction, % of improvement in time-to-marker or a % reduction in process duration). In the case of strategic innovation, client firms should also relate targets to Key Performance Indicators (KPI) and Key Success Factors (KSF) at the industry level. The contract should also have a clear reference to how the supplier will be rewarded if it improves the measurements further (e.g., bonus as % of additional cost savings that result from process improvement). As part of the design of measurement instruments, the client firm should assess its internal innovation and change capabilities and the mechanisms available to collaborate with its supplier network.

Step 3: Assessing supplier's innovation capability

Risk 3: Client firm does not possess supplier selection methodology that assesses the supplier's ability to innovate.

Method: Having carefully crafted the measurement requirements for the desired innovation, it is now the time to develop a set of criteria upon which the innovativeness of the bidding suppliers will be assess. While our research suggests that many client firms consider the innovativeness of their suppliers as one of the selection criteria, to our knowledge, no study has so far revealed what these criteria were, as well as how they should be applied in the context of innovation.

There are various ways to seek proven evidence of innovativeness from a supplier. Some of the examples we have come across are in the form of referral letters from existing and past clients, supplier's case studies about innovation delivered and evidence of the supplier methodology to deliver innovation. There is also a need to understand the supplier's relationship capabilities as an indicator of its collaborative approach and commitment. These inputs will allow the client firm to systematically compare between bidders when selecting an innovative supplier.

Step 4: Designing a relational contract for innovation

Risk 4: The contract does not include the facilitation of relational governance

Method: Once the supplier selection phase has been concluded, the attention of the parties involved should shift to the design of a relational contract. Our results clearly suggest a collaborative approach is the best basis for developing a contract at facilitates innovation. Firstly, in order to define a win-win situation, supplier and client firms need to allow sufficient time prior to signing the contract to reach a shared understanding of each other business goals and objectives, and to discuss their potential shared interests in innovation. Apart from such an alignment of goals and objectives, trust and open communication obviously help in laying open the innovation needs and potential cost saving on both sides. These early negotiations should also include securities for the supplier for the case that they suggest innovations. By building flexibility into the agreement, deliverables can be modified following innovative ideas, without requiring a renegotiation of terms and clauses. Such securities in turn facilitate the necessary openness and proactivity on the side of the supplier. However, not only the supplier but also the client needs to be open about their needs. Similarly, significant proactivity and effort are required not only by the supplier but also the client to follow up and implement innovative ideas. This effort is somewhat alleviated through a well-defined innovation methodology than can be part of the contract. For example, the steps, timing, and responsibilities for piloting and implementing an innovation, and certain times for innovation days can be defined in the contracting phase.

Step 5: Designing a pricing model for innovation

Risk 5: The parties apply rigid and risk-mitigating pricing models

Method: One very clear result from this study is that the pricing model chosen for an outsourcing engagement in which innovation is sought should be carefully considered. It appears that a stand-alone fixed-price or time and materials pricing model is unlikely to deliver innovation mainly because these pricing models offer little incentives for the supplier to engage in a higher risk and sometimes ill-defined innovation projects. On the other hand, an outcome-based pricing model offers clarity with regard to the expected results thus motivating the supplier to consider engaging in innovation. Further, gain-sharing clauses in any pricing model are also likely to motivate the supplier to engage in innovation, as the returns on the investment are clear. The challenge for most client firms lies in moving away from the traditional pricing models that currently rely heavily on fixed-price and time and materials models, and consider more complex pricing models that combine some degree of flexibility within the traditional well defined clauses.

Step 6: Measuring innovation performance

Risk 6: Parties assume positive impact on the client's business from any innovation delivered by the supplier.

Method: There is a general belief that innovation improves business performance; however, in the context of outsourcing it appears that many firms do not measure its impact. Client firms, therefore, should invest more in understanding the impact of innovation delivered on the firm's operations and strategic positioning. We believe that most firms can, in fact, measure the return on the outsourcing investment, in a quantifiable form, should they follow steps 1 and 2 of the Innovation Ladder in which the objectives and measurement instruments have been defined. Measurement instruments may have to be revisited during the project lifecycle, however, their impact can still be assessed.

Measuring strategic innovation is more challenging to measure; however, the client firm should seek both qualitative and quantitative inputs regarding performance. In terms of qualitative feedback, the client firm should seek input regarding the quality of the network created to arrive in strategic innovation. Periodical surveys among members of the joint effort regarding the quality of collaboration, motivation to contribute, assessment of each partner's contribution and intention for future collaboration can provide an indication regarding the 'health' of the relationships and the will to innovate. Quantifiable measurement tools to assess the impact of the strategic innovation on business performance should be in the form of benchmarks against industry performance. In particular, as strategic innovation was sought to improve the competitiveness of the firm either through operational excellence or strategic positioning, the client firm should judge the impact of this innovation through industry-wide performance indicators. For example, the quality of service provided, represented through various measurable indicators such as customer satisfaction, is one performance indicator that can be used by service firms.

Step 6 is not the last step in the innovation ladder. If anything, it is a step that calls for reflection and a stage that offers an opportunity redesign the innovation framework. Feedback collected during these six steps should serve the client firm in its journey to achieve innovation in outsourcing.

An Accounting Firm Perspective of Offshoring

Silvia Caratti[✉], Brian Perrin, and Glennda Scully

School of Accounting, Curtin University, Perth, WA, Australia
{silvia.caratti,b.perrin,g.scully}@curtin.edu.au

Abstract. Offshoring is increasingly being adopted by professional accounting firms of all sizes and has become a component of the larger Business Process Outsourcing ("BPO") industry. The traditionally conservative accounting profession operates in an environment subject to an intense and dynamic regulatory oversight. There is increasing competition and a pressure to reduce costs and manage staffing shortages faced by the profession. Offshoring presents itself as a solution to these pressures and as such is a key motivator for adopting offshoring. This suggests that offshoring in accounting firms is worthy of being examined in its own right.

Whilst offshoring generally has been the subject of much research, the use of offshoring in accounting firms, and in particular, research on the human resources aspect of offshoring for the domestic firm is scarce. This paper attempts to fill this void by investigating how the unique features of accounting firms apply to the general offshoring research through a rich case study approach. It demonstrates that "buy in" and human resourcing issues are important in ensuring the success of offshoring in accounting firms. This research in progress also examines the different offshoring ownership models adopted by accounting firms. Importantly, this paper introduces different interaction frameworks that firms can adopt, aiming to develop a model for firms to help them decide which is the most appropriate model and framework for them. In addition, this paper looks at the impact offshoring has on both the recruitment and development of domestic graduates in primarily Australian accounting firms and seeks to provide guidelines to assist firms in this area.

Keywords: Accounting firms · Offshoring · Offshoring ownership models · Offshoring interaction frameworks · Graduate skills · Graduate employability

1 Introduction

A 2008 global industry report found that the total number of finance and accounting services outsourced was expected to increase by 70 % over the next few years [2, 3]. Similarly, a 2014 survey of worldwide organisations also found that general accounting outsourcing was expected to grow at 12 %–26 % [4]. This general accounting trend has also impacted professional accounting firms who now are increasingly offshoring part of their compliance work. In fact, it is estimated that around 37 % of accounting firms offshore some of their work [5] and that 1.6 million tax returns would have been prepared in India in 2011 [6]. Previously just the domain of the Big 4 accounting firms, this trend is now a growing practice amongst some of the medium to smaller firms [7]. The type of work offshored by accounting firms includes basic bookkeeping, audit testing and cross-adding and the preparation of financial statements and tax returns.

Whilst Business Process Outsourcing ("BPO") has been studied extensively in recent years, very little of that research has focused on accounting firms which is a growing and significant component of BPO. This represents a gap in the literature as the accounting profession which does not consider accountings unique characteristics.

They operate in an environment that is heavily regulated. For example in Australia, accountants need to comply with regulations from their professional industry bodies, the Australian Taxation Office, Australian Securities and Insurance Commission ("ASIC"), the Tax Agents Board and various other bodies. Traditionally, labour intensive tax returns and financial statements is a core service offering of many accounting firms [8]. Software development and enhanced technology allows these to become a routine task [9]. According to the resource based view in the general offshoring literature, companies do not usually outsource activities that are part of their core competency [10]. The fact that accounting firms are doing this differentiates them from traditional BPO.

Using a qualitative approach, the research program proposed in this paper looks at the impact of offshoring from the perspective of domestic accounting firms who are all using Indian vendors. All of the domestic accounting firms used will be Australian. The paper focusses on two key issues relating to offshoring, the first being consideration of the most appropriate offshoring business ownership model and interaction framework. Depending on the type of model or interaction framework adopted by the accounting firms, the human resource ("HR") impact of offshoring differs. The second issue will focus on how the domestic firm interacts with the offshore provider and on the impact on domestic graduates and their development.

Specifically, the objectives of the study are to:

(a) Develop a model to assist accounting firms decide which offshoring business ownership model and interaction framework is appropriate to them; and
(b) Identify key skills and attributes required in domestic graduates of accounting firms to assist in their recruitment and training practices to support their offshoring model and framework.

The consequential scaffolded research questions are as follows:

(a) In accounting firm offshoring arrangements, what critical factors influence the successful management of business ownership models and interaction frameworks?
(b) Are there differences in the skills required in domestic graduates between accounting firms that adopt offshoring and those that do not?

A summary of the structure of the research is depicted below (Fig. 1).

The paper will be structured as follows. Firstly, a literature review is presented which addresses the use of offshoring in accounting firms, the models that are adopted and the resultant impact of offshoring on domestic graduates. The proposed research method follows and progress to date is provided before the significance and potential limitations of the paper are examined.

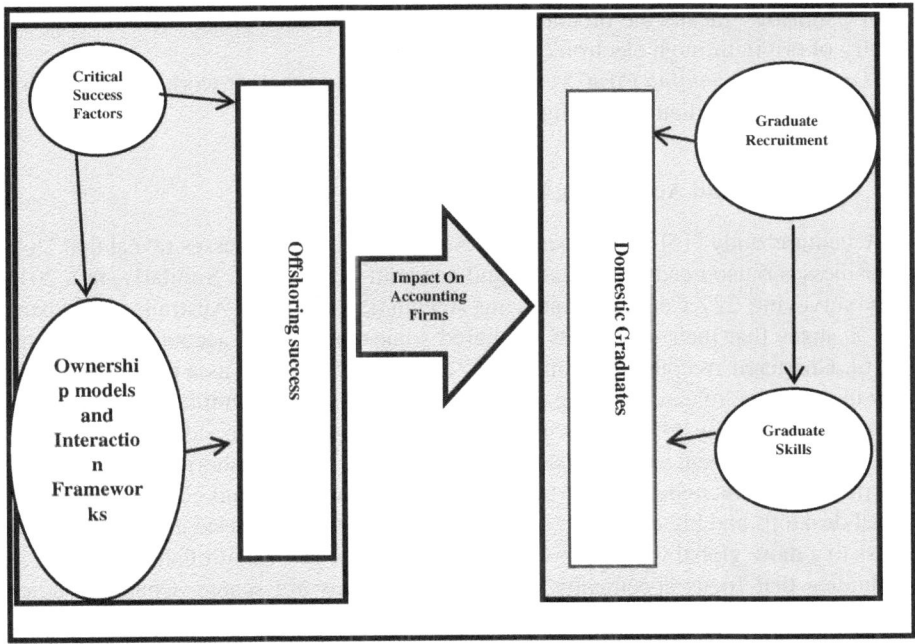

Fig. 1. Summary of the research

2 Literature Review

This literature review comprises four parts. First, the definitions adopted in the paper are presented. Background information on the use of offshoring in accounting firms is discussed, together with an overview of the critical success factors for offshoring within accounting firms. A review of the offshoring models and interaction frameworks adopted by accounting firms are then detailed. Finally, the impact of offshoring on domestic graduates is examined. This literature review draws heavily from the BPO and Information Technology Outsourcing ("ITO") literature due to the lack of specific literature on offshoring in an accounting firm context. This represents a significant gap in the literature.

2.1 Definitions Adopted

For the purposes of this paper, the following definitions in relation to accounting firms are used:

"BPO" means handing over a part or all of an organisations business processes to a third party [11].

"Outsourcing" means contracting any service or activity provided by an accounting firm to a third party [12].

"Offshoring" means the procurement of services by accounting firms outside the country of origin through electronic media [2, 13, 14].

"Domestic Accounting Firm" is the firm that is offshoring their work to India, which is the client of the Indian offshoring vendor.

2.2 Offshoring and Accounting Firms

An Accenture study [15] of European and North American businesses reveal that 26 % of businesses outsourced their finance and accounting functions. Similarly, in a 2010 study surveying 227 Certified Practicing Accounting ("CPA") Australian members, 11.7 % states that their employers offshored some finance and accounting functions [2, 16]. Chartered Accountants And New Zealand ("CAANZ"), as a peak accounting body in Australia, released a white paper in 2015 discussing the future of offshoring in accounting generally [17]. They highlighted that globalisation, technology, Asian economic development and skills shortages are key drivers of offshoring in accounting. Specifically, the increased use of technological advances in cloud computing, hosted virtual desktops and big data were described as facilitating increased globalisation and access to a more global workforce which would fuel the growth of offshoring.

Studies that focus specifically on accounting firms are scarce. Chaplin studied Australian accounting firms finding that 21 % of these firms outsource some of their services [9]. The Big 4 now have a large presence in key offshoring locations in India. For example, Deloitte's staff in India now total 27000, with approximately 800 of these servicing Deloitte Australia and they expect to hire another 12000 staff in India in the coming year to service Deloitte internationally in [18].

This emerging trend is attracting the attention of regulators [19]. In Australia, various government bodies have issued discussion papers relating to their concerns over the controls that accounting firms put in place when they engage in offshoring accounting arrangements [12, 20, 21]. For example, a specific guidance note on risk management strategies for firms who offshore has been produced by Australian accounting professional bodies which details some of the practices that firms should adopt in order to comply with their binding ethical obligations [21]. In the United States, certification is required of the controls used by all company providers as part of their statutory audits with various accounting body standards to assist auditors in completing these audits [19].

What Tasks Do Accounting Firms Offshore? General accounting services that are outsourced range from highly transactional activities such as accounts payable or payroll to processes that require more sophisticated knowledge such as tax strategy or analysis [22]. Bandyopahyay and Hall [5] determined that sending routine functions offshore has been increasing in accounting firms, mainly due to improved electronic data transfer capabilities and the abundance of less expensive English speaking accounting staff. Cloud computing and big data analysis in recent years has also had a significant impact on the uptake of offshoring by accounting firms.

A comprehensive review of the BPO literature finds that the main drivers for entering into a BPO relationship are the desire to reduce costs, the desire to improve performance, focus on core activities, ability to scale their business and access to skills and expertise [3, 23]. For accounting firms specifically, some of the cited reasons are the same, although there is an increased focus on the use of offshoring to allow accountants to focus on more complex work and to resolve staff shortages to assist with client service [4, 6, 9, 13, 17]. Young financial graduates are increasingly unwilling to engage in mundane tax compliance work when considering their employment options so offshoring is seen as a way to fill this staffing void [12].

Specific examples of activities that are offshored by accounting firms include:

(a) Preparation of financial statements and tax returns
(b) Specialist tax advice
(c) Self-Managed Superannuation fund ("SMSF") audits and financial statement preparation
(d) Bookkeeping services and management accounting
(e) Substantive audit testing and financial statement cross-adding
(f) Payroll and fixed asset accounting
(g) Business activity statements
(h) Debtor collection

Many of these activities are considered core activities of some accounting firms. A simple example of how offshoring could be used in the preparation of a tax return is shown in Fig. 2 [2]:

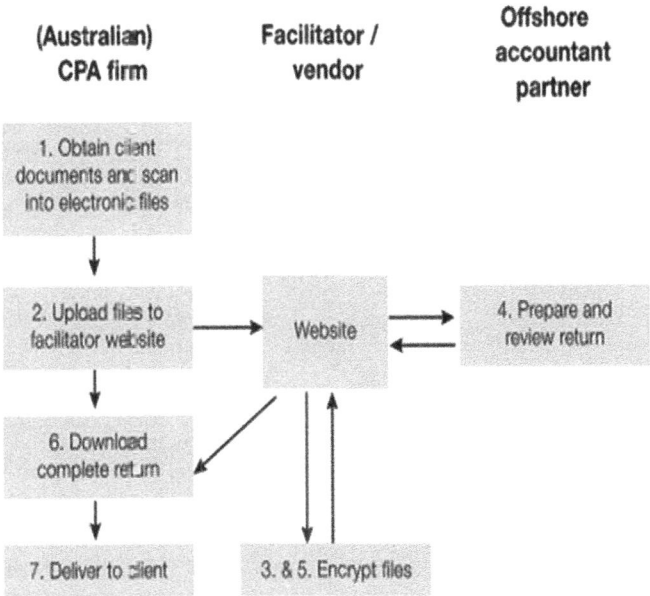

Fig. 2. Stages in the preparation of a tax return in an offshoring environment

There are numerous variations of this process depending on the interaction framework and ownership model adopted.

2.3 Critical Success Factors for Offshoring in Accounting Firms

One of the areas that managers are generally most concerned with is why some organisations fail and others succeed with offshoring [24]. This concern equally applies to accounting firms. A consistent definition of offshoring success has been elusive in the BPO/ITO literature as it is in the accounting firm literature [25]. Whilst there is no one specific construct for successful offshoring, potential measures of success identified include performance improvements, client satisfaction levels and cost savings [3].

Lacity and Willcocks provide a useful starting point to identify critical success factors in the ITO literature [1]. They categorise some of the critical offshoring success factors into contractual governance, relationship governance, client retained capabilities and provider capabilities. This model has been expanded and adapted in Fig. 3 to break down the client retained or domestic accounting firm critical success factors. In this context, the client is the domestic accounting firm whilst the vendor is the Indian offshore provider. These critical success factors are broken down into

(1) People related factors
(2) Skills related factors
(3) Process related factors

These additional factors are developed from the authors' review of the literature in both the offshoring and accounting fields, as well as from the author's personal experiences.

The key categories for this paper are those of contractual governance, relationship governance and client retained capabilities as they relate specifically to the research questions in this paper as shown in Table 1 below;

Table 1. Critical success factor categories

Research question	Category of critical success factor model
Research question one (ownership model)	Contractual governance
Research question one (interaction Framework)	Relationship governance
Research question two (domestic graduates)	Client retained capabilities (especially people and skills related)

Contractual governance between the vendor and domestic accounting firm will differ depending on the ownership model adopted. Different models are appropriate for different accounting firms [17]. For example, if there is no direct ownership interest, then greater reliance and importance is placed on the service level agreement. For accounting firms, there is specific guidance as to what should be included in such contracts in the professional body regulations [21]. A high level of contract detail and exception reporting with the right offshore vendor has also been shown to be critical [2, 3, 16, 22, 31].

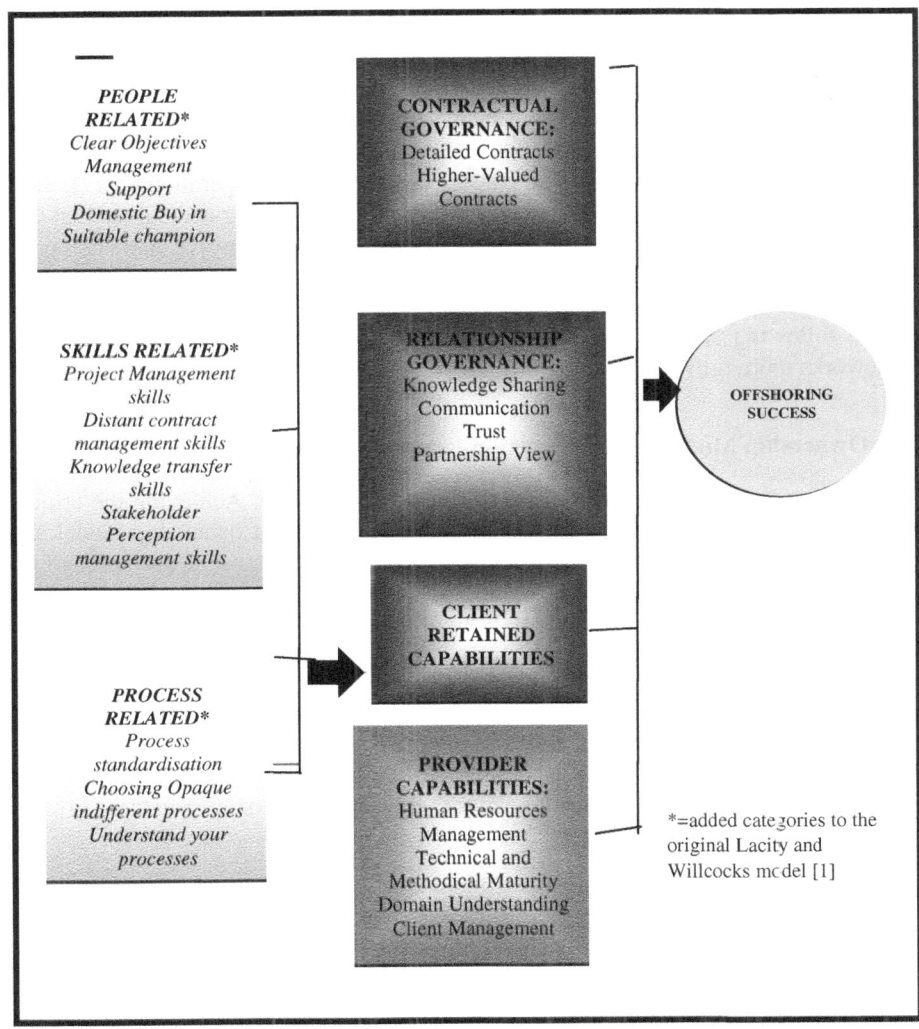

Fig. 3. Critical success factors for offshoring in accounting firms

Various relational governance factors are also viewed as critical to successful offshoring. Specifically, good communication leading to effective knowledge sharing, having a partnership view and relationship specific investments are seen as important [3]. Partnership attributes, a collaborative attitude, trust and co-operation are identified as positively influencing the success of IT outsourcing [26–28]. A true partnership relationship with the vendor can also assist to reduce vendor attrition which is traditionally quite high by encouraging loyalty [29].

Skills related capabilities of the domestic client organisation are critical to offshoring success in accounting firms. Strong supplier management capabilities and business process management capabilities are seen as key [3, 27, 30]. If the domestic accounting firm staff do not have the skills to successfully manage or understand the process of activities themselves, then how can they expect their offshoring vendor to do this [2, 3, 16]?

People related capabilities are also seen as key. A CPA survey concluded that gaining support from domestic employees and management was the most important success factor in offshoring [2]. Disgruntled domestic employees who try to ensure that offshoring fails are the greatest threat to a successful offshoring operation [2, 17]. Staff buy in is critical in interaction frameworks which are highly integrated. Given that one of the key drivers for accounting firms to adopt offshoring is to resolve staff shortages, it would be expected that domestic buy-in would be one of the most important critical success factors for accounting firms.

The following section describes the different ownership models and interaction frameworks more fully.

2.4 Ownership Models and Interaction Frameworks Adopted

This section of the paper addresses the first research question. Achieving the critical success factors discussed above is influenced by the choice of ownership model and interaction framework. There are broadly two distinct decisions that an accounting firm needs to make in structuring their offshoring operation, that being the ownership model and the interaction framework to adopt. Both of these are now examined in turn.

Ownership Models. This refers to legal ownership of the offshoring vendor and can range from zero to having a 100 % ownership interest. The models are continuously evolving and with no one model suites all users [16, 24]. The exact classification of ownership models varies slightly according to different authors [32, 33]. Much of the literature on the models of offshoring relates to this legal ownership structure [34].

Ownership models include:

(a) <u>External ownership models</u> - These include external, outsource offshoring, open market, arm's length ownership, third party service provider models. They are generally referred to as "arm's length ownership models".
Here, the focus is more on the output (for example, the completed tax return) and this model is commonly adopted by smaller accounting firms. Typically, the Australian firm has no real control over the process but merely receives the output (e.g. completed tax return), paying for a result. Arms-length ownership models have the advantage of visibility of costs and ability to participate in best practice but they can also provide greater risks with the lack of quality control oversight [2]. There are often multiple players in this market [16].

(b) <u>Co-operative Ownership models</u> - These include strategic alliances, partnerships, joint ventures, shared captives, partial captives, and relationship alignment.
These are like a partnership or joint venture where there is shared control and involvement in the operation of the offshoring arrangement. It can include joint ventures, brand service companies or a best of breed consortium [16]. This is often based on a sharing of costs and savings. There are various forms of this and they are often used by mid-tier accounting firms to gain both some control over the process and manage economy of scale issues. There can be single or multiple

vendors and clients [27]. The relationship and trust between the vendor and client is of the utmost importance here. Some argue that this partial or partnership type of model is the most appropriate due to the stronger relationships required in these models [27].

(c) Captive ownership models - these include captive offshoring, collaborative virtual organisations and internal subsidiaries.

These are often used by larger accounting firms to gain full control where the firm essentially creates their own offshore vendor which is owned by the client through a subsidiary. This requires larger scale operations to make it economical but does give full control to the domestic accounting firms. In some of these models, clients set up their own operations and then sell some of their ownership interest once it is functioning well [2, 32]. It has been estimated that captive models account for approximately 60 % of the overall BPO market in India [32, 35]. Whilst captive models can be less risky and allow more control although they can have increased fixed costs. They are becoming the most common model in the general BPO environment [2, 25, 28].

The accounting firm's required level of control over the processes is one of the factors that determines which ownership model they adopt.

Accounting firms, like the BPO industry, use a range of different models which do change over time. The large Big 4 accounting firms generally use more of a captive model whilst smaller firms will use either external ownership or co-operative models. A growing number of firms that have been offshoring for at least three years are adopting a blended model, retaining direct control of some activities whilst completely outsourcing other activities [36]. There is currently limited research on when it is appropriate to use a particular model for accounting firms and there is no "one size fits all" solution [16].

Interaction Frameworks. This section describes the different ways in which the vendor offshoring organisation interacts with the client accounting firm including how and who in the vendor and client accounting firm interact. The range of interaction frameworks are shown below in Fig. 4.

At one end of the continuum, there is the segregated framework where one person in both the vendor and client firm that interact with each other and pass on information to their respective teams. This model has the advantage of clear and consistent lines of communication between the client and the vendor but is considered high risk if one of either of these individuals leaves their respective organisation.

The other extreme is a highly interactive framework where many people in both organisations communicate with each other. Each framework has implications for knowledge transfer, communication, contractual and relational governance, client skills required and client domestic buy in.

Trust is an important element of successful offshoring and the quality of the relationships between client and vendor is an important determinant of trust [28, 34, 37]. The interaction framework is governed initially by the ownership model adopted and by the *contractual relationship* that exists. It has been shown that promoting internal acceptance and buy in of offshoring drives success in captives [37]. In ITO, allowing

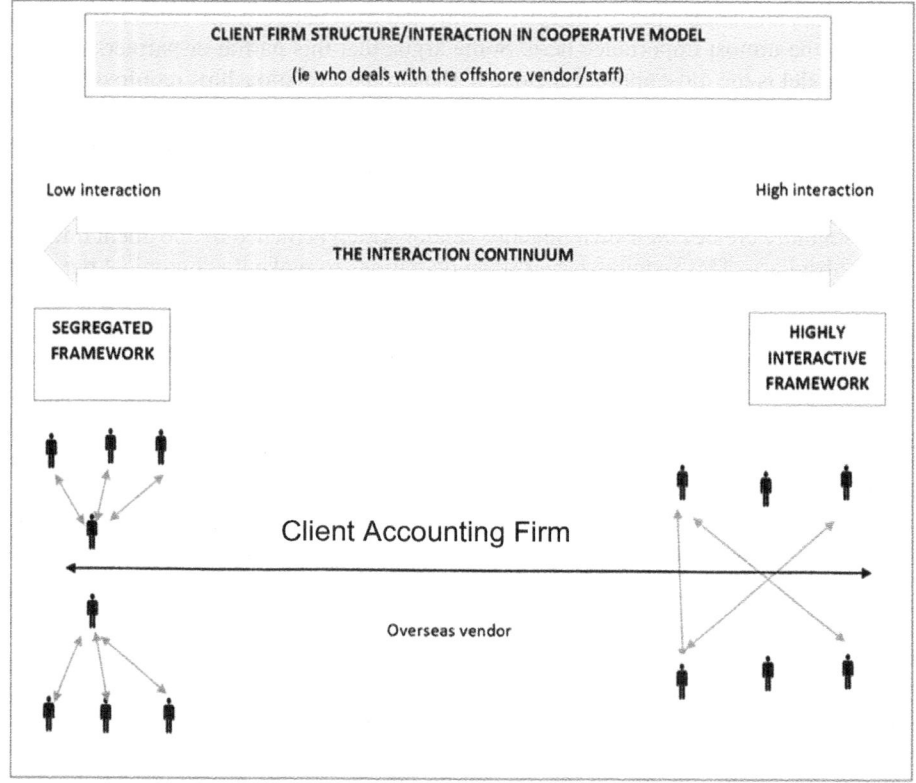

Fig. 4. Interaction frameworks

the client employees to be involved in each stage positively affects the success of offshoring which suggests that a higher degree of interaction is appropriate [27]. Different interaction frameworks also allow different relational controls to be implemented to reduce risk. A combined culture and shared vision can reduce risks associated with offshoring. However, there is the risk that disgruntled domestic employees can sabotage the offshoring operation in a highly integrated framework [2].

There appears to be limited research on how the types of ownership and more importantly interaction frameworks impact the engagement of and skills required of domestic employees in accounting firms involved in offshoring. It would be expected that highly interactive frameworks where graduates and accounting staff are constantly in contact with the offshore vendor would require different skills in there staff compared to a segregated framework. This is discussed in the next section of the paper.

2.5 Impact of Offshoring on Accounting Graduate Skills

This section of the paper addresses the second research question. There is a substantial amount of research on employability and required accounting graduate skills [38]. Given that business degrees usually provide the prerequisites for commencing professional accounting body accreditation programs, accounting firms generally employ graduates of university accounting degree programs.

There is already a well-documented *expectation gap* of employer requirement to the perceived actual graduate skills produced with many arguing that the rising graduate unemployment is at least partly due to a mismatch between supply and demand and "*fractured lines of communication*" between the profession and academia [39–42]. Employers have indicated that accounting courses are not keeping up with the changes in the profession [43]. Studies frequently identify that universities are not producing work ready graduates [4, 39, 44–46]. Employers were usually happy with the graduates technical skills, but the soft skills were considered to be inadequate [46, 47]. This expectation gap is exaggerated in an offshoring environment due to the expected change in role of the accounting graduate which includes building relationships and trust with offshore teams and the associated upskilling required. This is now discussed.

2.5.1 The Role of the Graduate in an Offshoring Environment

If the traditional tasks of a graduate are being offshored, then by default the role of the domestic graduate will need to be different. Their role will turn to more non-offshorable tasks. A non-offshorable role is one that "*requires face-to-face contact with end users*" [48]. Routine and mundane tasks such as preparation of tax returns that were traditionally performed by graduates and were the *training ground* for those graduates no longer exist in an offshoring environment [9, 17, 49–51].

This therefore means that instead of doing the basic tasks, graduates may be starting at a higher level and will be expected to value add at a much earlier level. Rather than doing the basic work, they may be involved in reviewing the work of their offshore counterparts which requires a different set of skills. They may be in client facing roles much earlier than their predecessors who were often protected from these roles for their first few years [52].

2.5.2 Skills Required by Graduates in These New Roles

The enhanced skills that graduates require in an offshoring environment can be broadly categorised as per Fig. 5. Each of these items will now be discussed in turn.

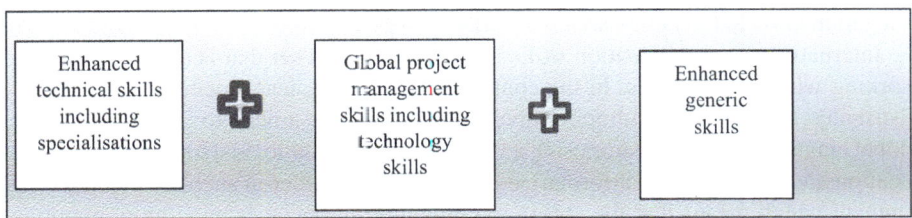

Fig. 5. Summary of enhanced skills required by new graduates in an offshoring accounting environment

If graduates are to commence at this higher level, then their core technical skills will need to be much stronger when they leave university [7]. The type of technical skills required may also be different. Increasingly complex transactions by clients and accounting standards require a much higher level of technical skills in audit graduates [53]. In other areas of accounting, they will need to be able to read and interpret a set of financial statements if they are going to get more involved in advisory work, not necessarily be experts in the preparation of accounts [54].

Given the evolution of accounting offshoring from ITO, it is worthwhile examining some of the IT graduate skills literature for potential application to accounting firms. In a 2014 study of new IT working graduates, the ability to work with people from different cultures and communicate in an appropriate manner in this environment was identified as a significant gap [55]. Offshoring introduces the concept of "global domestics" or "glocals" into accounting firms which are defined as *"employees that work across cultures without leaving home"* [56]. How individuals communicate with each other in multicultural environments is increasingly being discussed [57]. Both the offshore team and the remaining domestic team both have cross-national job responsibilities which require interaction with virtual teams over borders [56].

Offshoring requires a change in the way that accounting firms deliver traditional services and a move from actually doing the routine services, to project managing them. For example, a tax return for a client may commence with an initial meeting in Australia, be packaged up for sending over to India for completion, reviewed in Australia and then a meeting held with the client in Australia. This process usually involves an element of project management, which is can be *"procedure for controlling outcomes of a project objective"* [58]. This is a skill that is not traditionally associated with accounting firms.

If accounting graduates are involved with virtual teams across borders, then their technology skills will need to be enhanced. A virtual team can be defined as *"a group of geographically, organisationally and/or time dispersed workers brought together by information and telecommunication technologies to accomplish one or more organisational tasks"* [59]. The use of IT to process and communicate information has become vital, as has the knowledge of at least some accounting packages as clients also become increasingly technology focused [60]. In particular, familiarity with communication technologies such as video conferencing, email and instant messaging has become more important [7]. IT security, backups, operating systems, network management, and project management software are also seen as important. It has been suggested that there is a gap in knowledge in this area [61, 62].

International communication skills are a specific skill set that is directly related to working with virtual teams. In the context of offshoring, team members are globally distributed and are often culturally diverse [63]. There is a need to communicate in a global language in global teams using a variety of new technological tools [60]. Communication and production of information costs are often higher in such an offshore environment which means that the ability to communicate becomes even more important [14]. Accountants may be dealing with people whose English is not their native language. If a graduate's communication skills are below par, then this simply increases the potential for miscommunication. Often, there are time differences between virtual teams which therefore result in greater importance being placed on written communication in the form of emails [64].

In addition to the skills discussed above, certain other generic skills take on greater importance for graduates. If there is to become more client facing, then customer relationship and interaction skills become far more important [2, 7, 16, 44]. The new breed of accounting professional will require enhanced generic skills such as communication skills, co-operation, team collaboration, leadership, reasoning, judgement, problem solving, analytical and interpersonal skills [24, 46]. Analytical ability to ask the right questions and interpret information becomes critical in this environment as accountants are no longer preparing the information themselves. They need critical thinking skills to question the information they are receiving and to make judgements when not all of the relevant information is available.

3 Theoretical Framework

As the different primary research questions are examining different components of offshoring in accounting firms, there are different theories that will be used for each phase. No one theory can be used to explain this complex area with sufficient richness. In the same vein, Anderson [56], in her review of theories underpinning international human resource development suggests that different theoretical concepts apply to different elements of offshoring manifestations and also to different stages of offshoring.

The different theories appropriate for the different research questions are summarised in Table 2 below and are described in the following sections of this paper.

Table 2. Theories adopted in each research question

Research question	Theory adopted
(RQ1) Offshoring and business ownership and interaction models	Institutional theory [67]
(RQ2) Impact of offshoring on domestic graduates	• Resource Based View [24] and • Human Capital Theory [70]

3.1 Theories Relating to Ownership Models and Interaction Frameworks and Critical Success Factors

There are two dominant theories adopted in the traditional offshoring literature, Transaction Cost Economics ("TCE") and the Resource Based View ("RBV").

TCE has been applied to early outsourcing research in the 1980's and 1990's [24]. It is argued that if lower transaction costs can be achieved by using other markets, then a good or service should be outsourced [27]. Governance modes are used with different transactions so as to minimise transaction costs [14]. This theory implies that the firm will adopt the model that minimises their overall cost.

RBV suggests that resources related to human knowledge and skills as a valuable resource [62, 65]. Intellectual and human capital of organisations, both at a micro and macro level, produce sustainable competitive advantages for organisations and offshoring can assist by providing such resources [35, 65, 66].

However, an accounting firm is ultimately a network of clients, staff and suppliers and is a social structure consisting of people that interact. This is the main reason that this phase of the research extends beyond TCE and RBV to the strategic management theories.

A more appropriate theory in this context is Institutional theory. This theory looks at offshoring and the different models of offshoring through the lens of regulatory, normative and cognitive pillars [29, 67]. It seeks to explain organisational behaviour as a product of values, norms, beliefs and regulations [68]. The regulatory lens, which refers to the regulative processes and rules of law, clearly relates to the ownership models that different accounting firms adopt whilst the normative and cognitive pillars refer to the various relational controls that exist between the vendor and the client. The normative pillar refers to the social rules that are not legislatively based whilst the cognitive pillar refer to culturally supported habits and customs [29]. Effective knowledge sharing and having a strong partnership view has also been espoused as being a critical success factor in the literature [3]. This relates clearly to the normative and cognitive pillars of an organisation. Penter et al. [68] also argue that institutional theory plays a greater role in explaining offshoring trends in highly regulated industries, such as in the accounting profession.

3.2 Theories Relating to the Impact on Graduate Skills

Graduates are an accounting firm resource so a combination of Resource Based View Theory ("RBV") and Human Capital Theory ("HCT") will be used as the grounding theory for this primary research question. Developing graduate skills is developing a resource for the organisation with specific competencies that should be useful in the accounting firm. The combination of these theories in relation to strategic HRM has also been adopted by Wright and McMahan [65].

RBV suggests that some resources are a source of competitive advantage and so should not be outsourced. When an organisation does not have the resources that it requires, then outsourcing and offshoring can assist by filling the void [24, 69].

Human Capital Theory deals with the optimum amount to be invested in areas such as training in human capital by organisations. It suggests that employers and staff will invest in training up to the point of equalisation between marginal returns and costs [70, 71]. Local graduates are expected to complete higher level work earlier so their initial technical skills are required to be more advanced. This means that firms either need to change the type of training that they provide their graduates to be able to complete this work or pay a premium for staff that already have these skills.

4 Methodology

This paper adopts a predominantly qualitative firm based case study approach which is deemed appropriate due to the contemporary nature of this topic and the lack of detailed and rich literature in the area being addressed, especially in relation to accounting firms [72]. A key determinant of success of this research is the researcher's ability to build trust with the respondents which is easier to obtain by using a predominantly qualitative approach [5, 28, 73–75]. The focus will be on building a trusting relationship with a smaller number of accounting firms and respondents within these firms. The more in-depth case study approach is also deemed appropriate given that offshoring is a contemporary phenomenon and needs to be explored more fully [76].

Data collection will be primarily through in-depth interviews, as well as reviewing the documentation of firms' offshoring processes where available. As suggested by Yin [72], this will assist with the triangulation of the data. Interviews were chosen as the primary means of data collection because it allows a deeper repour to be developed. Pilot interviews were conducted with respondents involved in offshoring. As a result of these pilot interviews, a short survey component was added to the interview to provide some more measurable information in relation to graduate attributes and skills that accounting firms look for in their graduates. The interviews will include the collection of basic demographic information as well as details of their current and past level of involvement with offshoring. Depending on the role of the respondent within the firm, the interview questions either related to the first, second or both research questions. For example, the human resource manager in the firm is generally not involved in the offshoring process so their questions were limited to those related to research question two.

4.1 Sample Selection

The initial purposeful sample for the interviews is drawn from the researcher's professional networks. Cases were chosen to allow theoretical replication which is appropriate in this case due to the varied sizes of accounting firms. It is envisaged that there will be a sample of between 20–30 respondents in total from these firms. This is based on purposeful sampling which suggest that studies should have between 20 and 30 interviews and single case studies should contain between 15 to 30 interviews [77]. Broadly, accounting firms can be classified as either small, mid-tier or large (the Big 4). Mid-tier firms are often independently owned in each state but part of an international association. The selection of cases needs to be theoretically guided and the goal should be to generalise theories [72]. Cases are limited to Australian accounting firms that use India as their offshoring location.

In total, approximately nine firms will be used as cases which will result in around 30 individual interviews [76, 78]. By having a smaller number of cases, there is an opportunity to interview different hierarchical and functional positions within each firm, which will provide a richer picture than if one was to interview fewer respondents in a greater number of firms [29].

This will comprise six firms that do offshore for the first research question as described in Fig. 5. These will include small, mid-tier and Big 4 firms. For the second research question, the number of firms will be extended to nine to include an additional three firms that do not offshore. This inclusion of firms of different sizes that do not adopt offshoring is important as it allows a comparison in the graduate skills area. For example, graduate skills in a mid-tier that offshores and one that does not will be compared. This can be done for all size firms except the Big 4 accounting firms as all of them are involved in offshoring so a direct comparison of the graduate skills between those that do and do not offshore is not possible.

In relation to the second research question on graduate skills and development, each case study will be examined longitudinally at two separate points in time. Once, when the graduates are initially hired and then a year later to see their comparative progress. The aim of this is to compare the progression of the graduates in an offshoring and non-offshoring environment.

4.2 Research Phases

The preliminary phase of the study includes a detailed literature review. Once this has been completed, there will are two distinct phases as described in Fig. 6 below.

	PHASE ONE INTERVIEWS	PHASE TWO INTERVIEWS
TIMING	November 15 – September 2016	July – September 2017
FOCUS	• Critical success factors influencing different ownership and interaction frameworks and • Differences in graduate skills between firms that do and do not offshore	Differences in graduate skills between firms that do and do not offshore
SAMPLE SELECTION	Six firms involved in offshoring consisting of - 2 Big 4 firms - 2 Mid-tier firms - 2 smaller firms Three firms not involved in offshoring consisting of 1 mid-tier and 2 smaller firms	Same nine firms as used in the Phase One interviews (ie six that do offshore and three that do not)

Fig. 6. Summary of the data collection process

Phase One Interviews. This component of the paper focuses on the critical success factors of the different ownership and interaction frameworks adopted by accounting firms that do offshore and on the different graduate skills required by firms that do and do not offshore.

Lincoln [79] argues that one of the measures of rigour in qualitative research is that of reciprocity. Given the importance of trust between the researcher and the respondents in this research, this particular type of rigor is vital in this paper. Therefore, a key requirement of the interviews is to provide each of the respondents with a tailored summary of the results to meet the "what's in it for me" test [76]. Many of the respondent firms that have agreed to participate to date have already expressed a keen interest in receiving these generalised results.

Due to the location of some of the respondents, interviews will be conducted either face to face or through Skype if the respondents are overseas.

Phase Two Interviews (Graduate Development). This phase of the study focuses on the research questions in relation to the difference in accounting graduate skills developed by accounting graduates once they start working. This will be conducted via in-depth interviews of the same respondents as used in Phase one. It will be longitudinal in nature and held approximately one year after the initial interviews so that the progress of the graduates can be determined.

4.3 Research Analysis

Interview findings will be recorded, transcribed and provided back to each respondent for checking. Responses to each interview question will then be coded using Nvivo to assist in coding and indexing data. With the index system, each node is organised into trees, in order to organise the concepts into categories and sub-categories [80]. Guided by the research questions initially, a minimal codebook of themes were explored and organised in the data set. As the understanding of the data grew, this was modified.

The coding will be conducted using the same open coding themes as used in the coding of the literature during the literature review process to ensure consistency [81]. This process began by identifying approximately 155 themes in the open coding stage which was then reduced down to around 70 in the later stages of coding. The identified themes can be broadly categorised as falling into the categories of accounting firm specific themes, impact of offshoring, critical success factors, offshoring models, graduate roles, graduate employability and graduate skills.

5 Progress to Date

Whilst it is still early in the study, several respondent firms agreed to participate with four pilot interviews completed. All of these firms are part of a co-operative ownership model where they own a portion of the Indian operation. In addition, a number of other firms have agreed to participate in the study. Given the number of respondent firms that have already agreed, it is not envisaged that there will be any difficulties in securing a sufficient sample size that is theoretically guided.

A sample of the initial results firms where data has been collected is discussed below. Each of the respondents are involved in tax and accounting. Figure 7 provides a description of the cases.

	Firmlarge1	Firmmidtier1	Firmsmall3
Total no of respondents	9	3	3
No of partner respondents	1	1	1
No of champion respondents	3		
No of manager respondents	4	1	1
No of graduate respondents	1	1	1
Ownership model	Captive	Co-operative (no direct ownership interest)	Third party provider

Fig. 7. Description of cases

Whilst these interviews have not yet been fully analysed, preliminary findings are interesting and support the choice of research questions address in this study. A background on each case and a brief description of the preliminary findings are provided below.

5.1 Firmlarge1

Whilst other parts of this Big 4 firm adopted offshoring earlier, the private enterprise division was relatively slow to get involved and has only established its offshoring captive centre in India two years ago. All of the Australian private enterprise division used this centre which had approximately 25–30 Indian staff employed. Whilst they had 100 % ownership of the offshoring operation through the Big 4's Indian firm, all communication, workflow management and co-ordination was strictly controlled through a central shared services centre in one of the Australian city offices. The captive had a series of Australian secondees working in the offshoring operation for rolling periods of 3–6 months.

The first research question addresses the business ownership and interaction frameworks that accounting firms adopt in offshoring and some of the critical factors that influence the management of these. Firmlarge1 adopts a captive business ownership model and a segregated interaction framework. The interaction framework would be considered segregated in this case due to the limited communication that staff have with the offshore workers and the fact that all communication is filtered through a shared service centre. The respondents from this firm were all asked how they viewed their current model and interaction framework. As can be seen below, all both partner and champion respondents acknowledged that there were significant teething problems and a fair amount of frustration was expressed, mainly around the lack of direct communication that they had with their offshore staff. That is, they did not like the segregated approach to interacting with their offshore team, but wanted a more interactive framework. This would indicate, as supported by the comment below, that there is a potential preference for the interaction framework to be adopted, not a segregated framework approach.

> *"well the feedback that we get back is that things are getting missed because they are not able to talk directly to the person who is actually working on the job. There is inconsistency from one job to the next because different people over there are working on them. Um, and they are working for all these different offices and obviously every office wants things done slightly differently. So there is not always that consistency between offices so. But we are already looking at a few ways to work around that or improve I should say so there are things in the pipeline there." (Champion 4)*
>
> *"communication definitely needs to improve. And I also think, some of the work that is coming up, I do think that onshore do need to do a quick review."* (Champion 3)

> *"Yes, so the model that we have at the moment, it's a bit like a hourglass. You starts at I don't know 700 accountants, in the Australian practice. It drives through a couple of people in who run some sort of central centre in Australia, and then it spreads out to I don't know 40 accountants in India. And no-one knows where their work is, no-one knows what is happening." (Partner 1)*

The second research question considers the recruitment, skills required and development of graduates in an offshoring environment. Comments from respondents support the position that the impact of offshoring on graduates was also a concern for respondents in this firm. The reduced level of graduate recruitment appeared to be of greater concern to the respondents. Respondents both at partner and graduate level raised their concern over the reduction in number of graduates recruited in an offshoring environment.

> *"I know our graduate intake um has dropped a little bit, um. It's not, you know, when we had a grad not come on board, we decided not to worry about it. Sorry, they accepted an offer, they were going to come and then they, we gave them the offer before India actually kicked off. When they didn't come, we didn't replace them. We didn't get another grad, we just said India is going to replace that role." (Partner1)*
>
> *"Kind of less than 50% that have jobs in the profession at least. I reckon less than 50%. ......They would be, you know, bright as anything, even. They were the first person I would expect to get picked up. But just because they slipped through the cracks the first time, they are moving on and doing another degree".(Graduate1)*

In addition to the impact on graduate numbers, some respondents discussed the impact on the development of graduates in an offshoring environment which also forms part of the second research question. This confirms some of the literature discussed above which suggests that there is a hollowing out of some of the basic skills in the graduates. However, as noted in the respondent quotes below, there was also acknowledgement that offshoring did assist in exposing junior staff to higher level work sooner which would assist in their development.

> *"You go into our office today, you will find 2 managers and, ... one AM who knows SMSF and then xxxx, myself and (Partner name inserted) to a lesser extent. Um, for me that is, no one knows anything about pension funds, how is the decision making, how you can help clients and can add value to a client. So that is a massive gap. " (Partner 1)*

> *"From a local point of view here of seeing probably lower level type work being taken offshore, it has freed up a lot of the younger accountants here, sort of senior accountant type level, assistant manager level to um do some more higher level work, advisory work. They can get out of the office a bit more and meet with clients. So I think it helps to almost push people. Some goes before they are ready, doing more of that advisory type and relationship type work as opposed to sitting at a desk and doing tax returns. So I think from that point of view it is a good thing. To sort of see evidence of that here, or even just not getting it done or getting the work reviewing rather than doing it themselves. Sort of promotes that development a little sooner that would normally be the case. On the downside though, we have probably found, which is probably a little bit of the resistance to offshoring comes from, that perhaps for the grad or new people coming in, they don't necessarily have the lower level work to get started on, to cut their teeth on so much. So it's a little bit of a balancing act but overall though I say that the benefits outweigh the negatives." (Champion 4)*

5.2 Firmmidtier1

This firm had quite a different internal structure to a traditional accounting firm and was essentially built with offshoring in mind. They were using a co-operative model, although they did not directly have an ownership interest in this. Therefore, in terms of the first research question, this case provides an interesting insight. The respondents in this firm viewed their offshoring model as broadly successful, despite not having any direct ownership interest in the offshoring operation. This would indicate that they did not view having an ownership interest as a critical success factor for their offshoring.

This firm was relatively new, being a break away from a Big 4 accounting firm three years previously. The partners had involvement with offshoring in their prior roles, although they did speak positively about their previous experiences. Therefore, they were in an unusual position to structure their offshoring ownership model and interaction framework in a way where they could learn from their past experience with offshoring,

An Accounting Firm Perspective of Offshoring   157

without any inherited legacy issues. It is interesting that they deliberately chose not to have an ownership stake in the offshoring operation and that they structured the interaction framework as highly interactive. In fact, in the first year, they had structured their staffing with only principals who each had one offshore team member working for them directly to do the day to day tasks whilst they would deal with the client facing role as described below;

> *"So 22 staff altogether with a mixture of guys that are transitioning into retirement so we've got two guys that are here part-time transitioning into retirement. And then the rest are managers. We've got 2 below managers and the rest are managers or above. So we are top heavy which is why we rely on the India team More junior staff in India than what there are here." (Manager 1)*

At least initially, this meant that the interaction framework directly influenced the level of graduate recruitment which forms part of the second research question. As the firm used their offshoring operation to the extent that they, there was not as much of a need to hire graduates locally, but rather hire more senior client facing managers.

With succession planning in mind, the firm's structure has changed in the last year or so with graduates and other junior staff now being employed. Key skills considered when employing graduates are that they are good communicators, and have strong critical analysis and client-facing skills. As Firmmidtier1 focuses on making their domestic staff client-facing, these skills are considered important as can be seen from the following quotes.

> *"We needed the managers to come through to grow, to grow to get new fees so we needed a Canberra office is growing that has that capability to continue to grow. Junior managers to come through so definitely and client facing people so our recruitment I guess is all based good communicators and good client facing people rather than good technical, sheltered, or shy people that will be probably really struggling. So, it's evolved, it was probably always part of the plan." (Partner 1)*

> *"I think there will be a big need for, probably less of the processing but more of the business analytics and yeah, being in front of clients a lot more. I think, there will be a need for someone that knows about business rather than accounting. The accounting I think will be offshored, the cloud is getting so much better. The whole industry, there is going to be a big shift in the industry. We will still need a lot more people here to do the business analytics rather than the processing." (Manager1)*

5.3 Firmsmall3

This firm is also relatively new and comprises two young partners, two principals and a bookkeeper as well as two staff in India. They are a relatively progressive firm, putting all of their clients on the cloud which has allowed them to operate predominantly from home for the first few years and minimise overheads. Most of the current staff received their initial training in a mid-tier firm that had been heavily utilising offshoring for many years.

In terms of the first research question and the ownership model in particular, this firm is quite similar to Firmmidtier1. Viewing their offshoring as successful, they do not see having an ownership interest in the offshore provider as critical to their success in offshoring, but rather saw it as a constraint in many ways as is evidenced by the below quote.

> "It doesn't interest me to be heavily involved in that ownership side. I just like using them, they do a job. We tick it off and pay our monthly fee" (Partner 1)

Their focus of this firm has been on being flexible and innovative. This flexibility, driven partly by the lack of ownership interest, had allowed them to trial several different providers previously before settling on their current provider. This offshore provider acts as a type of shared service centre for numerous firms in Australia and New Zealand for which each firm pays a fee for a particular staff member. Unlike a traditional external ownership model, they encourage an interactive framework and personal relationships with the Indian team which is one of the features that attracted this firm to this offshore provider. This interactive mindset is also reinforced by the fact that Firmsmall3 pays for the particular staff member, not just for their output as with many external ownership models. This is demonstrated in the quote below;

> "I try to talk to him like he is a junior accountant so he gets to know the job and understand the business, rather than just. I can't imagine just sending the work up and getting just as good quality if I don't have any communication with them to explain what they are doing, or why they are doing it, or what the business does or just be aware of this time of business that are GST free or whatever it is. I can't see how that training would be as effective if I didn't have that communication channel." (Partner1)

Again, as with Firmmidtier1, this firm has been slow to hire graduates and the team domestically has a focus on experience. The focus on flexibility in this firm has also meant that to date, they have not hired any graduates although it is expected that growth in the firm will mean that they will do so shortly. Graduates are effectively seen as a fixed as opposed to a variable cost, thereby reducing flexibility as demonstrated by the quote below.

> "Um, it would have been harder for us just because of the whole recruitment and HR management we would have had to be doing. I don't think it would have been hard to find people, it just would have been a bigger cost and more administration that we would have to be doing I think to have people in-house and space obviously. We couldn't have grown to where we are without being able to offshore because where we were operating before we were so squished but we could manage to get through more work because we were using offshoring." (Partner1)

This quote again shows that the interaction framework and offshoring model adopted influences the graduate recruitment policy of the firm and demonstrates that research question one and two are linked. The second research question also addresses the impact on the development of graduates in an offshoring environment. Interestingly, one of the current principals in this firm commenced her career in a mid-tier accounting firm five years ago which was heavily involved in offshoring. As can be seen in the following quote, she credits her rapid career progression at least partly to her involvement with offshoring.

> " It's really good because it actually allows grads and others with less experience to deal more complex stuff and to learn faster. But still have some touch as a grad that is how they can grow into the more complex things. But I think offshore accounting is a great things because it allows people to have hands on on different areas on things they never do before, like would had never had done if um, if they would just go really really slowly. It would take them years to get them to the same place within 2 years. And I'm talking as well from personal experience. " (Manager 2)

5.4 Summary of Initial Findings

Whilst in the early stages of data analysis, the preliminary findings have provided some interesting observations in relation to the research questions. These research questions are;

(1) In accounting firm offshoring arrangements, what critical factors influence the successful management of business ownership models and interaction frameworks?
(2) Are there differences in the skills required in domestic graduates between accounting firms that adopt offshoring and those that do not?

In relation to the first research question, firmmidtier1 and firmsmall3 who both viewed their offshoring operation as broadly successful, did not have any direct ownership interest in the offshore provider. They also did not see this as an issue. However, the interaction framework was seen as important, in particular as a means of communication to achieve a good result in terms of the work produced. In contrast, respondents within firmlarge1 which operates a very segregated interaction framework, found this lack of communication frustrating and generally viewed their offshoring operation as not very successful. All firms viewed having an interactive framework with their staff engaging with the Indian team as important.

There was a clear link demonstrated between the first and second research question. For example, both firmmidtier1 and firmsmall3 were relatively new firms where the partners had seen offshoring used in prior roles, and they both chose to structure their firms domestically in similar ways. They both used highly interactive frameworks and they both had limited or no domestic graduates in their early years. This could have been because they either wanted to operate with lower fixed overheads and the skills required by domestic staff in this environment were not readily available in domestic graduates but in more experienced staff.

The development of the graduates was also seen to be influenced by the use of offshoring. Firmlarge1 recognised that offshoring forced their domestic graduates to undertake more difficult work earlier and one of the respondents in firmsmall3 even attributed her involvement with offshoring from her initial employment to relatively fast career progression. However, respondents in firmlarge1 there was an acknowledgement that this could produce a hollowing out of skills within the firm.

6 Significance of the Paper

The initial preliminary findings and the literature review support the direction of this research as outlined in the research questions. More generally, they support a call for additional research in this area specific to the growing area of offshoring in accounting. Whilst there is growing research on offshoring with an IT perspective and BPO generally, very little of this is aimed at accounting firms. It is not simply the "back office" peripheral tasks that are being offshored by accounting firms, but rather some of their traditional core tasks. Offshoring within accounting firms is also considered far more taboo given that firms are dealing with their clients' private financial information. This has been identified as a future research area by some authors, especially in the form of in-depth qualitative research which this paper will do [9, 64].

Whilst the critical success factors initially may be similar to those identified in the current ITO literature, there are some expected differences. It is expected that gaining buy-in of domestic staff will be considered far more important for accounting firms.

The first research question looks specifically at the different interaction frameworks and business structures that are suited to offshoring and their critical success factors. The majority of the literature on models used in offshoring relates only to the ownership structure. However, this is not where most of the work is in the domestic organisation. Who allocates the work to the offshoring entity? Who communicates with the offshoring team and completes the training? How does the organisation ensure domestic buy-in? Initial findings of this research indicate that at least for the three cases discussed, the ownership model was a key component of their success in offshoring. There is a surprising lack of research in the area of how to gain the support of domestic employees. These important questions remain largely unanswered and this paper will attempt to address this.

This research will extend the offshoring literature to the training and recruitment of graduates and domestic staff in an offshoring environment. Whilst there is a vast array of research on graduate skills generally, none of this is specifically aimed at organisations that offshore. Are there different skills required in those organisations? If so, how does the firm ensure that these are provided in their training programs? With the incidence of offshoring increasing in the accounting profession, this has significance to firms, as they seek to recruit the most appropriate domestic staff. For the firms, how then do they develop the core technical skills required in their graduates if most of the work that was previously used to develop these is now being done offshore? There is likely to be a altered training approach in firms that offshore. Also, is there a difference in the type of work that graduates complete in accounting firms that do offshore and those that do not and does this convert to ultimately different skill levels?

These questions are significant not only for the accounting profession but also universities as they design industry relevant business degrees for the future that improve the employability of their graduates and meet industry requirements.

7   Potential Limitations and Strategies for Addressing Them

Whilst the use of a case study approach will provide richer research results, it means that the research will be exploratory in nature with limited ability to generalise the results [82]. The paper will be looking at the graduate skill requirements and critical success factors within the domestic accounting firm, not in the vendor firm.

The most significant potential limitation of this paper is gaining access to the information and ensuring that the accounting firms are willing to contribute in a constructive way. Accounting firms by their very nature are conservative and do not easily share their experiences in relation to topics considered taboo such as offshoring [11]. Often, the offshoring relationship is seen to be the source of an imitable advantage so firms may be reluctant to discuss their offshoring capabilities [26]. Other studies have noted similar resistance with some accounting firms fearing a sales pitch or fearing negative fallout [5, 9].

Networking and building trust in the industry will be a key strategy to resolve this limitation. Providing industry presentations is one way of demonstrating knowledge in the area, whilst building trust and credibility and networking opportunities. To date, this has proven to be a very successful strategy with all of the respondent firms being sourced from the audience of two presentations already completed. It will be stressed that their involvement in the paper will provide them with some value in terms of the results and outcomes that is difficult for them to obtain elsewhere. It will also be made absolutely clear that the researchers are not aligned to any vendor of offshoring services and is totally independent. The use of university branding will assist with this process. Given the success of obtaining respondent firms involvement so early in the paper, it would appear that this strategy is working.

8 Conclusion

Although there is a growing amount of research on the use of offshoring generally, there is little research on the impact of offshoring on domestic accounting firms, and in particular on the "human side" of offshoring within the domestic accounting firm. This research in progress primarily focuses on Australian domestic accounting firms and is divided into two parts. The first examines the critical success factors of different ownership models and interaction frameworks that domestic accounting firms can adopt in implementing offshoring. There is very little research on the interaction frameworks adopted in offshoring in particular.

As a result of offshoring, there is also an effect on the domestic accounting firm staff. Therefore, the second part of the paper examines the impact of accounting firm offshoring on the skills that are recruited, required and developed in domestic graduates. Offshoring is expected to have a significant impact for educating, recruiting and training domestic accounting graduates and this paper is expected to be significant for both accounting firms and university educators.

Further areas of study include comparing the graduate skills required for the staff in the domestic and vendor firm and extending this research into other professional services industries that are starting to adopt offshoring.

References

1. Lacity, M.C., Willcocks, L.P.: Outsourcing business and IT services: the evidence of success, robust practices and contractual challenges. Legal Inf. Manage. **12**, 2–8 (2012)
2. Terjesen, S.: Offshoring: impact on the accounting profession, pp. 1–34. CPA (2010)
3. Lacity, M., et al.: Business process outsourcing studies: a critical review and research directions. J. Inf. Technol. **26**, 221–258 (2011)
4. Crawford, F.: Out of office. In: Acuity 2015, pp. 52–54, October 2015
5. Bandyopadhyay, J., Hall, L.A.: Offshoring of tax preparation services by US accounting firms: an empirical study. Adv. Competitiveness Res. **17**(1/2), 71–89 (2009)
6. Cervantes, P.: Sarbanes-Oxley and the outsourcing of accounting. Mich. J. Bus. **2**, 99–139 (2008)
7. Daugherty, B.E., Dickins, D., Fennema, M.G.: Offshoring tax and audit procedures: implications for US based employee education. Issues Account. Educ. **27**(3), 733–742 (2012)
8. Balint, B.: Process frameworks in service offshoring: implementation thoroughness, tax complexity and process improvement. Int. J. Inf. Syst. Serv. Sect. **7**(4), 47–64 (2015)
9. Chaplin, S.: Outsourcing income tax returns: convenient and/or controversial. J. Aust. Taxation **15**(2), 279–312 (2013)
10. Bierstaker, J., et al.: Obtaining assurance for financial statement audits and control audits when aspects of the financial reporting process are outsourced. Audit. J. Pract. Theory **32**(Supplement 1), 209–250 (2013)
11. Lahiri, S., Kedia, B.L.: The effects of internal resources and partnership quality on firm performance: an examination of Indian BPO providers. J. Int. Manage. **15**(2), 209–224 (2009)
12. Accounting Professional & Ethical Standards Board. Discussion paper: Issues impacting the Accounting industry from outsourcing (2012)
13. Aman, A., et al.: Transaction costs in finance and accounting offshore outsourcing: a case of Malaysia. Strateg. Outsourcing Int. J. **5**(1), 72–88 (2012)

14. Nicholson, B., Jones, J., Espenlaub, S.: Transaction costs and control of outsourced accounting: case evidence from India. Manage. Acc. Res. **17**, 238–258 (2006)
15. Accenture: Accenture high tech solutions: outsourcing the finance and accounting function, pp. 1–15 (2006)
16. EY&ICAA: Business Briefing series "20 issues on outsourcing and offshoring", pp. 1–32 (2011)
17. Chartered Accountants Australia & New Zealand. What is the future for offshoring?, pp. 1–43. CAANZ (2015)
18. King, A.: Deloitte dives into India's growth with equity deal. In: Australian Financial Review (2016)
19. SSAE 16: Overview of a service organisation. The SSAE Resource Guide 2015, May 2015
20. Delpachitra, S., Ralston, D.: Will draft prudential standard SPS 231 outsourcing reduce investment outsourcing risks in superannuation funds? pp. 1–24 (2012)
21. Accounting Professional & Ethical Standards Board). APES GN 30 Outsourced Services. 2013
22. Maelah, R., et al.: Accounting outsourcing turnback: process and issues. Strateg. Outsourcing Int. J. **3**(3), 226–245 (2010)
23. Jathanna, V.: Outsourcing. CMA **65**(10), 25 (1992)
24. Eriksson, T., Hatonen, J.: 30+ years of research and practice of outsourcing - exploring the past and anticipating the future. J. Int. Manage. **15**, 142–155 (2009)
25. Wreford, J., Davidson, F., Pervan, G., Penter, K.: Opaque indifference and corporate social responsibility a moral licence for offshore BPO. In: Oshri, I., Kotlarsky, J., Willlcocks, L.P. (eds.) Advances in Global Sourcing Models, Governance, and Relationships. LNBIP, vol. 163, pp. 192–209. Springer, Heidelberg (2013)
26. Nicholson, B., Aman, A.: Offshore accounting outsourcing: the case of India, pp. 1–54. Centre for Business Performance (2008)
27. Dibbern, J., et al.: Information systems outsourcing: a survey and analysis of the literature. Database Adv. Inf. Syst. **35**(4), 6–103 (2004)
28. Davidson, F., Wreford, J., Pervan, G., Penter, K.: Opaque indifference and corporate social responsibility: a moral licence for offshore BPO. In: Kotlarsky, J., Oshri, I., Willcocks, L.P. (eds.) Governing Sourcing Relationships. A Collection of Studies at the Country, Sector and Firm Level. LNBIP, vol. 195, pp. 98–113. Springer, Heidelberg (2014)
29. Nicholson, B., Aman, A.: Managing attrition in offshore finance and accounting outsourcing. Strat. Outsourcing Int. J. **5**(3), 232–247 (2012)
30. Nugroho, H., Afghani, G.A., Hodosi, G., Rusu, L.: Key factors in managing IT outsourcing relationships. In: Lytras, M.D., Ruan, D., Tennyson, R.D., Ordonez De Pablos, P., Garcia Peñalvo, F.J., Rusu, L. (eds.) WSKS 2011. CCIS, vol. 278, pp. 58–69. Springer, Heidelberg (2013)
31. Maelah, R., et al.: Accounting outsourcing practices in Malaysia. J. Asia Bus. Stud. **6**(1), 60–78 (2010)
32. Oshri, I., Kotlarsky, J., Liew, C.-M.: Four strategies for offshore captive centres. Wall Street J. Eur. **2**, 1–2 (2008)
33. Diversified Business Communications. Twelve Models for Business Process Outsorcing (BPOs), pp. 1–2. Institute of Finance & Management (2014)
34. Wreford, J., Penter, K., Pervan, G., Davidson, F.: Seeking opaque indifference in offshore BPO. In: Kotlarsky, J., Oshri, I., Willcocks, L.P. (eds.) Global Sourcing 2012. LNBIP, vol. 130, pp. 175–193. Springer, Heidelberg (2012)
35. Penter, K., Pervan, G., Wreford, J.: Offshore BPO at large captive operations in India. Inf. Technol. People **22**(3), 201–222 (2009)

36. Deloitte, Global financial services offshoring: scaling the heights (2005)
37. Wreford, J., et al.: Opaque indifference, trust and service provider succcess in offshore business process outsourcing. In: ACIS 2011 (2011)
38. Yorke, M.: Learning & Employability: employability in higher education: what it is - what it is not, T.H.E. Academy, York, UK (2006)
39. Abdullah, Z., et al.: Measuring student performance, student satisfaction and its impact on graduate employability. Int. J. Acad. Res. Bus. Soc. Sci. **4**(4), 108–124 (2014)
40. Osmani, M., et al.: Identifying the trends and impact of graduate attributes on employability: a literature review. Tert. Educ. Manag. **21**(4), 367–379 (2015)
41. Bunney, D., Sharplin, E., Howitt, C.: Generic skills for graduate accountants: the bigger picture, a social and economic imperative in the new knowledge economy. High. Educ. Res. Dev. **34**(2), 256–269 (2015)
42. Jackson, D., Sibson, R., Riebe, L.: Delivering work-ready business graduates - keeping our promises and evaluating our performance. J. Teach. Learn. Grad. Employab. **4**(1), 2–22 (2013)
43. Sithole, S.T.M.: Quality in accounting graduates: employer expectations of the graduate skills in the bachelor of accounting degree. Eur. Sci. J. **11**(22), 165–180 (2015)
44. Crawford, F., Mind the skills gap. In: Acuity 2016, pp. 48–51. CAANZ, Australia (2016)
45. Jackson, D., Chapman, E.: Non-technical skill gaps in Australian business graduates. Educ. Train. **54**(23), 95–113 (2012)
46. Low, M., et al.: Accounting employers' expectations - the ideal accounting graduates. Int. J. Learn. Teach. Educ. Res. **13**(2), 142–167 (2015)
47. Naidoo, M.: Using group work to improve generic skills of management accounting students in preparation for their accounting careers. Asia Pac. Manage. Account. J. **9**(2), 107–139 (2016)
48. Barbu, E., Song, X.: The effects of offshoring on employer-provided training. J. Int. Trade Econ. Dev. **25**, 1–25 (2015)
49. Bandyopadhya, J., Hall, L.A.: Off-shoring of tax preparation services by US accounting firms: an empirical study. Adv. Competitiveness Res. **17**(1&2), 71–89 (2009)
50. Smith, M.: Can Australian accounting graduates survive offshoring?, p. 1. Accountants Daily (2012)
51. Oliver, B., Whelan, B.: Building course team capacity to enhance graduate employability - Final report 2011. In: Graduate Employability Indicators. Curtin University (2011)
52. Turner, M.: Outsourcing and technology impacting graduates. Accountants Daily (2016)
53. Turley, S.r., et al.: Skills, competencies and the sustainability of the modern audit. ICAS and FRC (2016)
54. Turner, M.: Offshoring to impact jobs market in 2016. Accountants Daily 2016 (2016)
55. Nagarajan, S., Edwards, J.: Is the graduate attributes approach sufficient to develop work ready graduates? J. Teach. Learn. Grad. Employ. **5**(1), 12–28 (2014)
56. Anderson, V.: International HRD and offshore outsourcing: a conceptual review and research agenda. Hum. Res. Dev. Rev. 1–20 (2015)
57. Shamsuddin, A., Ibrahim, M.I.M., Ghazali, M.H.: Employers' level of satisfaction towards accounting graduates. South East Asia J. Contemp. Bus. Econ. Law **7**(1), 22–31 (2015)
58. Hassan, M.G., Ojeniyi, A., Razall, M.R.: Practices project management strategies in outsourcing best practices. Jurnal Teknologi **77**(5), 35–41 (2015)
59. Moe, N.B., Cruzes, D.S., Dyba, T.: Coaching a global agile virtual team. In: 2015 IEEE 10th International Conference on Global Software Engineering, pp. 33–37. IEE Computer Society (2015)
60. Lashine, S.H., Mohamed, E.K.A.: Accounting knowledge and skills and the challenges of a global business environment. Manag. Fin. **29**(7), 3 (2003)

61. Rai, S.: Gender diversity in boardrooms: comparative global review and India. J. Strat. Hum. Res. Manage. **1**(2), 16–24 (2012)
62. Poston, R.S., Dhaliwal, J.: IS human capital: assessing gaps to strengthen skill and competency sourcing. Commun. Assoc. Inf. Syst. **36**(34), 669–696 (2015)
63. Jebli, F., Vieru, D.: Interculturalality and virtual teams in it offshoring context: a social regulation theory perspective. In: Kotlarsky, J., Oshri, I., Willcocks, L.P. (eds.) Governing Sourcing Relationships. A Collection of Studies at the Country. LNBIP, vol. 195, pp. 1–17. Sector and Firm Level. Springer, Heidelberg (2014)
64. Nicholson, B., Aini, A.: Offshore accounting outsourcing: the case of India, pp. 1–17 (2008)
65. Wright, P.M., McMahan, G.C.: Exploring human capital: putting human back into strategic human resource management. Hum. Res. Manage. **21**(2), 93–104 (2011)
66. Jackson, D.: Undergraduate management education: its place, purpose and efforts to bridge the skills gap. J. Manage. Organ. **15**, 206–223 (2009)
67. Powell, W., Di Maggio, P.: The iron cage revisited: Institutional isomorphism and collective rationality in organisation fields. Am. Soc. Rev. **48**(2), 147–160 (1983)
68. Penter, K., Wreford, J., Pervan, G., Davidson, F.: Offshore BPO decisions and institutional influence on senior managers. In: Oshri, I., Kotlarsky, J., Willcocks, L.P. (eds.) Advances in Global Sourcing. Models, Governance, and Relationships. LNBIP, vol. 163, pp. 93–116. Sector and Firm Level. Springer, Heidelberg (2014)
69. Ali, S., Green, P.: Effective information technology (IT) governance mechanisms: an IT outsourcing perspective. Inf. Syst. Front. **14**, 179–193 (2012)
70. Becker, G.S.: Investment in human capital: a theoretical analysis. J. Polit. Econ. **70**(5), 9–49 (1962)
71. Hahn, W.: Accounting research: an analysis of theories explored in doctoral dissertations and their applicability to systems theory. Account. Forum **31**, 305–322 (2007)
72. Yin, R.K.: Case Study Research Design and Methods, 5th edn. Sage Publications, London (2014)
73. Lyubimov, A., Arnold, V., Sutton, S.G.: An examination of the legal liability associated with outsourcing and offshoring audit procedures. Audit. J. Pract. Theory **32**(2), 97–118 (2013)
74. Forman, A.M., Thelen, S., Shapiro, T.: Domestic versus offshore service providers: the impact of cost, time and quality sacrifices on consumer choice. J. Serv. Manage. **26**(4), 608–624 (2015)
75. Lacity, M.C., Rottman, J.W.: The impact of outsourcing on client project managers IT systems perspectives. Computer **41**(1), 100–102 (2008)
76. Darke, P., Shanks, G., Broadbent, M.: Successfully completing case study research: combining rigor, relevance and pragmatism. Inf. Syst. J. **8**, 273–289 (1998)
77. Marshall, B., et al.: Does sample size matter in qualitative research? a review of qualitative interviews in IS research. J. Comput. Inf. Syst. **54**(1), 11–22 (2013)
78. Flyvbjerg, B.: Five misunderstandings about case-study research. Qual. Inq. **12**(2), 219–245 (2006)
79. Lincoln, Y.S.: Emerging criteria for quality in qualitative and interpretive research. Qual. Inq. **1**, 275 (1995)
80. Jackling, B., De Lange, P.: Do accounting graduates' skills meet the expectations of employers? A matter of convergence or divergence? Account. Educ. Int. J. **18**(4–5), 369–385 (2009)
81. Miles, M.B., Huberman, M.A.: Qualitative Data Analysis, 2nd edn. Sage, Thousand Oaks (1994)
82. Cavaye, A.: Case study research: a multi-faceted research approach for IS. Inf. Syst. J. **6**, 227–242 (1996)

Offshoring in the Wrong Direction?

Paul Alpar[✉]

School of Business and Economics, University at Marburg,
Universitätsstr. 24, 35037 Marburg, Germany
alpar@wiwi.uni-marburg.de

Abstract. Outsourcing of IT-related work to an offshore (or nearshore) location takes almost always place from a developed country to a less developed country. One of the reasons is that wages of IT workers in the less developed country are usually significantly lower but additional reasons for such a move may exist (e.g., better availability of skilled personnel). While there are meanwhile complex sourcing arrangements and even cases of backsourcing from offshore to a developed country, a relatively new phenomenon can be observed where IT-based services are outsourced from less developed to more developed countries. These are cases of services with a high amount of automation or complexity. In our research on the service of Internet traffic exchange, we find that it is not only the costs that drive the decision to acquire the service from a supplier in a developed country.

Keywords: Offshoring · Internet exchange points

1 Introduction

After years of offshoring of low-skilled work, meanwhile even services that require a high amount of skills and specialization are being efficiently offshored. This is possible, among other reasons, because of relatively abundant and cheap telecommunication facilities. For example, Friedman reports in his bestseller "The world is flat" [1] that US tax returns are being prepared in India just as X-rays from patients in USA are being interpreted there. Nowadays, such work can be completely automated in some cases so that even specialists are barely needed and there is no need for offshoring. In other words, the efficiency and effectiveness of service delivery in the home country has improved so that the service can be sourced back [2]. But service provisioning may also be offered in the other direction. An example where a service for less developed countries is actually prepared in a developed country is credit scoring and granting. The company Kreditech from Hamburg, Germany (www.kreditech.com) offers loans to people in Peru, the Dominican Republic, Kazahstan and so on. Their competitive advantage is a sophisticated algorithm, developed and run in Germany, which calculates a credit score for an individual based on thousands of data points of which most are collected on the Internet. People can apply for a loan at Kreditech via Internet instead of at a local bank. In a way, the credit service is offshored to Germany in that case.

In this paper, we analyze another service that companies in less developed countries can offshore to developed countries; it is the service of Internet interconnection and peering. Each private Internet user and each business use this very specialized, highly technical service every day, often without being aware of it. There are more than 600 public Internet exchange points (IXPs) used by thousands of internet service providers (ISPs), telecommunication carriers, content suppliers, content delivery networks, and other companies to exchange their Internet traffic. This infrastructure currently serves more than three billion Internet users. Its importance is continuously growing with the growth of traffic and business on the Internet. The size of the industry in terms of the size of its workforce, if only the interconnection business is considered, is not big but the huge amount of Electronic Business (EB) would not be possible without it. Without efficient and reliable Internet connections, EB could only be conducted on "electronic islands."

We analyze the reasons why some companies in less developed countries are offshoring this service to developed countries, in a way in the "opposite direction" of usual offshoring streams. For example, an ISP in India can bring all his traffic to an IXP in India and receive all the traffic for his customers at the same IXP. However, the same ISP may also decide to exchange his traffic or some of it at IXPs in Europe and/or USA. While telecommunication specialists in India still earn less than their Western counterparts, the question is what drives the ISPs in that or other less developed countries to tilt the direction of offshoring in the other direction. Are these the differences in

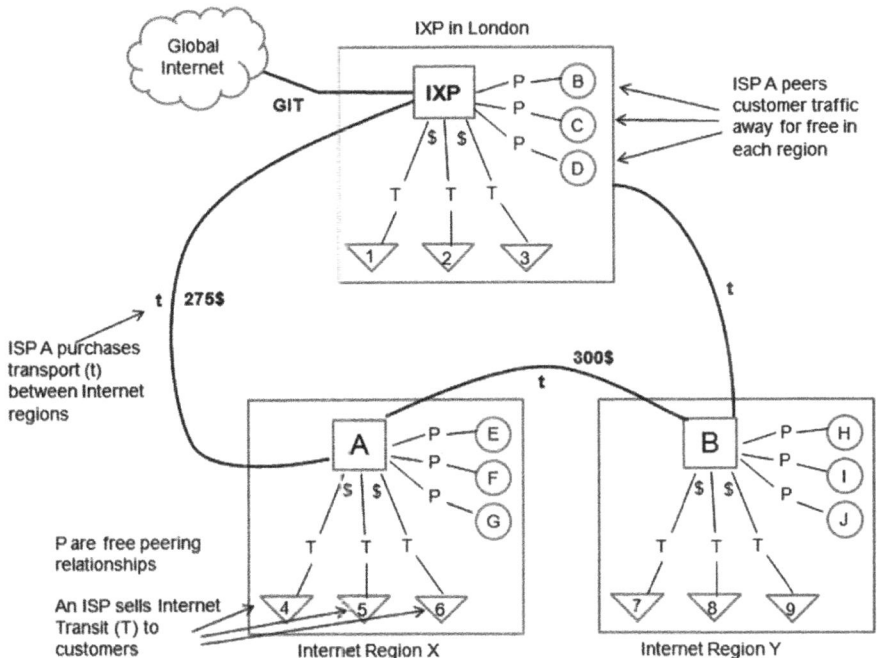

Fig. 1. Peering alternatives across regions from the point of view of ISP A (adapted from [3]).

telecommunication infrastructure and costs? One simple answer could be the costs. "Data highways" in developed countries usually have more capacity than in developing countries and the costs for using them are much cheaper due to competition. Therefore, ISPs, for example, in developing countries may find it cheaper to route their traffic for their region through an IXP in Europe. This is illustrated in Fig. 1, which is based on the example of two remote regions in Africa and an IXP in London [3]. A carrier in Africa may charge 300$ per Mbps for Internet transit between regions in Africa while another carrier may charge 275$ per Mbps for transporting data packets to London. There, ISP A may be able to peer his traffic away for free. Given such payment structures in the business, it can be cheaper for ISP A to connect to ISP B through London than to connect with him in Africa.

However, other factors besides cost may also play a role in the decision to offshore interconnection services. The size of the potential exchange population or the independence of an IXP from other companies or institutions may be also driving factors. This will be analyzed in the next sections.

2 Model and Hypotheses Development

We are trying to determine the factors for offshoring Internet connection services from less to more developed countries. However, there is little known why customers of IXPs choose a particular IXP. Therefore, we first develop relating hypotheses and an overall model. Then, we conduct a survey of customers of a big IXP (in developed and less developed countries). However, rather than directly inquiring why they chose the particular IXP, we analyze which factors contribute to their intention to continue buying the service from the IXP. This way, the respondents do not need to retrieve from their memory a decision making process from the past (that is often not explicit and not well documented) but can focus on their current evaluation of the arrangement and their experience with it. Interestingly, the success of outsourcing in general has not been often measured via the construct of continuance intention although this construct has often been used in IS research (e.g., [4]). We found only five publications that studied continuance intention in the context of outsourcing, including application service providing and software-as-a-service. Our research model has its conceptual roots in marketing where repurchasing intentions [5] or customer loyalty [6] have been extensively studied. In much of the research in the area, loyalty or intention to continue a business relationship are assumed to be influenced by perceived satisfaction and directly or indirectly influenced by perceived value. Perceived value involves a cognitive evaluation of monetary and non-monetary costs compared to the perceived benefits. In this context, satisfaction does not relate to a specific transaction but the whole relationship. It can be described as cumulative or overall satisfaction with services received and the company delivering the service.

Our first hypothesis relates to the effect of overall satisfaction of customers on the intention to continue acquiring the service from the same provider. It is obvious to expect that:

Offshoring in the Wrong Direction?   169

H1: Overall satisfaction with the IXP has a positive impact on the customer's continuance intention.

We assume that overall satisfaction is driven by the value that customers perceive to derive from the service and variables that relate to specific aspects of the service under research. The hypothesis relating to the influence of perceived value on satisfaction is again straightforward:

H2: A high value perceived by the customers of the IXP has a positive impact on the overall satisfaction with the IXP.

In research on services, there are different views on the influence of value. In some cases, it is assumed that it impacts the intention to continue with the service only via satisfaction while in other cases, it is allowed to influence intention also directly. Since the latter influence is also conceivable, we test for it through the following hypothesis:

H3: A high value perceived by the customers of the IXP has a positive impact on the customer's continuance intention.

Since no previous rigorous research on the subject of Internet interconnection as a business service exists, we need to rely on writings by expert practitioners [3, 7] and discussions with practicing professionals. The latter work in technical and business functions of Internet interconnection and represent diverse views on this business. This assures content validity of the constructs developed below. Twelve items that form three latent variables were determined. The variables may influence the perception of value and the perception of satisfaction at the same time. In other words, these variables affect satisfaction directly and indirectly, mediated by perceived value.

The technical and organizational infrastructure at an IXP must function well because the IXP's customers would otherwise get into troubles with their own customers. This includes not just the daily operations and customer service during operation but also the many steps at the set-up of the relationship (transferring and installing equipment to/at the IXP, initiating the operations). A service that is difficult to set up, that is often interrupted, or which does not support customers when they experience problems with it would not satisfy customers. Since most customers do not have their own fiber cable (or other cables) connecting to the IXP, there should be enough telecommunication carriers, which can carry customer data into the IXP. We refer to all these operational aspects under the term "infrastructure" and hypothesize that

H4: Satisfaction with the IXP's infrastructure has a positive impact on the perceived value of the IXP and

H5: Satisfaction with the IXP's infrastructure has a positive impact on overall satisfaction with the IXP.

Customers of an IXP want to exchange Internet packages with other customers and need, therefore, good support for this exchange through IXP's equipment that is open to every customer (public peering) as well as through private equipment at the same location for exchange with individual partners based on special contracts (private peering). Private peering may make sense with partners with which a lot of traffic is being exchanged to make it quicker and cheaper. The more potential peering partners are connected to the IXP, both from the region and the whole world, the more attractive an IXP becomes. Since the number of potential interconnections grows over proportionally with each new customer, the community of all customers enjoys network effects. The more customers an IXP has the more likely it is that some of them will be relevant to a customer. Therefore, we refer to the second latent variable as network effects. It is formed by factors relating to peering locally and globally. The relating hypotheses are formulated as

H6: Satisfaction with the network effects provided by the IXP has a positive impact on the perceived value of the IXP and

H7: Satisfaction with the network effects provided by the IXP has a positive impact on overall satisfaction with the IXP.

The last latent variable relates to various factors that express hopes and expectations of customers for the future positioning of the IXP. If they are positive then the customers believe that their current investment into the IXP was not in vain. We name the variable, therefore, "security of investment." It is first formed by their belief that the IXP is going to grow and remain an important IXP. But it also relates to the independency of the IXP. If it is owned by a telecommunication carrier, for example, then it may follow business goals that are not seen as beneficial for the customer (in the given example, the customer could be another telecommunication carrier that brings Internet transit traffic to the IXP). The connection to an IXP consists of financial start-up costs and various organizational investments. Customers, therefore, will probably not just consider operating costs but also how secure their investments are for the future. This will depend on the future stability of the IXP in economic, legal, and political terms. The degree of independence of the IXP from other companies (e.g., telecommunication carriers) and institutions (e.g., state agencies) may also be important because this could have, for example, an impact on costs for data transportation into or out of the IXP or on data protection. In recent years, it has become known that government agencies sometimes have the desire to scan Internet traffic. Some business customers fear that such intelligence may compromise their legal business secrets.

H8: Satisfaction with the security of investment by entering a business relationship with an IXP has a positive impact on the perceived value of the IXP and

H9: Satisfaction with the security of investment by entering a business relationship with an IXP has a positive impact on overall satisfaction with the IXP.

The variables continuance intention, value perception, and overall satisfaction are modelled as reflective constructs. The indicators for their measurement are taken with little adaptation from research on continuance intention in marketing. The indicators for latent constructs that drive value and satisfaction in our specific case were developed from professional writings on Internet interconnection and repeated discussions with six experts from the industry. Most of the indicators were already mentioned in the explanation of latent constructs.

The complete model is depicted in Fig. 2. The items that form or reflect the constructs are given in the appendix.

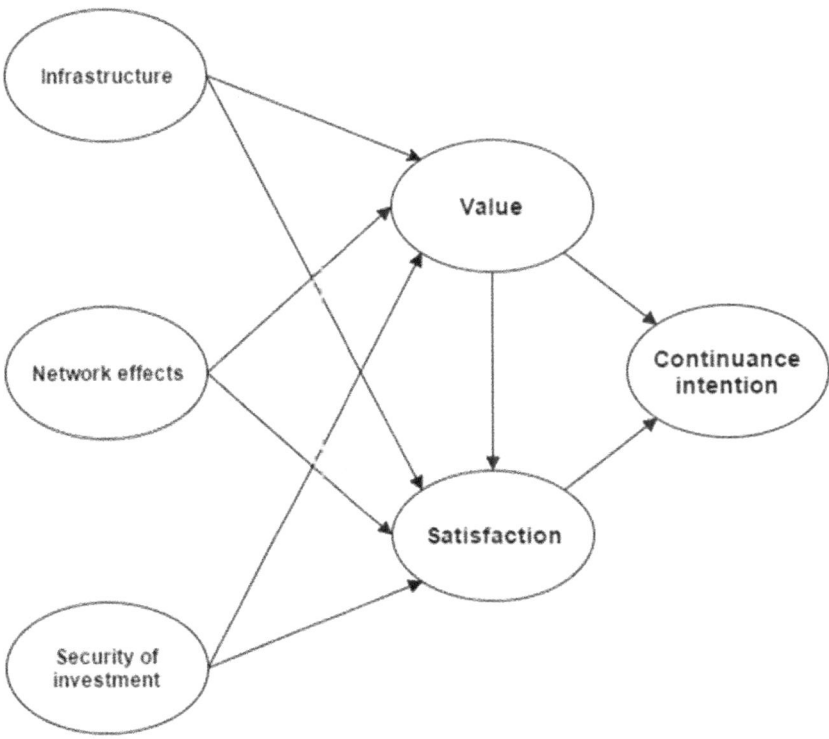

Fig. 2. Research model

3 Data Collection

Respondents were recruited from the customer base of a major IXP, which has clients from different countries and several continents. The questionnaire was administered in fall of 2015. First, a pre-test was run with eight respondents. This is too little for a quantitative assessment of the instrument but the purpose of the pre-test was to find out whether the questions were understandable, especially because the instrument was in English, designed for an international customer base. The feedback from the pre-test led to minor text changes only. Given the relatively small population and uncertainty about response behavior, we did not want to risk having too few answers in the main round. Of course, a full quantitative analysis of the data collected in the main test was carried out as reported below.

Since there is no common agreement what characterizes a "less developed" country, we take 50 % of the USA GDP per capita adjusted on the basis of purchasing power parity as the upper limit to consider a country to be "less developed." The survey was conducted through a web-based questionnaire. All items could be answered on a Likert type scale with seven alternatives ranging from least to strongest agreement. Two of the items are formulated in a negative way so that strong agreement means high dissatisfaction. Several respondents overlooked this. Based on this fact or other characteristics, e.g., all responses have the same value and completion time is extremely low, some answers were eliminated. The same is true for answers where major parts were missing.

4 Results

4.1 Measurement Models

We tested the model for the whole sample and for the two groups (developed and less developed countries) separately. Partial least squares (PLS) were used to test the research model in Fig. 2 because PLS is less demanding regarding sample size and distribution than confirmative SEM [8, 9], measurement models can be controlled for errors, and both reflective and formative indicators can be calculated simultaneously [10]. We received 150 useable responses of which 105 came from developed countries and 45 came from less developed countries. Thus, PLS can also be applied to the smaller subsample since the sample size fulfills the rule "10 times the maximum number of arrowheads pointing at a latent variable anywhere in the model" and the requirement based on power analysis (statistical power 80 %, $r^2 \geq 0.5$, $p \leq 0.005$) [11]. We report the results for the sample of less developed countries and results of a comparison between the two groups.

The formative constructs can be assessed by looking at multicollinearity and the significance of indicator weights [12–14]. The results of these tests are shown in Table 1. The variance inflation factor (VIF) measures multicollinearity and should not surpass the value of 5 [11]. This is true for all indicators attesting low multicollinearity. The weights are tested following the procedure in [11]. Weights of IS1, IS3 and IS4 are not significant but the loading of IS3 is significant and above 0.5. The loadings of IS1 and IS4 are 0.429 and 0.492 (i.e., < 0.5) but they are significant so we decide to keep them. NE4 does not have a significant weight but it has a significant loading above 0.5. NE2 is only significant at $p \leq 0.1$ but we keep it as the only departure from the above stated recommendation by [11]. It covers an important service part and clearly complements NE1. NE1 to NE4 all relate to network effects without doubt but perhaps two constructs (one for NE1 and NE2 and one for NE3 and NE4) that lead to NE as a second order construct would have revealed even better results. Indicators SI2, SI3, SI4 have significant loadings above or close to 0.5 so we keep them all. Since they cover distinct facets of the construct, this approach is also supported by [15].

The quality of the reflective measurement models is assessed in Table 1 by the criteria indicator reliability, composite reliability, and convergent validity [16]. Discriminant validity is tested by the Fornell-Larcker criterion [17]. All constructs fulfilled the criterion confirming that constructs are significantly different from each other. The recommended minimum value of indicator reliability is 0.7, which is easily reached by all indicators loads, except for Va4. However, since AVE and ICR of the construct *Value* are already well above the recommended thresholds there is no need to remove it. Composite reliability is calculated via the internal consistency reliability (ICR) and should surpass the value of 0.7 [18]. All constructs fulfill this criterion reaching ICR scores of above 0.9. Convergent validity is assessed using the criterion average variance extracted (AVE) as suggested by [17]. Sufficient convergent validity is reached if AVE is 0.5 or above [19]. All examined constructs reach an AVE score of above 0.7.

Table 1. Quality criteria of the measurement models

Formative constructs	Weights					VIF
	Item 1	Item 2	Item 3	Item 4		
Infrastructure (IS)	0.072	0.942*	0.410	−0.469		All VIFs ≤ 3
Network effects (NE)	0.537*	−0.351	0.789***	0.087		All VIFs ≤ 2
Security of investment (SI)	0.852***	0.128	0.031	0.138		All VIFs ≤ 2
Reflective Constructs	Indicator loadings					
	Item 1	Item 2	Item 3	Item 4	AVE	ICR
Value (Va)	0.901***	0.881***	0.951***	0.564***	0.702	0.901
Satisfaction (Sa)	0.893***	0.962***	0.929***		0.862	0.949
Continuance intention (CI)	0.911***	0.971***	0.933***		0.881	0.957

Notes: * = $p < 0.05$; ** = $p < 0.01$; *** = $p < 0.001$.

4.2 Structural Model

Table 2 shows the path coefficients of the structural model and their significances.

Table 2. Path coefficients

Hypothesis	Path	Path Coefficient	T-Value	P-Value
H1	Sa->CI	0.747	4.739	0.000
H2	Va->Sa	0.388	3.145	0.001
H3	Va->CI	0.119	0.843	0.200
H4	IS->Va	0.137	0.846	0.199
H5	IS->Sa	−0.023	0.180	0.429
H6	NE->Va	0.243	1.424	0.077
H7	NE->Sa	0.019	0.139	0.445
H8	SI->Va	0.480	2.289	0.011
H9	SI->Sa	0.570	3.186	0.001

There is no indication of collinearity between any two constructs based on VIF scores. The highest score is 2.522, well below the recommended upper limit of 5 [11]. Path coefficients relating to hypotheses H1, H2, H8, and H9 are strong and highly significant. This confirms the related hypotheses. The coefficient of the path from network effects to value is only significant at $p \leq 0.1$. However, the impact of network effects on value perception is confirmed by the f^2 statistic (0.075) that shows that the effect size of this construct lies between small (0.02) and medium (0.15) [20]. This means that it should not be omitted from the model. R^2 values of perceived value, service satisfaction, and intention to continue are 0.512, 0.783, and 0.710 respectively. They indicate a moderate or even substantial determination of these constructs by the exogenous constructs linked to them [11].

In the sample of developed countries, the coefficients of the paths IS->Va and NE->Sa are also significant and the path NE->Va has a significance of p ≤ 0.05. This is probably due to the higher sample size (n = 95). It is of interest whether the strengths of influence of variables (i.e., the values of path coefficients) differ significantly between the two subsamples. The multi-group analysis in PLS reveals that this is only the case for the path from SI to CI (via Sa) in such a way that the influence is stronger for companies from less developed countries. The same type of test for items shows that only the item *Equipment to ISP* is more important to customers from less developed countries than for their peers from developed countries.

5 Discussion

The model confirms observations from service science that continuance intention is strongly influenced by the overall satisfaction with the service. Value perception of the service influences satisfaction. It does not influence continuance intention directly but only indirectly through service satisfaction.

Perhaps surprising, the support for the set-up of the service and daily operations, labeled infrastructure here, do not have an influence on either value perception or service satisfaction. However, as discussed with experts from the IXP and other companies, it does not mean that they do not matter. It is probably as with most utilities, people expect them to function; one notices them only when there is a problem. In other words, this can be a source of dissatisfaction but not satisfaction, a hygiene factor in terms of [21].

Network effects have a slightly significant impact on value perception but not on service satisfaction. This makes sense since the bigger the population for peering the more cost can be saved by using the specific IXP. The indicator relating to the size of the population has the highest weight in forming the construct network effects.

The strongest and highly significant influence is exerted on value perception and service satisfaction by indicators forming security of investment, as we labeled this latent variable. We labeled it this way, because the connection at an IXP involves organizational and financial investment. While the financial amount may not be very big, the organizational and contractual involvement may be significant, especially if private peering arrangements exist. Therefore, customers will not like to change the relationship too often. Among the indicators, future importance of the IXP plays the most important role. The customers know that Internet traffic is growing and that their needs will probably grow. Therefore, they obviously want to use an IXP, which will be able to meet these needs. This creates an incentive, if not an imperative, for the IXP to grow. This can be accomplished in various ways as can be observed in practice: by creating or renting more data center space, by building "children" exchange points close to the customers, or by attracting more Internet transit carriers to the IXP. The growth enables an IXP in the same time to enjoy further economies of scale. The independence of an

IXP (from state institutions) and the legal and political stability in the country in which the IXP operates also play a role. While the same construct and indicators are also important for customers in developed countries, they are significantly more important for customers in less developed countries. The influence on satisfaction is even stronger than the one from value perception. The higher concern of companies in less developed countries for getting equipment to the IXP is obvious.

Our research shows that service providers in developed (high-salary) countries can be very competitive by offering highly automated high-skilled services, especially when they operate in a stable and trustworthy environment.

Appendix: Constructs and Items (Abbreviated)

The text of all items except SI 2 referred to the specific IXP. Reversed items are in cursive letters. The relationship between constructs and items (formative or reflective) is given in parentheses.

IS: Infrastructure (formative)

1. Easy to transport data to
2. Easy to transfer equipment to
3. Operates well
4. Easy to contact

NE: Network effects (formative)

1. Private peering support
2. Public peering support
3. Size of overall exchange population
4. Size of regional exchange population

SI: Security of investment (formative)

1. Future importance
2. Legal and political stability of location
3. Neutrality with respect to other firms
4. Independence from other institutions

Sa: Satisfaction (reflective)

1. Overall happy with service
2. Meets our expectations
3. Choice was right

Va: Value (reflective)

1. Provides best value
2. Reasonable price for quality
3. Better service at competitive price
4. *Lower quality for price*

CI: Continuance intention (reflective)

1. *Want to discontinue service*
2. Likely to continue using service
3. Expect to continue using service

References

1. Friedman, T.: The world is flat: a brief history of the twenty-first century. Farrar, Straus and Girou, New York (2005)
2. Oshri, I., Kotlarsky, J., Willcocks, L.P.: The attractiveness of western countries for outsourcing services and backsourcing. In: The Handbook of Global Outsourcing and Offshoring, Chap. 4, 3rd edn., pp. 105–128 (2015)
3. Norton, WB.: The Internet Peering Playbook: Connecting to the Core of the Internet. DrPeering Press (2014)
4. Bhattacheryee, A.: Understanding information systems continuance: an expectation-confirmation model. MIS Q. **25**(3), 351–370 (2001)
5. Patterson, P.G., Spreng, R.A.: Modeling the relationship between perceived value, satisfaction and repurchase intentions in a business-to-business, services context: an empirical examination. Int. J. Serv. Ind. Manag. **8**(5), 414–434 (1997)
6. Yang, Z., Peterson, R.T.: Customer perceived value, satisfaction, and loyalty: the role of switching costs. Psychol. Mark. **21**(10), 799–822 (2014)
7. Van Beijnum, I.: BGP: Building reliable networks with the Border Gateway Protocol. O'Reilly & Associates, Inc., Sebastopol (2002)
8. Chin, W.W., Marcolin, B.L., Newsted, P.R.: A partial least squares latent variable modeling approach for measuring interaction effects: results from a monte carlo simulation study and an electronic-mail emotion/adoption study. Inf. Syst. Res. **14**(2), 189–217 (2003)
9. Reinartz, W., Haenlein, M., Henseler, J.: An Empirical Comparison of the Efficacy of Covariance-Based and Variance-Based SEM. Int. J. Res. Mark. **26**(4), 332–344 (2009)
10. Streukens, S., Wetzels, M., Daryanto, A., et al.: Analyzing factorial data using PLS. In: Esposito Vinzi, V., Chin W.W., Henseler, J., Wang, H. (eds.) Handbook of Partial Least Squares. Springer Handbooks of Computational Statistics, pp. 567–587. Springer, Berlin (2010)
11. Hair Jr., J.F., Hult, G.T.M., Ringle, C.M., Sarstedt, M.: A Primer on Partial Least Squares Structural Equation Modeling (PLS-SEM). SAGE, Los Angeles et al. (2014)
12. Chin, W.W.: The partial least squares approach to structural equation modeling. In: Marcoulides, G.A. (ed.) Modern Methods for Business Research, pp. 295–358. Lawrence Erlbaum Associates, Mahwah (1998)
13. Diamantopoulos, A., Winklhofer, H.M.: Index construction with formative indicators: an alternative to scale development. J. Mark. Res. **38**(2), 269–277 (2001)
14. Tenenhaus, M., Vinzi, V.E., Chatelin, Y-.M., et al.: PLS path modeling. Comput. Stat. Data Anal. **48**(1), 159–205 (2005)
15. Cenfetelli, RT., Bassellier, G.: Interpretation of formative measurement in information systems research. MIS Q. **33**(4), 689–707 (2009)
16. Henseler, J., Fassott, G.: Testing moderating effects in PLS path models: an illustration of available procedures. In: Esposito Vinzi, V., Chin, W.W., Henseler, J., Wang, H. (eds.) Handbook of Partial Least Squares. Springer Handbooks of Computational Statistics, pp. 713–735. Springer, Berlin (2010)

17. Fornell, C., Larcker, D.F.: Evaluating structural equation models with unobservable variables and measurement error. J. Mark. Res. Am. Mark. Assoc. **18**(1), 39–50 (1981)
18. Nunnally, J.C., Bernstein, I.H.: Psychometric Theory. McGraw-Hill Series in Psychology, 3rd edn. McGraw-Hill, New York (1994)
19. Götz, O., Liehr-Gobbers, K., Krafft, M.: Evaluation of structural equation models using the partial least squares (PLS) approach. In: Esposito Vinzi, V., Chin, W.W., Henseler, J., Wang, H. (eds.) Handbook of Partial Least Squares. Springer Handbooks of Computational Statistics, pp. 691–711. Springer, Heidelberg (2010)
20. Cohen, J.: Statistical Power Analysis for the Behavioral Sciences. Lawrence Erlbaum, Mahwah (1992)
21. Herzberg, F., Mausner, B., Snyderman, B.B.: The Motivation to Work, 2nd edn. John Wiley, New York (1959)

Contract Renewal Decisions in IT-Outsourcing: A Survey in the Netherlands

Erik Beulen[✉]

TIAS School for Business and Society, Warandelaan 2
PO Box 90153, 5000 LE Tilburg, The Netherlands
e.beulen@tias.edu

Abstract. Increasingly, outsourcing companies decline to renew their contracts automatically at the end of their duration [1, 2]. Furthermore, only a very few contracts are renewed in sole-source contract negotiations. Switching IT outsourcing suppliers is becoming more common [3]. Organizations send out Requests for Proposal instead and may select a new provider for their Information Technology (IT) services. The costs of selection and knowledge transfer processes, switching costs, are substantial [4–6]. Service delivery continuity is also under pressure when a transfer to a new provider is made [8, 9]. What are the considerations in contract renewal decisions for IT services? The findings presented will be useful for client companies facing contract renewal decisions. In the current, increasingly mature outsourcing market, qualitative factors are considered most important in deciding contract renewal versus switching suppliers, as outsourcing companies are now well capable of negotiating a market-conform price [10]. In this research project, we focus on qualitative as well as financial factors related to switching suppliers. Furthermore, termination provisions in contracts are important. How can service delivery continuity be assured while switching your supplier? This results in a framework for contract renewal decision making in IT outsourcing containing motives, switching costs, risks and contract good practices.

This research presents the findings of a survey on contract renewal decisions in IT outsourcing. Dutch-based customer organizations participated in this research project. The data for this research is collected via survey.

Keywords: Contract renewal · Exit management · IT outsourcing · Switching costs and transition

1 Introduction

In addition to IT service provisioning by internal IT departments, outsourcing is also an option. For decades, the IT outsourcing market has been growing; according to Gartner, the global market is 3.8 trillion US dollars, which is a 2.4 % increase from 2014 [11]. Contract renewal percentage has dropped significantly [1, 2, 7]. When switching suppliers, service continuity is at risk, and clients face additional costs: switching costs. These are both substantial [12–14]. Alternatively, the existing contact is renewed under improved conditions. Client companies have to explore both options. However, it is essential for client companies to understand IT outsourcing contract renewal decisions better in the operational and contractual context of IT outsourcing partnerships.

Outsourcing contracts must include exit clauses, but a plan for an exit *strategy* is also recommended [15: seventh deadly sin and 16: element 9]. In exit clauses, mutual obligations for contract termination are detailed. Contract termination can occur at the end of the contract term or prior to the contract term, due to, for example, poor performance [17–19], as well as termination for convenience [20]. The obligations for the incumbent supplier are predominantly in supporting the new supplier to perform the service. The handover of responsibility to perform the services to the new supplier requires "double staff." The client organization must also set up project organization. The new supplier will manage this transition project, which typically take two to three months [10, 21]. The transition project is followed by a stabilization period. After the stabilization period, the new service provider is responsible for providing the services according to the agreed service levels [9].

The incumbent supplier's exit management consists of knowledge transfer and potentially asset and staff transfer [22]. In contracts, intellectual property rights [23], not limited to a source code escrow account [24], require special attention, as this is important to ensure service continuity and avoid costs. The obligations for client organizations are predominantly related to the charges during the exit. These costs should not be underestimated [25]. Typically, the incumbent supplier is allowed to charge the additional effort required for supporting the supplier switch. The categories of additional effort and a rate card are detailed in the contract.

In addition to the terms and conditions related to exit, the reputation of the incumbent supplier might support exit management [14]. The network serves as a reputation system [8]. Relational governance, as defined by [26], also contributes to a proper handover to the new supplier. Incumbent suppliers have to fully support handing over IT services to a new supplier to avoid jeopardizing future work at the client company. However, most

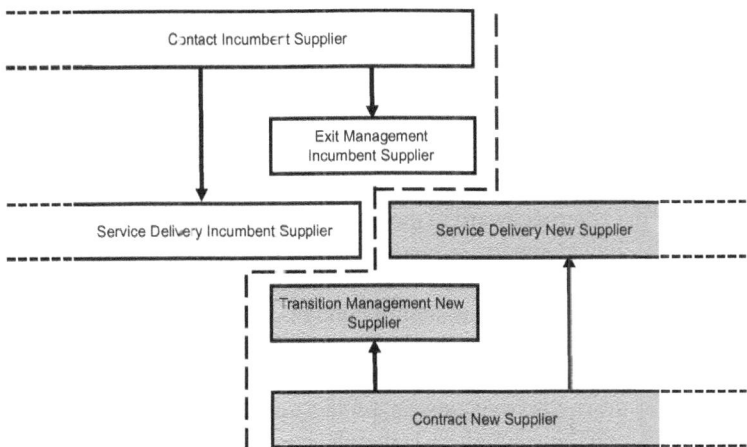

Fig. 1. Contractual and operational responsibilities in switching suppliers in IT outsourcing partnerships.

client organizations face high staff rotation. Therefore, a painful exit experience with a supplier has less impact on the chances of winning future work at the incumbent supplier. However, if an incumbent supplier chooses a hostile strategy of being uncooperative, the service continuity is in jeopardy and additional costs are to be expected [27] (Fig. 1).

2 Framework for Contract Renewal Decision Making in IT Outsourcing

Client organizations that are about to make contract renewal decisions need to re-align with their objectives first. At the start of the IT outsourcing partnership, objectives were set, which might have been adjusted over time. Is the current partnership still meeting the client company's objectives? Is there room for improvement? Are there alternative suppliers that might offer better service at a lower price? Client companies need to document their motives for switching suppliers. Typical drivers include lower costs and insufficient quality of service [1, 5, 7, 14]. The decision to switch suppliers can also be based on the limitations of the incumbent supplier to fulfill future requirements [28]. Examples are suppliers with immature cloud service offerings or limited mobile solutions capabilities. Furthermore, a deteriorating reputation of the incumbent supplier might tip the balance in contract renewal decisions [13, 29, 30]. The option of transferring IT services to a running contract with another incumbent supplier also might have an impact. IT service provisioning can be managed as a portfolio of contracts [31]. Client companies such as Shell have implement supplier ecosystems and manage the share of wallet of their key suppliers with dedication [32].

The costs of switching are important. Switching costs are the combination of the costs for exit management by the incumbent supplier and the costs of the transition by the new supplier. Additionally, the internal costs to support the incumbent supplier and the new supplier should not be overlooked. The costs of switching suppliers are substantial and range from 2 to 15 % of the total cost of the first year of the outsourcing deal [33]. These additional costs have no direct business benefit and have to be offset against improved services or lower operational costs for the service provisioning by the new supplier.

Client companies have to not only consider the costs of switching, but the risks related to switching as well [4, 7, 19, 21]. The biggest risk is the disruption of the service provisioning [1, 7, 9]. The disruption of service provisioning can start from the announcement of the contract award to the new supplier. The incumbent supplier might roll off their best technical experts in favor of other clients. This risk also applies to the exit management and transition period. Managing three-way contractual commitments, the incumbent supplier, and the new supplier and client organization is not straightforward [4, 13]. Finally, due to poor transition, service continuity can be in jeopardy after transition sign off. Over two-thirds of failed outsourcing relationships arise due to poor transitions [34]. Contractual provisions can protect client companies against these risks.

Another risk of switching suppliers is that the envisioned reduction in Total Cost of Ownership for the IT service provisioning will not be met. The predictability of costs is a general outsourcing risk [35–37]. This risk is predominantly related to the contract with the new supplier and not necessary the switching of suppliers per se; however, it obviously impacts the contract renewal decision. In the slipstream of the TCO for the service provisioning, there is also the risk of higher exit management costs and/or transition costs. These costs are sometimes overlooked during contract negotiations [7, 2011a, p. 45] and are difficult to manage [38].

During exit management, the risk of insufficient cooperation from the incumbent supplier might occur as well [5, 6. 39] Not only contractual provisions protect the client company for this risk, relational governance can mitigate this risk as well [25]. It is essential the incumbent supplier maintenance a transfer file of the term of the contract. The transfer file contains not only application and system management documentation but also processes, procedures and other knowledge documents, such as frequently asked questions databases and training material to onboard technical experts [9]. Having an exit plan in place is also helpful in mitigating this risk [4].

The impact of an extended transition deadline can be caused by issues in the knowledge transfer from the incumbent supplier to the new supplier or due to unexpected technical issues [7]. In the contract, the financial risk can be transferred fully to the new supplier. The agreed resource unit price for the services and service levels kick in after the end of the contracted stabilization phase. Transition struggles after this date will not impact the client company.

Table 1. Factors in the framework for contract renewal decision making in IT-outsourcing.

1. Motives for switching suppliers	1.1 Reduction Total Cost of Ownership IT service provisioning
	1.2 Poor performance
	1.3 The limitations of the incumbent supplier to fulfill future requirements
	1.4 A deteriorating reputation of incumbent supplier
	1.5 Transferring the IT services to a running contract with other incumbent suppliers
2. Costs of switching suppliers	
3. Risks of switching suppliers	3.1 Discontinuity of the service provision after contract award but prior to the transition
	3.2 Discontinuity of the service provision during the transition
	3.3 Discontinuity of the service provision after the transition
	3.4 Not meeting the envisioned reduction of the Total Cost of Ownership for the IT service provisioning
	3.5 Higher exit management costs and/or transition costs
	3.6 Insufficient cooperation from the incumbent supplier
	3.7 Longer transition timeline due to knowledge transfer issues
	3.8 Longer transition timeline due to unexpected technical issues

Finally, it is important to acknowledge the contracts with the incumbent supplier and the new supplier impact contract renewal decision making in IT outsourcing and the associated risks. The contracts detail the obligations of both the suppliers and the client organization. Contracts impact the costs and risks of switching. IT outsourcing contracts have to contain provisions for exiting [14, 15]. The contract renewal decision will be implemented through exit management by the incumbent supplier and by performance of the transition by the new supplier. The obligations are detailed in the contracts (Table 1).

3 Research Question

The research question in this explorative research is: what impacts contract renewal decisions in IT outsourcing? Here, the motives for switching suppliers, the switching costs and risks are investigated. In addition, an inventory of good contracting practices related to exit management is included. Finally, satisfaction with the contract renewal has been investigated (Fig. 2).

a. What are motives for switching suppliers?
b. What are the switching costs?
c. What are the switching risks?
d. What are good contracting practices related to exit management?
e. What factors contribute to contract renewal satisfaction?

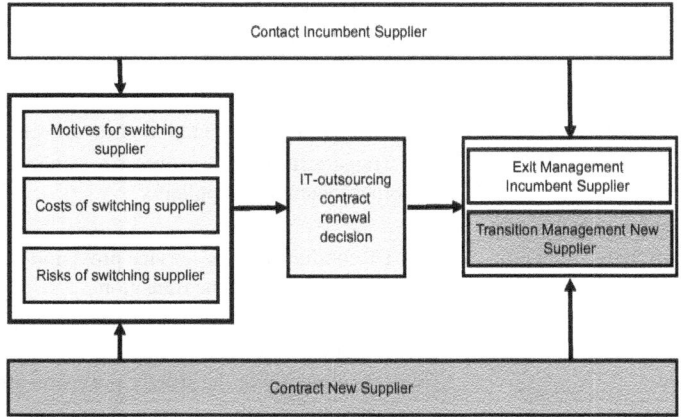

Fig. 2. Framework for contract renewal decision making in IT outsourcing

4 Research Method

The data for this research is collected by a survey. The survey was submitted to ICT Media[1] a Dutch organization that facilities IT decision makers in the Netherlands. The members of this community are Chief Information Officers and their direct reports. The response rate was 2 % (69 responses to 3,500 invitations). The survey was an anonymous survey; therefore, it is not possible to conclude the representativeness of the sample (69 responses versus total community of 3,500 members). However, the spread over the different sectors and spread of the size of the organizations the respondents represent do not indicate that the respondents are not representative for the community, which was also confirmed by ICT Media.

The survey was conducted in Dutch. The participants completed their response via a portal. The responses were collected from 4 and 8 October 2015. The potential participants received one friendly reminder the first week the survey was introduced.

The survey results will be used to perform analyses to better understand what impacts contract renewal decisions in IT outsourcing. The analyses will be structured according to the explorative questions related to the research questions.

Motives for Switching Suppliers. We expected the motives for switching suppliers to focus on the more obvious reasons for change, such as reduction of Total Cost of Ownership and poor performance. For the plus four generation of organizations, however, there is a higher valuation. We expected to see a higher valuation for the third

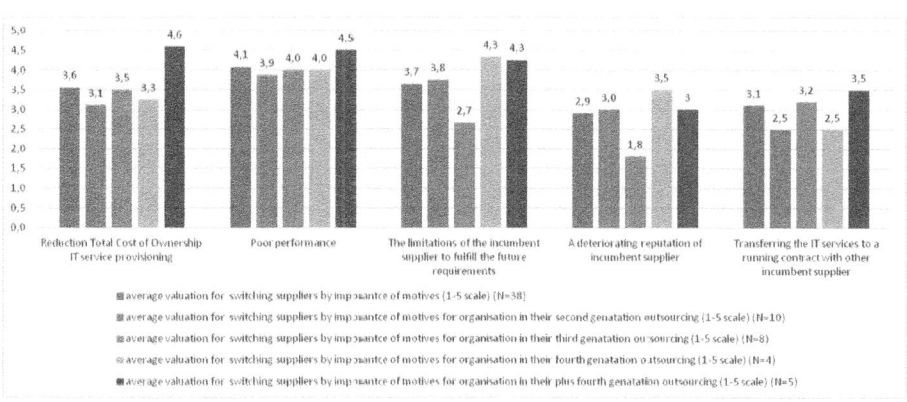

Fig. 3. Average valuation of motives for switching supplier by outsourcing generation.

---

[1] The mission of ICT Media is to facilitate Dutch IT decision makers. The community of ICT media consists of Chief Information Officers and their direct reports. The community is supported by a knowledge portal and business magazines. ICT Media also regularly facilitates round tables. ICT Media has an active community that represents the Chief Information Officers' community in the Netherlands.

and fourth generation outsourcing partnerships, as well. In general, an incumbent supplier's deteriorating reputation is not the most important motive for switching suppliers. Neither is transferring IT services to a running contract with another supplier (Fig. 3).

Switching Costs. In the survey, switching costs are addressed as a percentage of the expected costs of the first contract year. Only respondents 23 and 51 failed to provide those switching costs. The average switching costs are remarkable (N = 29):

a. 35 % of respondents report less than 5 % as their switching costs.
b. Nearly 30 % of respondents report 20 % or more as their switching costs (Fig. 4).

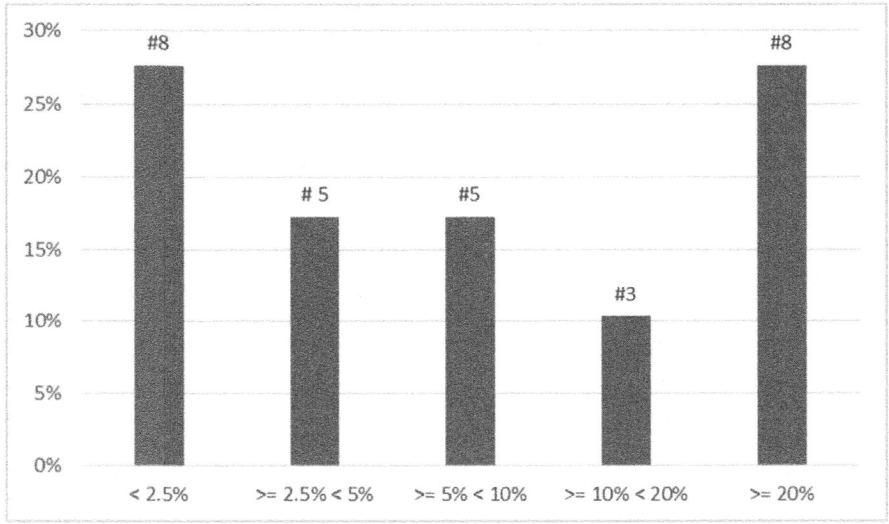

Fig. 4. Number of organizations by average switching costs as percentage of first contract year (N = 29).

We hypothesized the percentage switching costs for the network is high due to required site-specific transitions. To illustrate the spread, the low range (<5 %) and the high end (>=20 %) are isolated. The research data, however, indicate differently: only in the low range are organizations with network services lower than the average for all organizations. The difference for the high end is relatively small (Fig. 5).

We also expect the percentage switching costs for cloud services is low due to the standardized service provisioning. To illustrate the spread, the low range (<5 %) and the highend (>=20 %) are isolated. The research data again indicates differently. The difference for the high end is actually opposite of our expectation. The percentage switching costs for organizations with cloud services are significantly higher (Fig. 6).

Contract Renewal Decisions in IT-Outsourcing 185

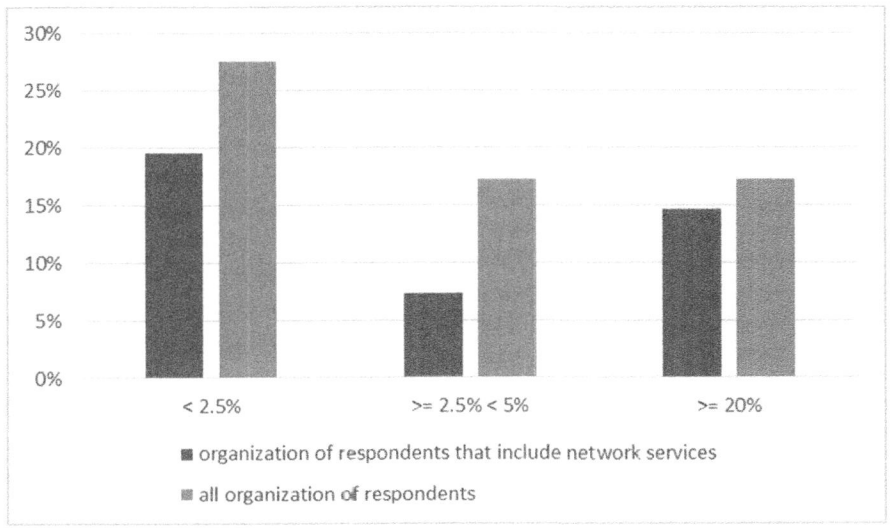

Fig. 5. Number of organizations by average switching costs as percentage of first contract year: only organizations of respondents with network services (N = 17 for organization with network and N = 29 for all organizations).

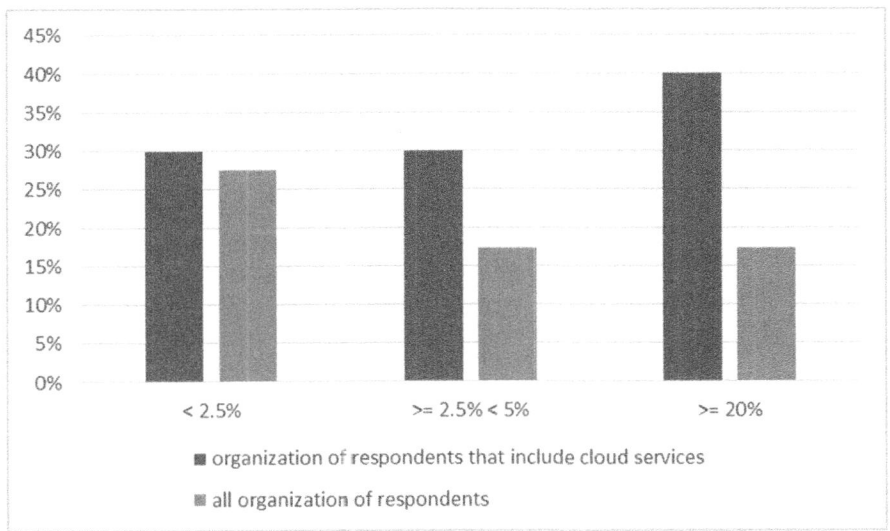

Fig. 6. Number of organization by average switching costs as percentage of first contract year: only organizations of respondents with cloud services (N = 10 for organization with cloud services and N = 29 for all organizations).

Switching Risks. The research data show that most organizations are not very concerned about additional exit management and/or transition costs nor about extended timelines of the transition. Remarkable are the relatively high scores of organizations with plus four generations of outsourcing experience. We expected their experience would strengthen their capabilities to mitigate switching risks (Fig. 7).

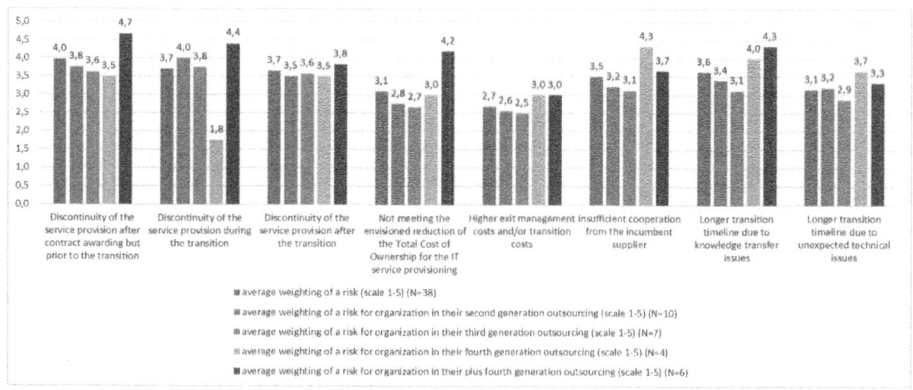

Fig. 7. Average weighted risk for organizations per generation.

Good Contracting Practices. The research data related to good contracting practices and their weighting provide insights into what is important to existing companies. The two most important lessons learned are to improve the contractual conditions with both the incumbent supplier (exit management) and the new supplier (transition). Remarkably, there is, over time, less concern about the duration of the transition period, the quality of the transfer file, and the availability of client organization staff to support the transition (Fig. 8).

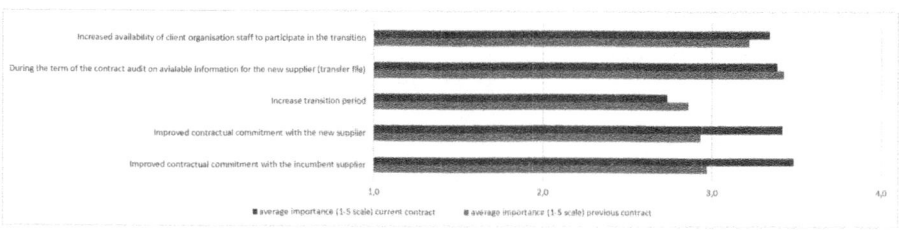

Fig. 8. Importance of good contracting practices.

Contract Renewal Satisfaction. In the survey, contract renewal satisfaction is addressed. From the total of 69 completed surveys, there are 31 respondents representing client organizations that have switched suppliers. The average satisfaction with this decision was remarkably high: 3.4 on a 1–5 scale, with a mode of 4 on a 1–5 scale. This indicates respondents are generally not unsatisfied with the outcome of the decision to switch suppliers. However, experience might be important in successful switching suppliers and thus affect the results. This pattern does not materialize in the data, however (Fig. 9).

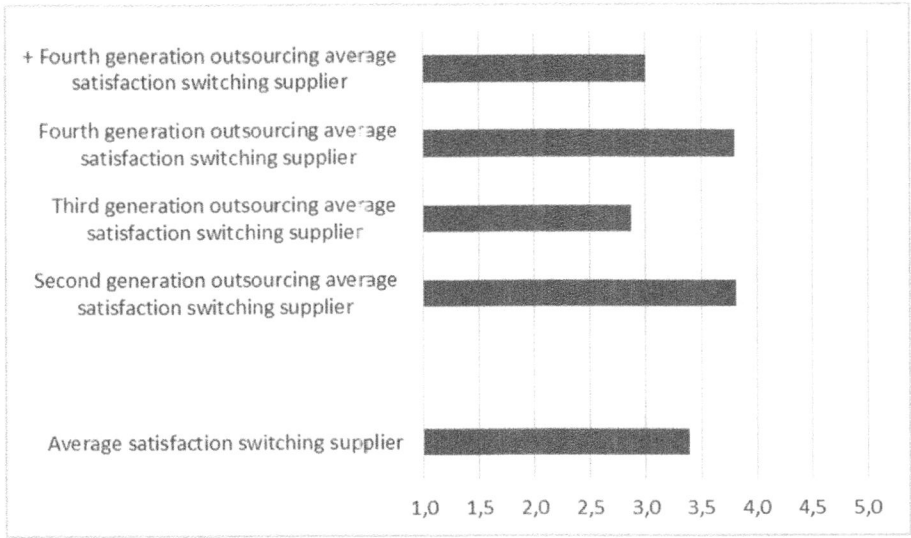

Fig. 9. Outsourcing satisfaction switching suppliers – average and by generation (N = 31).

There are six respondents with a satisfaction score of two and one with a satisfaction score of one. The following characteristics are used to explore potential explanations for a low outsourcing satisfaction rating in switching suppliers:

a. Percent revenue in the Netherlands: the expectation is that a low satisfaction score potentially can be explained by the additional complexity of global IT outsourcing contracts (low % revenue in the Netherlands)
b. Percent of outsourcing: the expectation is that low satisfaction potentially can be explained by the additional complexity of full outsourcing partnerships (high % outsourcing)
c. Size of the outsourcing contract: the expectation is that low satisfaction potentially can be explained by the additional complexity of large outsourcing partnerships (>10 m Euro TCV) note: respondents 19 and 20 did not indicate the size of the outsourcing contract

There are fourteen respondents with a satisfaction score of four and three with a satisfaction score of five. The following characteristics are used to explore potential explanations for a high outsourcing satisfaction score in switching suppliers:

a. Percent revenue in the Netherlands: the expectation is that high satisfaction potentially can be explained by the limited complexity of national IT outsourcing contracts (high % revenue in the Netherlands)
b. Percent of outsourcing: the expectation is that high satisfaction potentially can be explained by the limited scope of outsourcing partnerships (low % outsourcing) note: responded 25 did not indicate the percent of outsourcing

c. Size of the outsourcing contract: the expectation is that high satisfaction potentially can be explained by the limited complexity of the outsourcing partnerships (<=10 m Euro TCV) note: respondent 20 did not indicate the size of the outsourcing contract

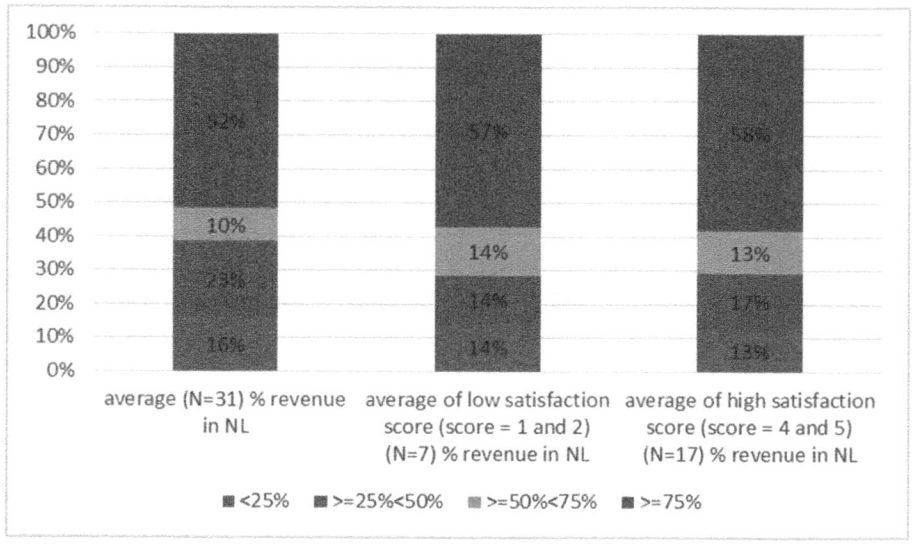

Fig. 10. Difference in percent revenue in the Netherlands to explore potential explanations for outsourcing satisfaction in switching suppliers.

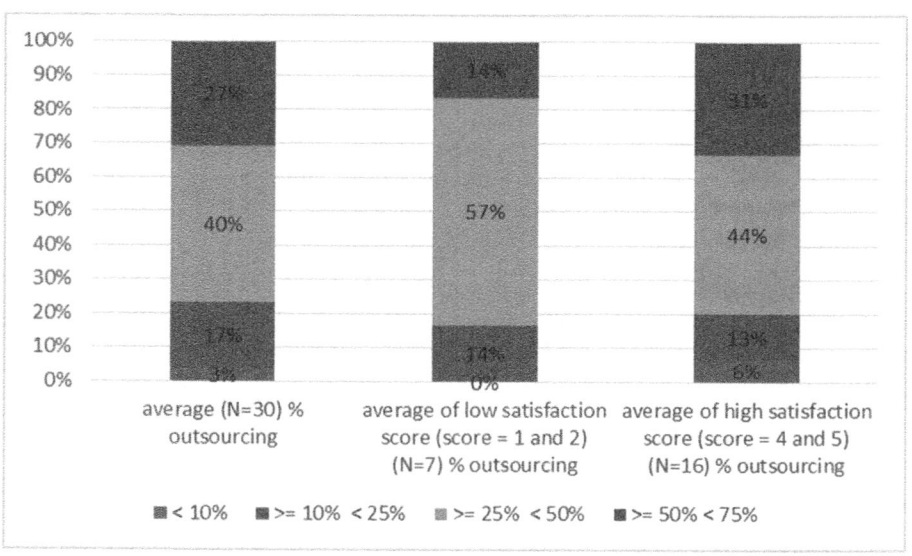

Fig. 11. Difference in percent outsourcing to explore potential explanations for outsourcing satisfaction in switching suppliers.

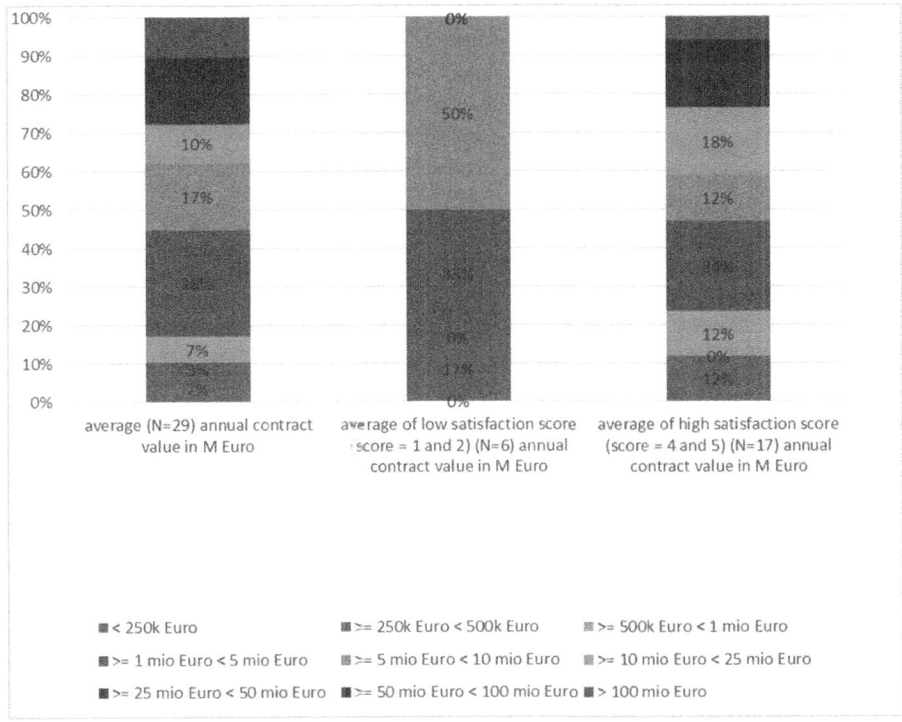

Fig. 12. Difference in the size of the outsourcing contract to explore potential explanations for outsourcing satisfaction in switching suppliers.

The above characteristics are detailed in the Figs. 10, 11 and 12 below.

Differences in the profile of high and low satisfaction scores is non-existing for the percent revenue in the Netherlands. The difference between the average profile and the high and low satisfaction profiles is fails to provide additional insight.

Differences in the profile of high and low satisfaction scores are not in line with the expectation that there is higher satisfaction for organizations with a low percentage of outsourcing. This is similar to the difference between the average profile and the high and low satisfaction profiles. We also expected that organizations with a low percentage between the low satisfaction and the high satisfaction.

Remarkably, there are high satisfaction scores for large deals: +10 m Euro TCV. The maturity of the organization might be an explanation for these unexpectedly high satisfaction scores. There may be other explanatory factors that are not taken into account in this survey.

5 Limitations

The survey does not include the transition plan of either the new supplier or the in-house IT department. This transition plan impacts the exit management of the incumbent. In the transition plan, the required involvement of the incumbent supplier is detailed. A transition plan potentially reduces the switching costs and the risk, although the new supplier or the in-house IT department are unknown at the time of the contract renewal decision. Including the transition plan in future research on contract renewal decisions might provide additional insights in exit management.

Due to the nature of any survey, it is very difficult to understand the terms and conditions of IT outsourcing contracts. To better understand the impact, more qualitative research might be required, such as case studies or expert interviews.

Finally, this research is conducted in the Netherland only and includes a low number of participants: 69 respondents. A larger and more international survey would mitigate these concerns. The supplier perspective of exit management also is missing in this study. Suppliers might be able to add additional insights in exit management.

6 Conclusions

The most remarkable conclusion from this research is the relatively high satisfaction with the contract renewal decision. This is different from the literature, which highlighted risks and exceeding transition budgets. However, the research data did not confirm the expectation that experience reduces the risks of switching suppliers. Not surprisingly, the contracts are the most important factor in mitigating risks and avoiding additional costs. The impact of the supplier's reputation and relational contracting are not acknowledged. The commoditization of IT services and the growing maturity in switching suppliers might reduce the impact of these soft mitigations.

The reduction of TCO for IT service provisioning and poor quality of service are confirmed as the most important motives for switching suppliers. The need for new technologies is not the most important motive for switching suppliers. Either the capabilities of most incumbent suppliers are at a sufficient level or the appetite for outsourcing new technologies is not strong.

The reported costs of switching suppliers of less than 5 % of the first contract year have to be questioned. The respondents might not have sufficient overview of all the costs related to switching suppliers, as a 5 % cost implies only 2.6 weeks of "double costs." Another explanation might be that in some outsourcing contracts, the transition costs are either absorbed or included in the monthly run costs.

Acknowledgements. The author would like to thank Rob Beijleveld, Diego Nendissa and Arnoud van Gemeren from ICT Media (www.ictmedia.nl) for inviting the members of the ICT Media community to participate in the survey and for facilitating the execution of the survey.

References

1. Whitten, D., Chakrabarty, S., Wakefield, R.: The strategic choice to continue outsourcing, switching vendors, or backsource: do switching costs matter? Inf. Manage. **47**, 167–175 (2010)

2. ISG, market research report, The ISG Outsourcing Index, second quarter and first half, 16 July 2015
3. Kien, S., Wee Kiat, L., Periasamy, K.: Switching IT outsourcing suppliers. MIS Q. Executive **9**, 23–33 (2010)
4. van Deventer, S., Harminder, S.: The impact of switching costs on the decision to retain or replace IT outsourcing vendors. In: Proceedings of the 23rd Australasian Conference on Information Systems, ACIS 2012 (2012)
5. Olzmann, M., Wynn, M.G.: How to switch IT service providers: recommendations for a successful transition. Int. J. Adv. Intell. Syst. **5**(1 & 2), 209–219 (2012)
6. Shi, W.: Entry and exit of service providers under cost uncertainty: a real options approach. J. Oper. Res. Soc. **67**(2), 229–239 (2015)
7. Beulen, E.: Contract renewal decisions in IT outsourcing: "Should I stay or should I go". J. Inf. Technol. Manage. **22**(4), 47–55 (2011)
8. Ravindran, K., et al.: Social capital and contract duration in buyer-supplier networks for information technology outsourcing. Inf. Syst. Res. **26**(2), 379–397 (2015)
9. Beulen, E., Ribbers, P., Roos, J.: Managing IT Outsourcing, Governance in Global Partnership, 2nd edn. Routledge, Oxon (2011)
10. Beulen, E., Tiwari, V., van Heck, E.: Understanding transition performance during offshore IT outsourcing. Strateg. Outsourcing Int. J. **4**(3), 204–227 (2011)
11. Gartner, Research report (2015). http://www.gartner.com/newsroom/id/2959717
12. Earl, M.: The risks of outsourcing IT. Sloan Manage. Rev. **37**, 26–32 (1996)
13. Argyres, N., Mayer, K.J.: Contract design as a firm capability: an integration of learning and transaction cost perspectives. Acad. Manage. Rev. **32**(4), 1060–1077 (2007)
14. Goo, J., et al.: The role of service level agreements in relational management of information technology outsourcing: an empirical study. Mis Q. **33**(1), 119–145 (2009)
15. Barthelemy, J.: The hard and soft sides of IT management. Eur. Manage. J. **21**(5), 539–548 (2003)
16. Vitasek, K., Manrodt, K.: Vested outsourcing: a flexible framework for collaborative outsourcing. Strateg. Outsourcing Int. J. **5**(1), 4–14 (2012)
17. Alaghehband, F.K., et al.: An assessment of the use of transaction cost theory in information technology outsourcing. J. Strateg. Inf. Syst. **20**(2), 125–138 (2011)
18. Lacity, M.C., Hirschheim, R.: The information systems outsourcing bandwagon. Sloan Manage. Rev. **34**, 13 (2012)
19. Gorla, N., Somers, T.M.: The impact of IT outsourcing on information systems success. Inf. Manage. **51**(3), 320–335 (2014)
20. Gurbaxani, V.: Information systems outsourcing contracts: theory and evidence. In: Karmarkar, U., Apte, U. (eds.) Managing in the Information Economy: Current Research, pp. 83–115. Kluwer, New York (2007)
21. Heinzl, A., Dibbern, J., Hirschheim, R.A.: Information Systems Outsourcing: Enduring Themes: New Perspectives and Global Changes. Springer, Heidelberg (2006)
22. Susarla, A.: Contractual flexibility, rent seeking, and renegotiation design: an empirical analysis of information technology outsourcing contracts. Manage. Sci. **58**(7), 1388–1407 (2012)
23. Parikh, M.A., Gokhale, G.: Legal and tax considerations in outsourcing. In: Hirschheim, R., Heinzl, A., Dibbern, J. (eds.) Information Systems Outsourcing, pp. 137–160. Springer, Heidelberg (2006)
24. Buhl, H.U., Fridgen, G., König, C.: Using financial derivatives to hedge against market risks in IT outsourcing projects–a quantitative decision model. J. Decis. Syst. **22**(4), 249–264 (2013)

25. Chou, D., Chou, A.: Information systems outsourcing life cycle and risks analysis. Comput. Stand. Interfaces **31**(5), 1036–1043 (2009)
26. Poppo, L., Zenger, T.: Do formal contracts and relational governance function as substitutes or complements? Strateg. Manage. J. **23**(8), 707–725 (2002)
27. Chua, C.E.H. et al.: Threat-balancing in vendor transition. In: International Research Workshop on IT Project Management (2008)
28. Kern, T., Willcocks, L.: Exploring relationships in information technology outsourcing: the interaction approach. Eur. J. Inf. Syst. **11**(1), 3–19 (2002)
29. Lacity, M.C., Willcocks, L.P., Feeny, D.F.: Capability: a framework for decision-making. In: Information Management: the Organizational Dimension, p. 399 (1996)
30. Levina, N., Ross, J.W.: From the vendor's perspective: exploring the value proposition in information technology outsourcing. MIS Q. **27**(3), 331–364 (2003)
31. Ward, J.: Joe, P: Strategic Planning for Information Systems. Wiley, West Sussex (2002)
32. Looff de, L.: McKinsey Insights (2010). http://www.mckinsey.com/insights/business_technology/managing_it_transformation_on_a_global_scale_an_interview_with_shell_cio_alan_matula
33. Ambrose, C., Matlus, R.: Following best practices to manage transitions in outsourcing relationships, vol. 124899. Gartner research report (2005)
34. Robinson, M., Iannone, P.: 9 ways to avoid outsourcing failure, a three-part approach to maximizing the value of an IT outsourcing deal. CIO Magazine, 5 July 2007. http://www.cio.com.au/index.php/id;28653977;pp;1;fp;4;fpid;15
35. Ketler, K., Walstrom, J.: The outsourcing decision. Int. J. Inf. Manage. **13**(6), 449–459 (1993)
36. Klepper, R.: The management of partnering development in I/S outsourcing. J. Technol. **10**(4), 249–258 (1995)
37. Currie, W., Willcocks, L.: Analysing four types of IT-outsourcing decisions in the context of scale, client/server, interdependency and risk migration. Inf. Syst. J. **8**(2), 119–143 (1998)
38. Beulen, E., Tiwari, V., van Heck, E.: Understanding transition during offshore outsourcing: factor model of transition performance. In: Global Sourcing Workshop. Keystone, Colorado (2009)
39. Ariño, A., et al.: Contracts, negotiation, and learning: an examination of termination provisions. J. Manage. Stud. **51**(3), 379–405 (2014)

Exploring Choices of Software Sourcing Methods Among Start-Ups

Björn Johansson[✉], Blerta Deliallisi, and Pien Walraven

Department of Informatics, School of Economics and Management, Lund University,
Ole Römers väg 6, 22363 Lund, Sweden
bjorn.johansson@ics.lu, blerta.deliallisi@gmail.com,
pienwalraven@gmail.com

Abstract. In the paper we discuss the following research questions: How do start-ups provide themselves with software and what are the motivations behind deciding on a specific sourcing option? The questions are motivated from the fact that acquirement of software is a challenging question, and it is especially interesting to explore how start-ups do, since they do not have a legacy to deal with. The research was conducted as a mixed approach including a survey among start-ups followed by interviewing decision-makers in some start-ups. The research indicates that motivations for choosing a specific software application include ease of use, compatibility, reliability, flexibility, and previous familiarity. Right now, sourcing of paid software mostly occurs in a single license set-up, although interviewed start-ups showed to prefer Pay-Per-Use, as it is more flexible and because they feel more in control over how much money they spend. The start-ups said to consider free software options in case alternatives that fulfilled their requirements were available. In the cases where start-ups paid for software the motivation was either because there were no other options available, or they felt that this sourcing method secured support.

Keywords: Acquisition · SME · Start-ups · Software · Sourcing

1 Introduction

Software sourcing is a challenging task for many organizations. It is a challenge from different perspectives as many variables should be taken into consideration, for instance: which business processes the software should automate, how to integrate it with software that is already in use, deciding on tailor-made software or using standard packages, finding a balance between quality and cost, and so on. The focus in this research is twofold: Firstly it focuses on which software sourcing options are used mostly by start-ups, and secondly it looks into motivations behind selecting these sourcing options. Researching start-ups is especially interesting since they have a unique situation regarding flexibility when it comes to software sourcing. For instance, start-ups do not have to take a large existing system architecture into consideration since they are only in the beginning of their business development. For the same reason, start-ups often do not yet have strictly established business processes [1] and are therefore also more flexible in terms of how these processes could be automated. From this perspective it is especially interesting to explore how start-ups actually source software, which option do they select and why do they select just that or those specific option(s). For academics it would be interesting to research this since there is no prior research done on this topic specifically and for businesses it can be very useful in order to better meet needs of start-up companies when targeting this group with software packages. In line with this, the following questions are discussed in this research: How do start-ups source software and what are the reasons behind deciding on a specific sourcing option? Start-ups are in this study defined as companies that were founded at most five years ago. The motivations behind this definition will be discussed later in this paper.

The rest of the paper is organized in the following way: Next section presents what we already know about start-ups and software sourcing. Section 3 then presents how the research was done, followed by Sect. 4, that presents empirical data, which then is analyzed and discussed in Sect. 5. Finally some conclusions are presented and possible future research is discussed in Sect. 6.

2 What Do We Know About Start-Ups and Software Acquisition?

Start-ups have been researched from different view-points for a few decades already. For instance, studies have been done about market entry determinants [2] and strategy differences compared to larger companies [3]. Furthermore, Carter, Gartner and Reynolds [4] researched what needs to be done in order to begin a new business. They also investigated the amount of steps that are taken and the order in which start-ups take these steps. They found that entrepreneurs that succeeded in starting a business do undertake specific activities such as: *"making their businesses tangible to others, looking for facilities and equipment, searching for financial support, forming a legal entity, organizing teams, buying facilities and equipment, and devoting fulltime to the business"* [4].

Thus, according to Carter, Gartner and Reynolds [4], arranging facilities and equipment is an important aspect for start-ups. Nowadays, a crucial form of equipment for more or less every organization is supporting software in the form of computer based Information Systems (IS). Several researchers have covered this part of the field as well. For example, Thong [5] wrote about aspects that affect Information Systems adoption within small companies while Davila and Foster [6] studied the rate of adoption of management control systems in early start-ups. Nelson, Richmond and Seidmann [7] focused on software acquisition decisions in particular, whereas other recent studies [8] discuss on a 'make vs buy' acquisition model in SMEs (Small Medium Enterprises) or in-house software development characteristics of start-ups [9].

Another aspect that has evolved over time, and not only in start-ups, is the way that companies source their software. Apart from the traditional Single License model, Open Source software, Freeware and Shared License, several other types of software sourcing methods have become widely adopted, like Software as a Service (including Pay-Per-Use and Subscription Licensing models), and Entrepreneur Licenses. In addition because a lot of emerging start-ups tend to be tech related and given the technical expertise of the initial staff, in such circumstances more opportunities for in-house developed products would exist [8].

Computer based Information Systems, otherwise referred to as software applications or just software, offer more efficient and effective methods to execute business processes and sometimes even is a way of gaining competitive advantage in the market [10, 11]. While computing capacities continually grow and digital services become ubiquitous, they become more viable even for limited budgets companies such as start-ups [5, 8]. The results from the study by Knight and Cavusgil [12] that start-ups are more often born globally, meaning that they target an international market from the point they are founded, makes software even more important. For example, communicating and working remotely is facilitated by software in these cases. Thong, Yap and Raman [13] discuss that because of the budget limits some companies make trade-offs to choose lower cost software that maybe are not the best option for what they want to achieve.

While technology evolves, it unfolds new possibilities to facilitate existing services. However, not all start-ups survive in the harsh environment of competition [14]: Actually 60 % of newly founded companies fail in their first five years [9], thus a risk always coexists with undertaking business initiatives [9]. Therefore, it can be claimed that start-ups would carefully assess different options, and financially measure each step and acquisition decision, to initially adopt only what is necessary and focus on launching core products or services [15].

It can be claimed that the biggest challenge faced during software acquisition is to choose the option and the system that will increase the efficiency and target different organizational needs [7]. In the specific case of start-ups an emphasis is given to their lack of resources and dependency on third party software application [9].

Giardino, Unterkalmsteiner, Paternoster, Gorschek and Abrahamsson [9] state that, in relation to software sourcing, the biggest advantage of start-ups is their ability to embrace the newest technology without any constraint from previous employed systems and issues in switching systems or data migration. However some drawbacks are also observed as many software applications have specific product features and start-ups do not know yet what they are going to need later thus careful software evaluations are also needed [9].

Because of unclear demands when start-ups want to embrace software systems for daily usage they generally settle for general purpose software systems that they feel can accommodate their future needs and specifications [15].

Daneshgar, Low and Worasinchai [8] did a study on software acquisition and came up with a description of decision-making in the field based on the well-known decision making model by Simon [16]. Following their work, the process of software sourcing typically undergoes four phases: (i) intelligence, (ii) design, (iii) choice, and (iv) implementation. In the first phase the company scans the market and explores for alternatives, during the design phase the alternatives are identified and some criteria for the optimal option is set. The choice process is when the actual alternatives are assessed and a decision is reached, and then implementation of the software follows in the final step.

2.1 Software Sourcing Methods

As shortly described before, not much research has been done on software sourcing methods by start-ups. The most relevant to our topic in particular being by Nelson, Richmond and Seidmann [7], who developed a framework for software sourcing. In their model, they distinguish between in-house and outsourced software acquisition teams, as well as custom software and packaged software acquisition approaches. Their model is visible in Fig. 1.

		Acquisition team	
		Insource	Outsource
Acquisition approach	Custom	Internal resources only for needs analysis, coding, etc.	Vendor performs needs, analysis, coding, etc.
	Package	Internal resources only for package selection, installation, etc.	Vendor performs package selection, installation, etc.

Fig. 1. Software acquisition model [7]

In this model, companies can follow an acquisition approach of obtaining software package or customize the software, which means that they either choose whether to make their own software applications or to acquire them from third parties. The acquisition team can be insource or outsource, either internal implementation of custom software is done or internal selection of which third party software to select or an external vendor (outsource) is assigned the task of developing a custom software solution or to take over provision and installation of readily available software. With a package insource approach, the company buys the software and makes the decision around it itself. With a package outsource approach, the company buys software from a third party but asks for help to do this, for example from a consultant. The custom outsource approach means that the company buys software that is custom-made for them. The development is done by an external party in this case.

In analogy to the traditional make vs buy decision, the *make* option is the custom insource approach of software acquisition, where the used software is custom made by the company itself. The *buy* option is in the package approach, both insource and outsource, and in the custom outsource approach. Within the Package software acquisition approach, there are different kinds of software licenses that are used. The most traditional, well-known type of software licensing is a Single-User license, meaning that one user pays for the software and only that user can use it on his or her device. Additionally, several other types of licensing are used for software distribution, including Open Source software, Freeware, Shared License, Pay-Per-Use and Subscription. Open Source software is software where not only the software is free but the code is freely available to adapt as well [17]. In the case of Freeware the code itself is not available but the software is free to use [18]. Shared License refers to cases where a limited amount of users can make use of the same license to use the application [19]. With a Pay-Per-Use licensing model, the company pays for each time they use the software [20].

Subscriptions are characterized by the fact that companies pay a specific amount of money for a certain period generally for each subscriber that uses the application [21]. Finally, another important type of license is Entrepreneur Licenses, such as BizSpark by Microsoft ("Microsoft supports your startup as you grow", 2013), which are offered by some companies and provide usually paid-for software packages to start-ups for free. Although we are conscious that there are a lot of illegal software packages easily accessible, we did not include this in our study since piracy is considered an illegal activity. This point of view is similar to that of previous studies with a comparable subject [8].

2.2 Prior Related Research on Software Acquisition/Sourcing in SMEs and Start-Ups

Except for the study by Thong [5], as described in the previous section, there are a few other studies that focus on software acquisition, although not many of them focus on start-ups specifically. However, they do focus on small companies and are thus at least for that matter comparable to start-ups. This is the reason that the results of these researches could be relevant for the current study.

An example is the study by Harrison, Mykytyn Jr. and Riemenschneider [22], who studied business executives' decision to adopt Information Technology. They based their research on the Theory of Planned Behavior [23] and studied 162 small businesses (which had between 25 and 200 employees) in different industries. They also looked at a wide variety of IS systems, focusing at systems that provided the companies with a competitive advantage. Results showed that attitude towards IT adoption, subjective norms about adoption and perceived control over adoption influenced the decision on adopting IT.

An important downside of the studies by Thong [5] and Harrison, Mykytyn Jr. and Riemenschneider [22] is that both of them are quite old, and that more recent research is lacking in this field. This is problematic since IT has evolved a lot since the 90s and therefore the results of these studies might be outdated. There are however a few articles on software acquisition in start-ups that are fairly recent: Davila and Foster [6] write about the rate of adoption of management control systems (MCS) within start-up companies. They found that financial planning and financial evaluation systems are the first to be adopted by start-ups (50 % respectively, 77 % of the companies that they studied adopted these systems by the end of their fifth year), followed by Human Resource Planning, Human Resource Evaluation and Strategic Planning. Despite the fact that their main focus does not lie on the motivations behind software acquisition, they do make some comments related to this: for example, they write that in their interviews, they found *"descriptions of specific MCS adoption being associated with the hiring of a particular manager"* [6] and also that *"Early-stage companies adopting product development MCSs sometimes referred to the "requirements" of third parties [...] when explaining why specific MCSs were implemented"* [6]. Important to note about this research is that their definition of start-ups is different from ours: Their research sample included companies which were at most 10 years old and which were independent with in-between 50 and 150 employees. This means that a large part of these companies fall outside of our definition of start-ups.

Another research that is more recent is that of Daneshgar, Low and Worasinchai [8], who studied Small and Medium Enterprises and what factors influence the decision making in terms of software acquisition within these companies. Results showed that these factors include requirements fit, cost, scale and complexity, commoditization/flexibility, time, in-house experts, support structure, and operational factors.

For a better understanding of existing research related to software acquisition in start-up or SME organizations discussed above, we created Table 1, where we show an overview of the key aspects of each of the identified research.

Table 1. Prior research on software acquisition in SMEs and start-ups

Author	Researched companies	Focus of research	Core findings
Thong [5]	Small businesses (<100 employees, fixed assets below $7.2 million, sales below $9 million)	Contextual variables as determinants of IS adoption	Determinants of IS adoption are: Decision-maker characteristics IS characteristics Organizational characteristics Environmental characteristics
Harrison, Mykytyn Jr. and Riemenschneider [22]	Small businesses (between 25–200 employees)	Business executives' decision to adopt Information Technology	Factors that influence the decision on adopting IS are: Attitude towards IT adoption Subjective norms about adoption Perceived control over adoption
Davila and Foster [6]	Start-ups (between 50–150 employees, age less than 10 years, independent)	Rate of adoption of management control systems within start-up companies	Financial planning and financial evaluation systems are the first to be adopted by start-up companies, followed by Human Resource Planning, Human Resource Evaluation and Strategic Planning.
Daneshgar, Low and Worasinchai [8]	SMEs (not specified more detailed)	Factors that influence decision-making in terms of software acquisition	Factors that influence decision-making in terms of software acquisition are: Requirements fit Cost Scale and complexity Commoditization/flexibility Time In-house experts Support structure Operational factors.

3 Research Method

As technology advances, the competitive environment of start-ups becomes highly dynamic and unpredictable, thus creating a need for academic literature to be updated as well. Considering that IS usage is present in almost every company to some extent, and keeping in mind the limited budget and growing needs of start-ups, it would be of interest to understand how software acquisition is handled within start-ups. This can be done both in terms of what kinds of software they acquire (for what usage purposes are applications engaged) as well as what software acquisition methods are applied for it and why. As the methods and the motivation are applicable to start-ups in general, while kinds of software could be for example industry-specific, the field of interest for this study is how start-ups acquire their software, and why.

Several authors have written about start-ups, but only few have explicitly defined the term. Blank [24] in his definition of start-ups focuses on their yet unknown business model. However, most prior research (Archibald et al.; 2002, Burgel & Murray, 2000; Carter et al., 1996) does not define start-ups explicitly but seems to focus on the time of existence and/or the number of employees. However a more recent study by Giardino, Unterkalmsteiner, Paternoster, Gorschek and Abrahamsson [9] completes the notion of start-ups as not just newly founded small organizations, but additionally describes the companies to operate in an unexplored and highly unstable market and attempt to solve previously unsolved issues. Another characteristic of start-ups is their unpredictable future, sometimes taking high risks in their first moves but other times expanding quite quickly [9].

Although the uncertain environment referred by Giardino, Unterkalmsteiner, Paternoster, Gorschek and Abrahamsson [9] is used as the pivotal point to differentiate start-ups from any other newly founded company, it clearly makes some distinction based on the innovativeness introduced by start-ups products. If we were to choose our participant companies based on innovativeness or uncertain environments it could turn out to be very complex to measure and moreover we are not interested in getting to know software applications and their acquisition methods in such specific conditions. Therefore, we decided to base our definition and selection of start-ups on company age, and in this research define start-ups as companies that are aged at most 5 years.

The specific approach for this study is mixed methods in the form of that we first did a survey and then semi-structured follow-up interviews to answer our research questions.

Initially we compiled a list with contact information of start-ups in Sweden and Netherlands to be included in our research. These companies were taken from websites such as Ideon Innovation Center (Ideon, n.d.) and SiSP catalogue (SiSP, n.d.) and several websites with start-ups from the Netherlands, like Dutch Startupmap (DutchStartupmap. n.d.).

The survey was sent out as an online questionnaire to start-up organizations in Sweden and Netherlands via e-mail. It was sent to 450 companies from which 63 responded by filling the survey, thus scoring a 14 % response rate. Approximately one week time was provided to companies before collecting the data and beginning the analysis phase. Of the 63 responses, 50 were considered valid and analyzed further.

Our main purpose of the survey was to gain an overview on acquisition trends of how software systems were acquired.

After ensuring that our data were clean, it was analyzed by doing descriptive analytics using QlikView. Since it could perform all the needed descriptive statistics and also provide rich graphics to better visualize results, the choice was easy. In order to make an analysis in QlikView possible, we transformed the data by putting it in two separate main tables: a software table and a company table, linked by a key that was based on the company.

The final data structure that we used for the analysis in QlikView is visible in Fig. 2.

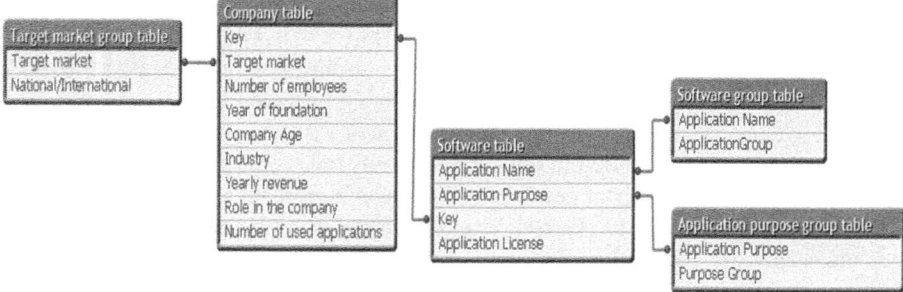

Fig. 2. Data structure used in QlikView

As priory stated our sample population was composed of start-ups that were at most 5 years old. Our final sample was on average 2.4 years old, with a median value of 2. An important metric to reveal company size is undoubtedly the number of employees working in a company. Our respondents consisted with an average staff size of 6,7 employees while variations in this variable ranged from having 0 employees (implying the founder is still on his own) to 36 employees.

Most of our participant start-upswere active in Information Technology & Service Industry (33 %). Following were Consultancy (10 %) and Media industries (8 %). In Fig. 3 a complete overview of the industry areas of all the participating companies is shown. Overall a wide variety of industries was represented in our sample population.

Half of the participating start-ups indicated that their target market was international (meaning not only Europe). 32 % of the companies targeted the Netherlands, 10 % targeted Europe and 8 % of the participants indicated Sweden to be their target market.

After analyzing the results of the survey, four follow-up interviews were done. The aim of these interviews was to investigate the motivations behind choosing a specific software acquisition method. The interviews were semi-structured.

To select companies for the interviews, we used the results of the survey. To make sure that the companies we interviewed represented as many types of companies present within the survey as possible, we chose to interview one company that uses (almost) only paid software, one that uses (almost) only free software (open source or freeware) and two that use a mix of the abovementioned acquisition methods. In that way we would be able to encounter all aspects from the software acquisition model. Furthermore, we made sure that all four companies were from different industries, to prevent the overall

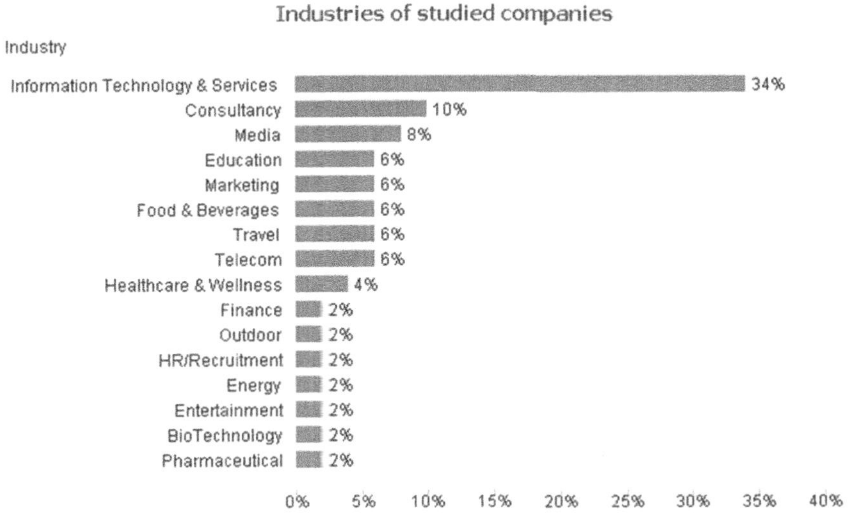

Industries of studied companies

Industry	Percentage
Information Technology & Services	34%
Consultancy	10%
Media	8%
Education	6%
Marketing	6%
Food & Beverages	6%
Travel	6%
Telecom	6%
Healthcare & Wellness	4%
Finance	2%
Outdoor	2%
HR/Recruitment	2%
Energy	2%
Entertainment	2%
BioTechnology	2%
Pharmaceutical	2%

Fig. 3. Industry areas of studied start-ups

interview results to be influenced by industry characteristics. All interviewed companies also participated in the survey and had indicated they wanted to participate in the interview. This way, we were able to analyze differences in motivations behind the choices that these companies made when acquiring their software. A complete overview of the interviewees is shown in Table 2.

Table 2. Interviewees profile overview

	Company 1	Company 2	Company 3	Company 4
Industry	IT & Services	Consultancy	Healthcare & Wellness	Communication & Content Creation
Foundation Year	2014	2011	2014	2012
Country	Sweden	Sweden	Sweden	Netherlands
Interviewee	Founder	CEO Founder	CEO	Owner
Acquisition Type	Open Source	Paid Software (Shared License, Single License)	Mix (Pay-Per-Use, Freeware)	Mix (In-house Developed, Freeware, Pay-Per-Use, Single License)

Although we had interviewed two companies that used a mix of acquisition methods, we still interviewed both of them as one of these companies had an in-house developed solution and the other one did not. In each category that we wanted to interview in terms of software acquisition methods (almost) only paid software, (almost) only free software, a mix of paid and free software), we had the choice between two or three companies that indicated that they would want to collaborate with an interview. We then proceeded to approach a random company from each of these categories, taking into consideration industry types so that we wouldn't interview companies from the same industry type. Below an overview of our interviewee profile is shown.

4 Findings About Software Sourcing in Start-Ups

As described earlier, our categorization of software sourcing methods was based on the Software Acquisition model by Nelson, Richmond and Seidmann [7]. This model differentiates four different types of sourcing methods, being "Custom Insource", "Custom Outsource", "Package Insource" and "Package Outsource". In this model, custom software refers to software that is custom-made for the company and package software refers to existing packages offered on the market. In case of the custom software, insource means that the software was developed in-house, and outsource means that the software was developed by a third party. In case of the package software, insource and outsource refer to the decision-making process around acquiring the software: Package Insource software is acquired by the company, with the decision-making and selection process done within the company. Package Outsource software is eventually acquired by the company, after the decision-making and selection process is done by a third party [7].

In the survey we asked about one dimension of this model, namely about the distinction between Package software and Custom Software. Since there are a lot of different options to acquire Package software, we also differentiated between different kinds of Package software, namely Freeware, Open Source, Single License, Pay-Per-Use, Shared License, Subscription, and Other. Freeware is software that is distributed for free, Open Source is software that is distributed for free and additionally has its code publicly available, Single License software is software that is paid for and that can be used by one user, Pay-Per-Use software is software that is paid for each time you use it, Shared License software is software that is paid for and that can be used by a predefined number of users, and Subscription software is software that is paid for every set period (e.g. month, year). In the interviews, we focused on the second dimension of the Software Acquisition Model [7], which is the differentiation between in-house and outsource.

In the following of this subchapter, firstly the survey results on software acquisition will be presented and secondly the interview results on software acquisition will be presented.

4.1 Survey Results on Software Acquisition

We found the top five used software acquisition methods being Freeware (68 responses), Single License (42 responses), Open Source (31 responses), Pay-Per-Use (23 responses) and Shared License (21 responses). We found no relation between a company's yearly turnover and their used acquisition method, with the most used methods being dominant in different revenue groups. In Table 3 the most widely used acquisition methods by distribution are shown.

Table 3. Distribution of software sourcing method

Software sourcing method	Frequency	Percentage
Freeware	68	31,8 %
Single license	42	19,6 %
Open source	31	14,4 %
Pay per use	23	10,8 %
Shared license	21	9,8 %
Subscription	13	6,0 %
Other	8	3,7 %
Entrepreneur license	4	1.9 %
In-house developed	4	1,9 %
Total	**214**	**100 %**

The least popular software acquisition methods were Subscriptions (13 response), other (8 responses), Entrepreneur License (4 response), and In-house Development (4 responses).

4.2 Interview Results on Software Acquisition

It was very crucial for our study to understand how the software applications are actually acquired by start-up companies: How potential software systems for usage are identified or implemented, who makes such decisions in the company or the extent of using external resources to help make such decisions.

It turned out that all interviewed start-ups admitted making the decision mostly internally, especially the interviewee themselves, or consulting with their colleagues in cases when such discussions are needed. For example, Company 1 stated: *"In the case we needed to collaborate...we did a five minute chat about which alternatives do we have, which is best [...] just the technical people [...] the ones that had to work with the tools"*.

Interesting to know was that all the interviewed companies owned internal IT expertise, developers, people that work with technology or somebody dedicated for gathering software requirements. Although, Company 2 admitted just being passionate on exploring software requirements, which is easy thanks to internet resources. The interviewee of Company 2 described himself as an above average user more than an IT professional, but still didn't hire external expertise to advise him which software to use. The companies that stated having IT expertise said that some of the applications they used were in use because of their previous experience with the systems and gained familiarity.

In general our interviewees, who mostly occupied high managerial roles in the company (CEO, founders), felt very comfortable in asking for advice from friends and colleagues and obtain information through social ties as to what other companies are using.

One of the start-ups (Company 2) had a custom made software for very specialized purposes, where an external consultancy was employed to do the job, however requirements analysis and testing were done by the start-up company itself through continuous and informal communication. The interviewee explained: *"collaboration, and interaction and iteration...it was not a formal work really that we had a long list of detailed specifications that must be fulfilled...it was just a talk over a cup of coffee"*.

Three of our interviewees (Company 1, 2 and 4) revealed not having any plans in the near future to buy software while company 3 admitted that they would re-evaluate a few software applications they were using and would acquire more while they were still expanding and 'scaling up'. We looked back if any relation could be drawn from our respondent regarding their foundation years and future acquisition plans, but we have two companies founded in 2014 that have different acquisition plans in the future. The other companies were founded in 2012 and 2011 making them generally fresh in the market but relatively saturated in terms of software systems since three out of four weren't planning on future acquisitions. However, they said that if they would acquire software in the future, they planned to make the decision of which software to acquire in the same way as they did before, maybe additionally asking for advice among friends and colleagues (Company 2, Company 3 and Company 4) or looking at commonly used software (Company 1).

4.3 Why Do Start-Ups Acquire Their Software in the Way They Do?

In terms of used software acquisition methods, interviewed start-ups were in a mixed situation, paying for what they should and getting cheap what they could, however they all agreed never compromising on software quality: such as ease of use and flexibility of open source (Company 1); Company 2 stated that *"it's not really the money"* implying if there are no free alternatives, accessing between paid version of software, a couple of thousand euros was not much of a difference, Company 3 stated that if the financial difference was insignificant they would settle for the software delivering the best value and Company 4 said that meeting their requirements was the most important and secondly the price.

Start-ups being charged for some of their software applications said that they chose paid software because it makes them feel more secured to demand support in case something went wrong or they needed updates (Company 2 & 3). Another important reason stated for paying for software applications was *"because no other available free option was identified yet"* (Company 3). Two of our respondents implied that they felt comfortable having to pay as they scale thus employing Pay-Per-Use where there are no upfront costs and one revealing to have more software applications that offered these type of licensing (Company 2 & 3).

Asked on what portion of their budget planning was dedicated to software acquisition, all interviewees implied that software acquisition was not a priority in their budget planning and thus that the importance of software acquisition in their budget planning was very low.

Only one of the respondents (Company 2) had custom made software for his company and that was due to the fact that they need very specialized software for their tools and the company paid for its development performed by an external party. Another respondent (Company 4) had in-house developed product due to the fact that available alternatives were too expensive and also didn't match entirely with their requirements. However since they had internal employees to deal with the implementation it was stated as not being a problem.

Company 1 which used mainly open-source software did so because they felt free but also owned the knowledge to change and customize functionalities and emphasized that they would be free of forced upgrades in the future.

Since we were particularly interested in the software acquisition method Entrepreneur license, as it is one of the newest and aimed to be targeted for a niche market such as start-ups we were surprised to see that very few companies from the surveyed ones admitted to using it. Therefore we were interested to know if there was any particular reason for this license not to have a wide usage yet. All of our interviews admitted not being informed on this type of licensing.

Additional comments interviewees had, regarding current software offering and how they felt the market targeted start-up needs, were also considered interesting in our research. Suggestions included that start-ups wanted more options for open source software, because they need a bigger level of freedom (Company 1), and more flexible licensing supporting growth (Company 2 & 4).

While Company 2 suggested for more Pay-Per-Use licensing, scaling more gradually from individual to business packages and feeling more in control of their budget, Company 4 stated that sometimes such billing method might get expensive as not all users need the same software to the same extent.

Company 4 suggested that the way software functionalities are communicated to the start-up market can be improved and that they felt the need to have some comparing tool in terms of software functionalities.

One of the respondents (Company 3) pointed out that it was important for them to have full functionalities offered from the start even for small companies and then scale up and pay according to their usage but not being 'forced' to switch the environment entirely because what works in the beginning does not work when they become bigger.

Furthermore, Company 3 mentioned that a smoother integration of different software applications would help them a lot. The interviewee explained: *"some of the software applications [...] could have easier integrations or automatic integrations from the beginning [...]. If you could get that in one package that would be pretty cool.."*. Later, the interviewee added to this that he expected start-ups to be willing to pay for this type of software as well: *"Eh, and I think most would be willing to pay for it as well."*

5 Why Start-Ups Acquire Their Software as They Do

Start-ups emphasize on the search for flexibility when thinking about software acquisition. However, despite that the data supports that they actually in a high extent goes for a quite inflexible solution (Freeware and Single license) when deciding on software acquisition method. From the survey data it is found that Freeware is the dominate method, followed by single license. Both could be seen as highly inflexible from a growth and cost perspective, since the software could be downloaded and used for free.

It is actually surprising that single licenses shows a higher frequency than both pay-per-use and subscription type, as it is not as flexible when the company needs to scale up.

One reason for why start-ups paid for their software (single licenses), especially in cases where the software served customers, was because they felt more secure to demand a higher level of support in case of facing problems. A likely explanation for the fact that some start-ups took into consideration free options first, if those existed, was that the budget dedicated to software acquisition was pretty low. However main reasons to settle for a specific software application include ease of use, compatibility (both internally and externally), reliability, flexibility, requirement fit and familiarity, even if start-ups had to pay for it. Furthermore an important aspect that was taken into consideration when selecting software is looking at the software that is used by competitors.

In-house development was very uncommon (2 %). However, one of the interviewed start-ups has actually developed their own ERP-system. The reason for doing this was because they felt like the software offered on the market was too expensive and did not meet their requirements. However, it should be mentioned that this is an exceptional case, since this start-up was one of the few that actually developed their own software. Furthermore, another case adapted Open Source software themselves to make it fit to their company. This was mainly done as they wanted the flexibility and freedom to grow and be independent of forced upgrades.

Regarding the Pay-Per-Use software acquisition method, interviewed start-ups were positive about it and especially the fact that no upfront costs were involved, they felt in control of how much money they were spending, and also that scaling and shifting to a business license felt more acceptable. However one company suggested that sometimes not all employees are using the software applications at the same extent therefore in those cases a more flexible pricing model would be beneficial.

Interviewed start-ups also did some suggestions to improve the current offering of software, which gives us information about their motivations behind software acquisition as well. These suggestions include firstly to have more open source software (free software with publicly available code), because it provides a certain level of freedom and flexibility in terms of software acquisition. It should be noted that the start-up that suggested this has a high level of IT knowledge and therefore was able to adapt the software in such ways that it suited their business better. A second suggestion done by another start-up was that of having more flexible licensing, so that a more gradual shift from individual usage to business usage can be made: The interviewee more specifically suggested to have plans that are particularly suited for smaller companies, with for example five employees. Another suggestion made by a third start-up was to provide easier integration or more package offerings of software that include features that are commonly needed by start-up companies. Finally start-ups also emphasized that software vendors need to communicate software functionalities more clearly.

Interviewed start-ups, although operating in different industries (IT & Services, Consultancy, Healthcare & Wellness and Communication & Content Creation), showed to have an extensive IT knowledge and they were very clear what they wanted to have from their software systems. The decision on how to acquire software by referring to the previously identified software acquisition model by [Nelson, Richmond and Seidmann [7]] in our study, made for the distinguishable associations to be Insource-Package or

Outsource-Custom while there is a vague existence of Outsource-Package relation slightly different in start-ups, who seek external advice through social networks/colleagues.

By Insource-Package they generally made the decision in-house or from the technical people which software to choose. In the case of specialized developed software (Outsource-Custom) the needs and testing were still done by the start-up itself, the latter being pretty clear in their requirements and needs. This reveals that start-up nowadays, no matter industry, are very conscious and informed on the software market offerings or generally have an employee/co-founder responsible for these operations from the beginning.

We slightly touched the case of Insource-Custom but in two different scenarios, one in the case of the company using open source software since they admitted that they changed the code to accommodate their needs and their ability to grow, suggesting for a slightly different model for start-ups regarding software acquisition. The other case was Insource-Custom in the sense that they developed an in-house software application as no available software packages satisfied their needs. As we did not find many companies using Insource-Custom solutions, we would suggest future research to further investigate this matter. It should be mentioned that in both Insource-Custom cases, economical factors constrained their choices in available software on the market.

In case of the economic category, it seems that cost is not necessarily the top priority when selecting software however it is still important. Start-ups said to consider free software options in case there were available alternatives meeting their requirements. Given the low budget dedicated for software acquisition it was still an important variable in consideration. Viable in this context means selecting budget wise options and considering the limitation of not being able to buy 'premium' products. In the cases where start-ups paid for software was either because there were no other options, they wanted the ability to demand support and then having found the right alternative they were willing to pay. Relating to costs, a preference for flexible licensing types or those without upfront costs was noticed, that made companies feel more in control of their spending.

6 Conclusions

Coming back to our main research question, "*How do start-ups acquire their software and why?*", we are able to say that the major part of software used in start-ups is freeware. The start-ups use freeware as a software acquisition method since this is a way of getting software without any direct financial consequences. However, start-ups are not totally convinced about the quality of the software that comes as freeware and that makes the single license being the second most used acquisition method. The main reason for why start-ups use this method is that they have a feeling that this option gives better support possibilities and that the software is more reliable. In other words, reasons for selecting a specific software acquisition method are related to reasons to choose specific software. This means that ease of use, compatibility, reliability, flexibility, and previous familiarity with the software influence the way the start-ups provide them with software. Most start-ups prefer free or cheap software, supported also by the fact of their lower budget planning for this purpose, although the start-ups clearly state that reliability and quality of the software should not be compromised, especially in the case of software that serves their customers. In these cases, start-ups confirm that they are willing to pay for their software. Right now, acquisition of paid software mostly occurs in a single license setup, although interviewed start-ups stated a preference for pay-per-use, as it is more flexible and because they feel more in control over how much money they spend.

References

1. Sutton, S.M.: The role of process in a software start-up. IEEE Softw. **17**(4), 33 (2000)
2. Burgel, O., Murray, G.C.: The international market entry choices of start-up companies in high-technology industries. J. Int. Mark. **8**(2), 33–62 (2000)
3. Archibald, T.W., Thomas, L., Betts, J., Johnston, R.: Should start-up companies be cautious? Inventory policies which maximise survival probabilities. Manage. Sci. **48**(9), 1161–1174 (2002)
4. Carter, N.M., Gartner, W.B., Reynolds, P.D.: Exploring start-up event sequences. J. Bus. Ventur. **11**(3), 151–166 (1996)
5. Thong, J.Y.L.: An integrated model of information systems adoption in small businesses. J. Manage. Inf. Syst. **15**(4), 187–214 (1999)
6. Davila, A., Foster, G.: Management control systems in early-stage startup companies. Account. Rev. **82**(4), 907–937 (2007)
7. Nelson, P., Richmond, W., Seidmann, A.: Two dimensions of software acquisition. Commun. ACM **39**(7), 29–35 (1996)
8. Daneshgar, F., Low, G.C., Worasinchai, L.: An investigation of 'build vs. buy' decision for software acquisition by small to medium enterprises. Inf. Softw. Technol. **55**, 1741–1750 (2013)
9. Giardino, C., Unterkalmsteiner, M., Paternoster, N., Gorschek, T., Abrahamsson, P.: What do we know about software development in startups? IEEE Softw. **31**(5), 28–32 (2014)
10. Ives, B., Learmonth, G.P.: The information system as a competitive weapon. Commun. ACM **27**(12), 1193–1201 (1984)
11. Porter, M.E., Millar, V.E.: How information gives you competitive advantage (1985). Harvard Business Review, Reprint Service, 1985
12. Knight, G.A., Cavusgil, S.T.: Innovation, organizational capabilities, and the born-global firm. J. Int. Bus. Stud. **35**(2), 124–141 (2004)
13. Thong, J.Y.L., Yap, C.S., Raman, K.S.: Top management support, external expertise and information systems implementation in small businesses. Inf. Syst. Res. **7**(2), 248–267 (1996)
14. Zalesna, A.: Intellectual capital and the SME life cycle model: a proposed theoretical link. In: Proceedings of the European Conference on Intellectual Capital, pp. 489–495 (2012)
15. Sutton Jr., S.M.: The role of process in software start-up. IEEE Softw. **17**(4), 33–39 (2000)
16. Simon, H.A.: The New Science of Management Decision. Prentice-Hall, Englewood Cliffs (1977). Rev. ed., 1977
17. Wang, H., Wang, C.: Open source software adoption: a status report. IEEE Softw. **18**(2), 90–95 (2001)
18. Liao-Troth, M.A., Griffith, T.L.: Software, shareware and freeware: multiplex commitment to an electronic social exchange system. J. Organ. Behav. **23**(5), 635–653 (2002)
19. Indenbom, E.: Methods of licensing software programs and protecting them from unauthorized use (2009). (Google Patents)
20. Michel, A.D., Reinke, R.E.: Software pay per use system (1997). (Google Patents)

21. Choudhary, V.: Software as a Service: Implications for Investment in Software Development (2007)
22. Harrison, D.A., Mykytyn Jr., P.P., Riemenschneider, C.K.: Executive decisions about adoption of information technology in small business: theory and empirical tests. Inf. Syst. Res. **8**(2), 171–195 (1997)
23. Ajzen, I.: The theory of planned behavior. Organ. Behav. Hum. Decis. Process. **50**(2), 179–211 (1991)
24. Blank, S.: Search versus Execute. http://steveblank.com/2012/03/05/search-versus-execute/. Accessed 7 Apr 2015

Author Index

Aggarwal, Shivom 1
Alpar, Paul 166
Arduin, Pierre-Emmanuel 19

Beulen, Erik 178

Caratti, Silvia 137

Deliallisi, Blerta 193

Herbert, Ian 51

Janssen, Marijn 77
Johansson, Björn 193

Kooijman, Christiaan 77
Kumar, Kuldeep 40

Lambert, Stephanie 51

Oshri, Ilan 118

Perrin, Brian 137
Plugge, Albert 77

Ravindran, Kiron 1
Ray, Gautam 1
Rosenkranz, Christoph 97
Rothwell, Andrew 51

Schmidt, Nikolaus 97
Scully, Glennda 137
Suri, Vipin 40

Vaia, Giovanni 118
van Hillegersberg, Jos 40
Vieru, Dragos 19

Walraven, Pien 193

Zöller, Bastian 97

The manufacturer's authorised representative in the EU is Springer Nature Customer Service Centre GmbH, Europaplatz 3, 69115 Heidelberg, Germany. If you have any concerns regarding our products, please contact ProductSafety@springernature.com

Printed and bound by CPI Group (UK) Ltd, Croydon, CR0 4YY

23/03/2026

02076674-0013